KEEPING GOD'S SILENCE

Challenges in Contemporary Theology

Series Editors: Gareth Jones and Lewis Ayres
Canterbury Christ Church University College, UK and Emory University, US

Challenges in Contemporary Theology is a series aimed at producing clear orientations in, and research on, areas of "challenge" in contemporary theology. These carefully co-ordinated books engage traditional theological concerns with mainstreams in modern thought and culture that challenge those concerns. The "challenges" implied are to be understood in two senses: those presented by society to contemporary theology, and those posed by theology to society.

Published

These Three are One: The Practice of Trinitarian Theology   David S. Cunningham

After Writing: On the Liturgical Consummation of Philosophy   Catherine Pickstock

Mystical Theology: The Integrity of Spirituality and Theology   Mark A. McIntosh

Engaging Scripture: A Model for Theological Interpretation   Stephen E. Fowl

Torture and Eucharist: Theology, Politics, and the Body of Christ   William T. Cavanaugh

Sexuality and the Christian Body: Their Way into the Triune God
Eugene F. Rogers, Jr

On Christian Theology   Rowan Williams

The Promised End: Eschatology in Theology and Literature   Paul S. Fiddes

Powers and Submissions: Spirituality, Philosophy, and Gender   Sarah Coakley

A Theology of Engagement   Ian S. Markham

Alien Sex: The Body and Desire in Cinema and Theology   Gerard Loughlin

Scripture and Metaphysics: Aquinas and the Renewal of Trinitarian Theology
Matthew Levering

Faith and Freedom: An Interfaith Perspective   David Burrell

Keeping God's Silence: Towards a Theological Ethics of Communication   Rachel Muers

Forthcoming

Christ and Culture   Graham Ward

Aquinas and Authority   Mark Jordan

KEEPING GOD'S SILENCE

Towards a Theological Ethics of Communication

Rachel Muers

Blackwell
Publishing

© 2004 by Rachel Muers

BLACKWELL PUBLISHING
350 Main Street, Malden, MA 02148-5020, USA
108 Cowley Road, Oxford OX4 1JF, UK
550 Swanston Street, Carlton, Victoria 3053, Australia

First published 2004 by Blackwell Publishing Ltd

Library of Congress Cataloging-in-Publication Data

Muers, Rachel.
  Keeping God's silence : towards a theological ethics of communication / Rachel Muers.
    p.   cm. – (Challenges in contemporary theology)
  Includes bibliographical references and index.
  ISBN 1-4051-1899-7 (alk. paper) – ISBN 1-4051-1900-4 (pbk. : alk. paper)
    1. Silence – Religious aspects – Christianity.   2. Spiritual life – Christianity.
  I. Title.   II. Series.

BV4509.5.M83 2004
241 – dc22

                                                                    2004007686

A catalogue record for this title is available from the British Library.

Set in 10.5 on 12.5 pt Bembo
by SNP Best-set Typesetter Ltd., Hong Kong
Printed and bound in the United Kingdom
by TJ International Ltd, Padstow, Cornwall

The publisher's policy is to use permanent paper from mills that operate a sustainable forestry policy, and which has been manufactured from pulp processed using acid-free and elementary chlorine-free practices. Furthermore, the publisher ensures that the text paper and cover board used have met acceptable environmental accreditation standards.

For further information on
Blackwell Publishing, visit our website:
www.blackwellpublishing.com

CONTENTS

Preface and Acknowledgments   vii

Sources   ix

List of Abbreviations   x

Introduction: Beginning with Silence   1

1 Assessing Silence   21

2 Who Hears?   49

3 Resurrection Silence   71

4 Hearing the Word?   102

5 Wisdom and Folly: Seeking Places to Stand   124

6 Hearing with God's Ears: Interpreting
Practices of Silence   143

7 Privacy, Omniscience, and the Silence of God   182

8 Openings   213

Bibliography   225

Index   239

To Jane and Robin
Who heard me first

PREFACE AND ACKNOWLEDGMENTS

This book began as a PhD project. It was convenient to have a one-word answer to the standard question "So, what is your thesis about?" – "Silence!" – and also very convenient to be able to predict the jokes – "So, what are you going to do in your viva?" or occasionally "So, are you going to leave the last few pages blank?"

Many would think, possibly with good reason, that trying to write 80,000 words about silence was an even stranger way to spend three years of one's life than are most pieces of research. Be that as it may, I have been fortunate enough to find a large number of people, during the initial period of research and since, who have been prepared to help bring the project to fruition. In acknowledging my enormous debts to them, I of course retain full responsibility for the defects of the final product.

The PhD was written under the supervision of David Ford, whose enthusiasm for the original idea has been followed by enormously generous help, guidance, and encouragement. Janet Martin Soskice acted as my supervisor at two important stages of the research, and has been another most valuable source of support throughout. Al McFadyen and Catherine Pickstock, the examiners of the thesis, offered important advice for its subsequent development, as did Dan Hardy.

During the genesis of the book I have been part of three academic institutions: Clare College, Cambridge, which provided practical and financial help during my PhD work; Girton College, Cambridge, where as a junior research fellow I was welcomed into a supportive and stimulating interdisciplinary work environment; and most recently the Department of Theology at the University of Exeter. I am grateful to all the members of these institutions who have helped to create the conditions within which this book could grow. My doctoral research was supported by the Arts and Humanities Research Board, formerly the British Academy.

I have been fortunate at every stage of the work to be surrounded by encouraging and inspiring colleagues, and am very grateful to all those whose interest and insights fed into this project in ways too numerous to list. Among them are Paul Janz, Peter Waddell, Julie Gittoes, Mike Higton, Alice E. Wood, Shannon Craigo-Snell, and Janet Scott. I owe particular debts of thanks to Jon Cooley, Chad Pecknold, and Susannah Ticciati, to whom I am bound by an ever more complex web of shared conversations, concerns, and experiences, and who have between them heard me to so many of the insights I have thought worth writing down in recent years.

Worship at Jesus Lane Meeting of the Religious Society of Friends (Quakers) is the context without which this work on silence would have been impossible. Members of that community have been consistently supportive. I have appreciated my stays at Woodbrooke, and would particularly like to thank Tim Peat for the "Serious about Silence" course and other collaborations.

Having a strong network of "small-f" friends has been equally important. Thanks are due especially to Angela Piearce, Chris Jordinson, Eleanor Coghill, Melissa Demian, Naomi Hetherington, Rachel Bearon, Alia Ganaposki, Angela Billington, and Doris Abbs. Copernicus and Kepler have saved work for other critics by occasionally tearing my drafts to pieces.

I would like to thank the anonymous readers whose comments on the manuscript initially submitted helped to shape the final version of this work. In the latter stages of its development, Lewis Ayres has been a most encouraging, and helpfully critical, reader and editor; I am very grateful to him, and to Gareth Jones, Rebecca Harkin, and Sophie Gibson for all their assistance.

My husband and beloved Ffriend Gavin Burnell is a true exemplar of patience, listening, and other virtues discussed in this book. I prefer not to ask him whether it takes more patience to cope with me or with my frequently recalcitrant computer. In any case, my gratitude to him is incalculable, and ever greater.

SOURCES

ABBREVIATIONS

New critical edition of Bonhoeffer's works

DBW   *Dietrich Bonhoeffer Werke*, ed. Eberhard Bethge et al., 16 vols. (Gutersloh: Kaiser, 1986–).

DBWE   *Dietrich Bonhoeffer Works*, ed. Wayne Whitson Floyd, Jr., 16 vols. (in progress) (Minneapolis: Fortress, 1995–)

Other editions of Bonhoeffer's works

GS   *Gesammelte Schriften*, ed. Eberhard Bethge (Munich: Kaiser, 1965–)

INTRODUCTION:
BEGINNING WITH
SILENCE

When the Lamb opened the seventh seal, there was silence in heaven for the space of half an hour. (Revelation 8:1[1])

The book of Revelation is full of sounds – crying voices, thunder, trumpets, harp-playing, singing – and of speech – proclamations, prayers, commands, prophecies. Carried along by the tumult of sounds and voices, the reader of Revelation is brought up short by the silence at the beginning of chapter 8. We are invited to pause and wonder, not only what will happen next, but what this silence means. Why is there "silence in heaven" just at this point, and for just this length of time? Who is keeping silent, and for what end? What wider meaning of silence is brought into play here – wonder or terror, meaninglessness or fullness of meaning, suspense or completeness? Having begun to ask these questions, the reader might ponder them indefinitely, because the unexplained silence opens up so many possibilities for interpretation. At the same time, since all that the text does is to state that the silent pause occurs, it is very easy for the reader to pass over it quickly to the next set of events and the next sound effect. What more can be said, she might ask, once one has said "there was silence?" By definition, there is nothing going on here that can be talked about; there is no action, no event, no Revelation, merely their absence.

A few commentaries on Revelation do pause in confusion at verse 8:1, and a few pass over it altogether; but generally they must attempt to speak intelligibly about its significance – as not just another sound, and not simply the absence of sound. Anyone trying to give a theological or philosophical account of silence must undertake a similarly difficult task. Speak-

---

[1] Revelation 8:1. All biblical quotations are from the New Revised Standard Version.

ing, or even writing, about silence may look like a paradoxical or self-contradictory enterprise; but its difficulties are not obviously greater than the difficulties of speaking about God, and in both cases ways of speaking have repeatedly to be found and rediscovered – perhaps, as Augustine put it, "not in order to say something, but in order not to be silent."[2]

This book is an attempt to reflect theologically on silence – on God's silence and on human silences – in a context in which we have been said to experience both too little and too much silence. "Where shall the word be found, where will the word/Resound? Not here, there is not enough silence,"[3] wrote T. S. Eliot in 1930, and his description of the communicative situation finds even more resonances in the contemporary world. The sheer amount of public speech, communication, and the transfer of information has increased and continues to increase exponentially. At the same time, however, the silence of the divine voice, the authorial voice, whatever voices could authoritatively interpret a puzzling world or cause it to speak to us, is proclaimed.

Doing theology in the present context, we encounter silences of many kinds. There are the silences of biblical texts, both those that are marked as such and those that are notable only as absences from the text. There are numerous practices of silence, liturgical and otherwise, that form significant parts of the lives of Christians. Most strikingly, there are theological texts that draw attention to silence – in the rereading of apophatic theology or debates over deconstructionism, in critiques of the historical silencing of particular theological voices, or in the characterization of the secular age as one in which God is silent. Theological concern with the powers and limits of language, shaped both by shifts in philosophical thought and on older theological tradition, produces reflection on the relationship between speech and silence.[4]

---

[2]   Augustine of Hippo, *On the Trinity*, book XV.
[3]   T. S. Eliot, "Ash Wednesday," V. *Collected Poems: 1909–1962* (London: Faber & Faber, 1962), p. 102.
[4]   Examples of recent work including extended discussion of "theological silence" in a specifically modern context are the collection of essays in Oliver Davies and Denys Turner, *Silence and the Word: Negative Theology and Incarnation* (Cambridge: Cambridge University Press, 2002); Kevin Hart, *The Trespass of the Sign: Deconstruction, Theology and Philosophy* (Cambridge: Cambridge University Press, 1989); Rebecca Chopp, *The Power to Speak: Feminism, Language, God* (New York: Crossroad, 1989); Jean-Luc Marion, *God without Being*, trans. Thomas A. Carlson (Chicago: University of Chicago Press, 1991); Eberhard Jüngel, *God as the Mystery of the World: On the Foundation of the Theology of the Crucified One in the Dispute between Theism and Atheism*, trans. Darrell L. Guder (Grand Rapids: Eerdmans, 1983).

These theological reflections on silence are specific to our historical situation. They draw, however, on a long tradition wherein silence is a focus, not only of theological reflection per se, but of the engagement of theologians with a social and political context. Silence, both as practiced and as theorized, can mark a withdrawal or separation from "the world," a radical interruption of it, or a submission to its demands. Theology can take up speech on behalf of those who have been politically "silenced," or call for silence so that the single and unifying word of God can be heard. Looking at theological uses of the theme of "silence" draws attention both to how theology constructs itself as a form of communication, and to the wider communicative environment in which theological discourse is placed. Thinking about silence theologically confronts us with ethical and political questions. Even the silence of Revelation 8:1 has its implications for such questions; is silence being kept so that the prayers of the "saints," who have been silenced within the kingdoms of the world, can finally be heard?[5]

In this book, I ask how attention to the significance of silence, and to the significance of God's silence, can reshape understandings and practices of communication in the twenty-first century. I consider how Christian theology can and should challenge the patterns of communication that produce "wars of words," cacophonies of competing voices within which the weakest are silenced and the silent are passed over. It can do so on the basis of a different understanding of *God's* communication, one that gives priority to a listening silence, the silence in which God hears the world and thus opens up the possibility of innerworldly freedom. I shall argue, further, that people can learn not only to recognize this silence but also to share in it – that a theological ethics of communication can begin from "keeping God's silence."

But does it make any sense to talk about silence in this way? What can we say about silence that does not rely entirely on treating it as the opposite, or the absence, of something else – of sounds or utterances? The analysis of silence has been pursued within many disciplines, other than theology, in the twentieth century. Such analyses can be helpful in our attempts to understand the many "theological silences" – and to see ways through the inherent difficulties of speaking about silence.

---

[5]   For an extended discussion of this view, see Richard Bauckham, *The Climax of Prophecy: Studies in the Book of Revelation* (Edinburgh: T. & T. Clark, 1993), pp. 70–83. See also G. B. Caird, *A Commentary on the Revelation of St John the Divine* (London: Black's, 1966), pp. 106–7.

Studies in Silence

"There was silence in heaven for the space of half an hour." Silence is both something we encounter or discover – the silence of a deserted place, an empty room – and something we do, and experience as done by others – conversational silences, silences in response to questions. Silence is found, and silence is made; but often these two appear difficult to separate. Even Revelation's "silence in heaven" is made by those who fall silent – the angels, the singers, all the others whose voices and sounds have been heard so far – but it is then encountered by the writer and the reader as something that exceeds any of those performances of silence. We hear, not "they fell silent," but "there was silence." When we speak of *keeping* silence, we point to this relationship between silence as a reality we find and silence as part of our communicative activity; silence, the idiomatic expression suggests, is in some sense "already there," for us to discover and keep.[6]

The fact that silence can be treated both as part of conscious communicative activity and as a feature we discover in the world makes a *phenomenological* approach particularly helpful at the start of an attempt to talk about silence; an approach that centers on silence as something intended and experienced by the human mind, without needing in the first instance to determine its "objective" and "subjective," its found and made, components. Examining silence from this perspective can give us a starting-point for talking about silence as something not reducible to speech – or sound – or to its absence.

Bernhard Dauenhauer's work on *Silence: The Phenomenon and its Ontological Significance*[7] includes the analysis of philosophical texts, but focuses on silence as a general feature of human existence. Dauenhauer's hypothesis is that silence is a positive phenomenon, not merely the absence of something else, "at least equiprimordial with utterance" (p. 4), and in fact capable of being regarded as *prior* to speech or utterance. Starting from the fact that silence happens, both as something we do and as something we think about, he treats silence as a conscious communicative activity

---

[6] For discussion of the distinction between "silence as the absence of noise and silence as the cessation of speech" – a distinction that many languages can denote more clearly than can English – see Oliver Davies, "Soundings: Towards a Theological Poetics of Silence," in *Silence and the Word: Negative Theology and Incarnation*, ed. Oliver Davies and Denys Turner (Cambridge: Cambridge University Press, 2002).

[7] Bernard Dauenhauer, *Silence: The Phenomenon and Its Ontological Significance* (Bloomington: Indiana University Press, 1980). Subsequent references in parentheses in the text.

that "makes sense." It is, in other words, an appropriate action within the world we inhabit, and it is part of how we make that world intelligible. If we understand why it makes sense to keep silence, Dauenhauer hypothesizes, we will understand something more, not just about silence, but about persons and the world they inhabit.

Dauenhauer begins with an analysis of some of the more obvious ways we *keep* silence, relating these silences at every point to the utterances – spoken or musical communicative activities – around and between which it occurs. For example, there is the phenomenon of "intervening silences" – the rests in a piece of music, the pauses between sentences or units of thought. Intervening silences divide the units of meaning-bearing sound one from another; but they also bind and join the parts of an utterance, each intervening silence bearing within it the meaning of both the preceding and the following "sound phrase" (pp. 6–7). The "fore-and-after silences" around an utterance, in turn, bind and join it to a wider field of speech and meaning, while at the same time "cutting" and setting a limit to the meaning-making of that particular utterance (p. 9).

Learning to appreciate silence as a positive phenomenon, even from the trivial examples of everyday speech, is learning that all utterance is surrounded by a "fringe of silence." So far, however, this analysis might leave silence subordinate to speech or utterance, as something that helps the latter along by rendering it comprehensible (where would be the sense in a constant flow of sound without silences to articulate it?), but that carries no significance of its own. Considering Revelation's "silence in heaven," by contrast, brings to mind the phenomenon of silences that are more significant than utterance – silences that appear, perhaps, to govern or determine utterance. When we begin to consider these deep silences – liturgical silences in many different traditions, the silence kept among intimates or at times of profound emotion – we are brought, as Dauenhauer sees it, closer to the "ontological significance" of this phenomenon. Silence – usually thought of in terms of its contrast with utterance – is found, when we consider "deep silence," to reflect a more general feature of all "mediating activity," all the activity by which people make sense of the world to themselves and to others (p. 16).

What is this general feature of our sense-making activity to which silence gives us particular access? Dauenhauer's analysis suggests that silence indicates the dependence of any utterance, any act of communication or making sense of the world, on something beyond itself and beyond *any other* determinate utterance. An attempt at making sense depends on something beyond itself to authenticate it in the claim it makes. Silences "interrupt" or "cut" the attempt, in utterance, fully to determine oneself or the world. At the same time, they open the way for further, new communications or mediating acts; utterance needs silence if it is ever to begin.

On this view, then, silence as a phenomenon reveals both our finitude and our freedom as communicating and interpreting beings (pp. 158–9). On the one hand, people do not determine their world, but engage in their various mediating activities "in response to a gift." Keeping silence recalls speakers and utterances to this situation of "givenness" – the "givenness" of a tradition or a context, of the natural world, of our own capacity for utterance that had to be learned before it could be used. The deep silences of intimacy – or of liturgy as Dauenhauer analyzes it – bring people closer to some central aspect of their world's "givenness." On the other hand, however, silence reveals freedom – because the "givenness" of the world or of previous mediating activities cannot fully close off the possibilities for future mediation. Silence opens up these further possibilities; the "intervening silences" between utterances make some different utterance possible, and "deep silences" do not prevent, but rather become the sources of, further mediating activity.

There are, however, some silences that are experienced, not to open up new possibilities of mediating activity, but to forbid them – silences that Dauenhauer analyzes as instances of the phenomenon of "terminal silence" (p. 75). The "terminal silence" declares in a particular situation that no further act of mediation is possible. It is, for example, the silence that refuses to add further interpretation to an utterance, an action or a decision – that declares communication or interpretation, on a particular subject, *closed*. Dauenhauer's choice of the silence of Abraham, in the story of the offering of Isaac as a sacrifice (Genesis 22), as an example of the "terminal silence," points clearly to its theological relevance (p. 112). Following the famous analysis by Kierkegaard,[8] Abraham's silence throughout the story – speaking only to reinforce his determination to keep silent – is the deliberate refusal of mediating activity, because no "mediation" of his solitary decision of faith is possible. His silence reveals the limited character of all discourses, all attempts at mediation or interpretation – they cannot encompass or comprehend Abraham's decision, and his silence challenges any claim on their part to completeness or self-sufficiency.

The idea of a "terminal silence" is particularly relevant in the context of contemporary thought, because it has so often been suggested that the twentieth century confronts Western languages or cultures with a termi-

---

[8]   Søren Kierkegaard, *Fear and Trembling; Repetition*, trans. Edna H. Hong and Howard V. Hong (Princeton: Princeton University Press, 1983).

nal silence. George Steiner's essays on *Language and Silence* uncover in various aspects of the twentieth-century experience the fragility of linguistic mediation and the possibility of its collapse into silence. Most importantly, Steiner discerns the pull towards a terminal silence – of "literature," but by implication of all new verbal mediations – in the face of the brutally unspeakable event of the *Shoah*.

> There is a widespread intimation, though as yet only vaguely defined, of a certain exhaustion of verbal resources in modern civilisation, of a brutalisation and devaluation of the word . . . The question of whether the poet should speak or be silent, of whether language is in a condition to accord with his needs, is a real one. "No poetry after Auschwitz," said Adorno.[9]

Steiner's account of the "silence of the poets," and of all the silences kept after the *Shoah*, raises very sharply the question of the "meaningfulness" of this silence. Is it a silence that "speaks" more profoundly than words do, that opens up another dimension of meaning, that is in some way "eloquent of God" as the silences of mystical poets are?[10] Or is it a silence that discloses only the "exhaustion of verbal resources," the collapse of all attempts at making sense of the world?[11]

While not discussing this historical context, Dauenhauer does suggest that the phenomenon of "terminal silence" pushes us towards questions about the ultimate ontological significance of silence. The terminal silence reveals the limitation of all particular utterances and of the whole "signitive domain" – the whole human enterprise of making sense of the world. It could thus be taken, he suggests, to signal either ultimate "futility" or "union with the Absolute" as the end to which all human utterances point. The phenomenon itself, he suggests, does not allow a decision for either, although it allows both possibilities to be entertained; a definitive conclusion about the significance of "terminal silence" would "outrun the available evidence" (pp. 160–1). Although he uses examples from religious practice and theological tradition – liturgical silence and silent prayer as examples of "deep silence," and Kierkegaard's reading of the silence of Abraham as an example of the "terminal silence," not to mention dis-

---

[9] George Steiner, *Language and Silence: Essays 1958–1966* (Harmondsworth: Penguin, 1969), pp. 67, 75.
[10] Ibid., p. 60.
[11] See Graham Ward, "In the Daylight Forever? Language and Silence," in *Silence and the Word: Negative Theology and Incarnation*, ed. Denys Turner and Oliver Davies (Cambridge: Cambridge University Press 2002) for a more extended reading of Steiner in terms of these two alternatives.

cussions of the place of silence in Buddhist and Daoist thought – Dauen-hauer is nonetheless clear that "nothing about silence itself . . . justifies the formulation of claims concerning God's existence or nature" (p. 172).

The phenomenology of silence suggests an initial framework within which "silence" can meaningfully be spoken about; but at the same time it declares its own inability to answer questions at the crucial point of the contemporary interrogation of silence – at the junction of theology, pol-itics, and ethics. Is it the case that our finite attempts at meaning-making give way only to "ultimate futility" or to wordless union with the "Absolute?" Or is this, perhaps, as has been suggested in response to Steiner's similar claims, a false dichotomy, based on an equally false deci-sion to absorb all attempts at sense-making into a "terminal silence?"[12] After all, Dauenhauer's own account suggests that the concept of a "ter-minal silence" is problematic; the phenomenon of silence, as ordinarily experienced, is such as to render questionable any attempt to make some utterance the "last word," or to forbid further speech.

Phenomenological analysis of silence cannot, of itself, give us a theol-ogy; nor does it seem to give us an ethics. Talking about silence as "binding and joining" and as "opening the way" for new mediating activ-ities, however, seems to leave open a set of questions about the agency of silence. Does it make a difference *who* keeps silence, and towards what end? Does it make a difference, to the nature of the silence or of the utterances it makes possible, to what "givens" one attends and responds? Does it make a difference if the given is a person – so that silence is a response, not to something, but to someone?

Questions like these lie behind the very different approaches to silence taken by those thinkers who begin their work, not from phenomenology and the study of general features of human experience, but from com-munication theory, conversational analysis and the study of what silence "means" in particular contexts. The meanings of silences, for those who follow this course, are only determinable within particular contexts – as is the fact that any particular silence is meaningful, or communicatively relevant, at all.

Even if silence is not just the same as speech, particular acts of keeping silence do "say" something. We know that, sometimes, "silence gives consent," and that sometimes it rather refuses consent; we encounter silences of approval, disapproval, rebellion, disquiet, contentment. Particular acts of keeping silence do not *only* indicate the element of the pre-given and of the nondeterminate in all communication; they are also, themselves,

---

[12]   See Ward, "In the Daylight Forever?"

communicative. Studying the enormous range of cultural and political significances of silence raises the question of whether there is any sense in talking about silence *as such* in abstraction from particular silences. What could be the justification, after all, for placing the silence kept with the bereaved in western Apache culture[13] together with the silence of a defendant refusing to answer questions in a British court[14] and the silence of a Quaker meeting for worship[15] as examples of a single "phenomenon?"[16]

An approach that focuses on the contexts – cultural, social, and political – in which the meanings of silence are determined also suggests the ethical questions that the simple investigation of "silence, the phenomenon" may tend to obscure. Silence can be a shield to protect the powerful from public scrutiny; or a condition imposed from above on the powerless; or a mask for conflicts that are never permitted to emerge or be resolved. If we think about the silence imposed by totalitarian regimes on their critics, the silence of the prisoner in solitary confinement, the silence of an abused woman too scared to cry for help – on what basis can we assert that the "true" significance of any of these silences has to do with human freedom, or with the acceptance of finitude? Is it not irresponsible to interpret "silence" as a single phenomenon, and hence to obscure its function in violence and abuse?[17] To call an interpretation of silence "irresponsible" then raises the question of how and whether silence itself can be a "responsible" act – an ethically significant response to the requirements of a particular situation or a particular other. Analyses of silence on these lines remind us again of the importance of asking *who* keeps silence, and in relation to whom.

What are the implications, for a theological ethics of communication, of the conflicting tendencies found within talk about silence? In the first

---

[13] K. H. Basso, "To Give up on Words: Silence in Western Apache Culture," in *Language and Social Context*, ed. Pier P. Giglioli (Harmondsworth: Penguin 1972).

[14] Dennis Kurzon, "The Right of Silence: A Socio-Pragmatic Model of Interpretation," *Journal of Pragmatics* 23, 1 (1995).

[15] Richard Bauman, *Let Your Words Be Few: Symbolism of Speaking and Silence among Seventeenth-Century Quakers* (Cambridge: Cambridge University Press 1983); see also chapter 6.

[16] See further Deborah Tannen and Muriel Savile-Troike, *Perspectives on Silence* (Norwood, NJ: Ablex 1985), and especially the introductory essay by Savile-Troike, for accounts of this differentiated approach to silence in communication studies.

[17] Langdon Gilkey, in responding to Dauenhauer's book, describes his experience in a Japanese prisoner-of-war camp, which included the extensive experience of solitary confinement. Silence in those circumstances, he writes, is "in no sense a form of *self-expression*," and appears as the absolute negation of communication. Langdon Gilkey, "The Political Meaning of Silence," in *Philosophy Today* 27, 2 (1983).

place, I shall affirm, within this study, the basic insight that silence is not the equivalent either of speech or of its absence; and the further insight, that to regard silence in this way requires some wider claim about the nature of existence. I have already indicated the presence of silence as a "phenomenon" both in theological texts and in Christian practice. I shall assume that the keeping of silence can be a right response to the prior givenness of a context of speech and action, a response that reveals and enacts human freedom. At the same time, I want to take seriously the distortions of communicative situations that can make such a "responsible silence" impossible; and I want to suggest that an undifferentiated statement about silence as such, that affirms it as a phenomenon with positive significance, would be politically and ethically irresponsible. This latter suggestion is particularly important in the light of twentieth-century critiques of acts of violent silencing, historical and contemporary.

Above all, the question about the "who" – "Who keeps silence?"– must, I shall claim, be central to the treatment of silence in the theological ethics of communication. An ethics of communication must ask about the persons whose silence is being theorized and evaluated; a theological account of silence must ask about the place of silence in the identity and the self-identification of God. In thinking about the latter point, however, we seem to go beyond the limits of both phenomenology and conversation analysis.

God's Silence

Nothing creaturely is so like God as silence. (Meister Eckhart, *Deutsche Predigten Und Traktaten*[18])

O Sabbath rest by Galilee!
O calm of hills above,
Where Jesus knelt to share with Thee

[18] Meister Eckhart, *Deutsche Predigten Und Traktaten*, trans. J. Quint (Munich: Carl Hanser, 1955), p. 367; ". . . *aber gleicht nichts in allen Kreaturen Gott so sehr wie Ruhe.*" The English translation of the Quint volume (Meister Eckhart, *German Sermons and Treatises*, trans. M. O'C. Walshe, 2 vols., vol. 2 (London: Watkins, 1981), p. 14.) translates *Ruhe* as "rest" rather than "silence;" accuracy would appear to lie somewhere in between, but the quotation is more widely known as referring to "silence" (for an example of its more popular usage, see Joachim-Ernst Berendt, *The Third Ear: On Listening to the World*, trans. Tim Nevill (Shaftesbury: Element, 1988), p. 102).

The silence of eternity
Interpreted by love!
(John Greenleaf Whittier, "The Brewing of Soma"[19])

The "deep silences" of which Dauenhauer speaks can be interpreted, as he himself realizes, as gestures toward God – God as the context in which the finitude and the freedom of human utterance is defined. Within theological tradition, there is a persisting claim that silence is a particularly appropriate gesture toward God; silence is that creaturely reality that is least unlike God.[20] Monastic writers associated the difficulties they encountered in speaking about their practices of silence with the difficulties of speaking about God;[21] a rich tradition of mystical theology takes up Pseudo-Dionysius' prayer for ascent to the "brilliant darkness of a hidden silence."[22] If we accept this, to say that "God is silent" is not only to describe our experience of a particular historical moment; it is to say something about how, or who, God is.

The phenomenological analysis of silence, discussed above, indicates certain respects in which it might be the case that "nothing is so like God as silence." To affirm God as Creator – as recent studies in mystical theology have recalled – is to affirm that God is different from the world, in a way that transcends all the ways in which things within the world differ one from another. Speech is appropriate for distinguishing created things one from another; but silence, in going beyond all the distinctions speech can make, is the best communicative "likeness" for the God who transcends all the distinctions between created things. We can go further; it is suggested that silence is neither the absence of speech nor its equivalent. It does not differ from utterances in the way that they differ one from another, and it does not differ from them as simply their negation or their absence, and yet it is in some way related to them. A very similar account of the relations of "difference" between God and creation under-

[19] John Greenleaf Whittier, "The Brewing of Soma"; reprinted in part in *Quaker Faith and Practice: The Book of Christian Discipline of the Religious Society of Friends (Quakers) in Britain*, (London: Quaker Home Service, 1994), extract 20.03.

[20] Noting that there is a difference between the claims "there is nothing so like God as silence" and "silence is like God;" the former continues to emphasize the *lack* of resemblance between God and creatures. Compare Denys Turner, *The Darkness of God: Negativity and Christian Mysticism* (Cambridge: Cambridge University Press, 1995), p. 35.

[21] See on this Paul F. Gehl, "Competens Silentium: Varieties of Monastic Silence in the Medieval West," in *Viator* (1987), 125–6.

[22] Pseudo-Dionysius, *Mystical Theology, in the Complete Works*, trans. Colm Luibheid (New York: Paulist, 1987), p. 997.

lies the practice of apophatic theology – not simply denying all creaturely attributes of God, but denying even their negation.[23]

The paradox here is that to say silence is in some way "like" God is apparently to say nothing of what God is "like." It is, rather, to indicate how God's nature transcends our ways of comprehending it. More than this, it is, within the patristic and medieval traditions of negative theology, to say that God's nature is *as such* incomprehensible; not, then, that we happen not to have the right set of verbal or conceptual tools, but that the subject matter itself cannot be spoken or conceived. Saying that God is silent, or that "nothing is so like God as silence," is, for these theologians, not only saying something about our own inability to comprehend God; it is saying something about who God is in Godself, even if it is a paradoxical "something," a something that does not enable us to claim comprehension of God.

I have said that I attempt, in this book, to articulate a way of thinking about silence, and especially about God's silence, that neither reduces it to an absence of speech nor absorbs it into speech. In doing this, I shall affirm the importance of acknowledging a silence of God that is *not* just the reverse side of the limitations of people's knowledge of God; and a silence of God that has something to do, not only with how God is in relation to the world, but with who God is in relation to Godself. Learning from the extended analyses of silence undertaken within non-theological disciplines, however, produces the need to ask further questions about the silence of God – what kind of silence is it, and what does it do? Most importantly, as the prerequisite for an answer to any of these questions – who is the God who keeps it?

The key insight I take from the studies in communication theory, used above to qualify the idea of silence as a single "phenomenon" with an "ontological significance," is that silence as communicative practice is relational and personal. In order to understand silence, we must ask: who keeps silence? And in relation to whom? Is any particular silence the denial of personhood, the suppression of a relationship, the closing off of all further possibilities of communication; or is it a silence that opens up such possibilities? The answer in any case, as this discussion has already suggested, cannot be given on the level of the analysis of silence as such. When we are talking about the silence that forms the ground of all our utterances, the context of their freedom and finitude, there is no particular reason, from the analysis of silence, to interpret it as a silence that relates to us rather than as a silence that cuts off – as if uttered into a void

[23]   On which see Turner, *Darkness of God.*

– all our attempts at meaning-making. In fact, everything depends, in this matter, on whether and how the silence of eternity is truly "interpreted by love."

I shall be exploring here, in conjunction both with philosophical and ethical accounts of silence and with biblical and theological tradition, what it means for the "silence of eternity" to be the silence of the God who is love. There is, however, a problem with an account of divine silence that would make it in some way fundamental to who God is. How can such an account be given in the light of the far stronger biblical and traditional assertion that God *speaks*? God does – so it is repeatedly asserted within Christian theology – reveal Godself within creation in ways that both have the character of speech and can be spoken about, and does not hide in silence; and this speech of God in creation is grounded in the identity of God. In the context of the belief that God speaks and has spoken a definitive Word in which God is fully revealed, the attribution of silence to God can easily appear misleading, erroneous, even dangerous.

Such a challenge from the perspective of Christian theology is mirrored by external challenges to "poor little talkative Christianity."[24] Raoul Mortley, in an important historical account of the philosophical and theological meanings of silence, argues that Christian theology was never able to appropriate the great "leap into silence" taken by the Neoplatonic philosophers.[25] Silence, he claims, both as a practice and as a supposed divine attribute, was too anti-institutional, too subversive of any given way of knowing God, for a theology grounded in a definitive and comprehensive revelation. As I shall explore in my next chapter, an implicit and explicit critique of the supposed inability of Christian theology adequately to think silence is articulated in contemporary feminist thought. Here, the critique is linked to a specifically ethical and political concern. Christian speech, and Christianity's emphasis on speech, is interpreted as an attempt to seize and maintain control, not only over the expression and conceptualization of divinity, but thereby over the capacity to shape social structures and values.

A theology, and especially a theological ethics, that takes silence seriously has to respond to these challenges. In response to the suggestion that it is wrong to focus on divine silence in the context of Christian assertions that God speaks, it would be possible simply to say that this work is a correction of the theological balance. If God has so often and

---

[24]   E. M. Forster, *A Passage to India* (London: Arnold, 1929).
[25]   Raoul Mortley, *From Word to Silence*, 2 vols., vol. 2 (Bonn: Hanstein, 1986), p. 254.

consistently been named and thought as one who speaks, we need to disturb the predominance of that way of naming and thinking God – lest a limited understanding of God and God's action be substituted for the fullness of God's mystery. Since both "speech" and "silence" as we know them are inadequate representations of God's reality, the dominance of either of them as a characterization of God needs to be questioned.

More than this, and taking up the challenges put forward in feminist thought, I argue that the dominance of certain models of God's communication, based around the claim that God speaks, has significant and problematic ethical implications. It is not simply a matter of theorizing how God is to be named; the naming of God as a speaker, and the ways in which that speech is conceptualized, has direct implications for practices and structures of communication. If women have been silenced by the naming of God as a speaker, that is reason enough to question that naming of God.

In the final analysis, however, I am not only *using* the idea of "God's silence," either as one metaphor among many to demonstrate the inadequacy of all our words for speaking about God, or as the starting point for a better theological ethic of communication. Recalling the basic insight gained above from earlier Christian theological accounts of the silence of God, I am claiming that we cannot speak rightly about who God is without speaking about God's silence – as "the silence of eternity interpreted by love."

How can this claim be made within Christian theology? It is around the person of Christ, as Word of God, that theological reflection on God's communication – with all its ethical and political implications – has centered. I shall suggest that it is also in Christology that the basis for an understanding of God's silence is found. Subsequent chapters develop, in conversations with contemporary theology, the interpretation of the silences of the incarnate Word. We should remember, however, that from the early centuries of Christian theology we can find examples of reflection on the idea that the one who is himself the Word may keep silent – or may be rendered silent. For some interpreters, the silence of the dead Christ is the completion of the incarnation – the point at which the Word becomes most fully flesh. At the same time, Christ's silence can mark the hiddenness, weakness and foolishness of the Word of God in the world. Christ is made not only silent, but mute and passive. Christ's silence in one sense conceals nothing; but at the same time it apparently claims no power to communicate itself.

In this book I develop an account of the silence of God to which Christology, and reflection on the silences of Christ, is integral. My account focuses around the idea of God's listening. It is appropriate, I shall claim, to understand God as one who keeps a *listening* silence, and that this is the silence that forms the determinative context for human freedom and finitude. I develop, then, the claim that God listens, that God's listening is integral to understanding who God is both in relation to Godself and in relation to the world, and that this listening in turn shapes who people are in relation to God and to each other. In naming God as one who listens, I focus attention on God's hearing of God's own Word – the Word silenced within the world but heard by God. I characterize the resurrection as God's hearing of God's Word and of creation, and link this with the recognition that this hearing in love is intrinsic to who God is.

The claim that God listens, and that God's listening can be basic to our understanding of God, has, as I shall indicate, biblical and traditional antecedents, and has been restated in Christian feminist theology. Its wider significance for theological ethics, which is all the greater in the contemporary situation, has never been fully recognized. Considering the activity of listening enables us to articulate theologically both the hope for a communicative situation not dominated by the "war of words," and the ethical importance of aspects of communication often neglected in theorizing about such a situation. The silence of those who listen, and the formation of the capacity for listening and discernment, is central to the theological ethics of communication I shall put forward here.

In developing this focus on listening, as will become clear in the first two chapters, I am in fact seeking to avoid the dichotomous division of "speech" and "silence" assumed in accounts such as Mortley's – and in a range of (particularly, modern) attempts to impose "silence" on particular topics. A "silence" set in unmediated opposition to speech and other communicative activity – as opposed to a silence that admits, gives rise to, and is nourished by communication – can rightly be criticized as ethically, politically, and theologically inadequate. Simply to think about "keeping" silence, an activity of persons over time with a relational context, is already to think beyond such a dichotomy.

Listening to Whom?

Any theological text reflects its author's own acts of listening, through the ways in which others are heard contributing to or questioning the argument. Among the various such acts of listening reflected in this book, two are particularly significant. One has already been discussed – attention to the feminist thinkers, both within and without theological discourse, who put the key questions about the contemporary meanings of silence and the ethics of communication, and whose answers to those questions I seek to develop. The other is my extended consideration of the theology of Dietrich Bonhoeffer.

Why listen to Bonhoeffer, rather than anyone else, on the subject of silence and the theological ethics of communication at the beginning of the twenty-first century? The English-speaking theological world knew him first, and perhaps still knows him best, as the proponent of a "religionless Christianity" appropriate to the "godless" world. His famous reflections about the need for a radical shift in, among other things, the communicative practices of Christianity arise, however, from a much longer engagement with questions about the theology and ethics of communication, centered throughout on Christology – thinking about what it means for the Word of God to be silent, about what Christian practices of silence can mean, and about what ethics of communication were appropriate to a political situation dominated by the power of a single voice. More than this, as my discussion will show, his thoughts about silence are integrally related, both to his understanding of who God is and to the way he relates theology and ethics. In essence, I claim that Bonhoeffer's theology provides the starting point for a Christologically-focused theological ethics of communication centered on silence.

Reflecting on Bonhoeffer's thought in this area requires, however, a particular approach to reading his work. I try, in my discussion, to listen to the silences in Bonhoeffer's texts and in the other texts I read. Thus, I pay particular attention in my reading to little-developed claims that appear to counterbalance or contradict what is said elsewhere; to statements the significance of which is never made apparent; and to unfinished or fragmentary discussions. This is, in itself, not unusual; but listening to a theologian's silences is commonly undertaken with one of two purposes in mind – to expose the defects in his or her system, possibly with a view to showing how the system can be complemented; or to explain those silences by reference to the theologian's life or other works.

In my reading, I do identify points at which the "silences" in Bonhoeffer's theology open it to criticism – particularly from the perspective of the feminist thinkers to whom I also listen – and vice versa. I do, also, read each text in the context of others, both earlier and in the light of the historical and personal circumstances within which it was produced. My aim is, however, to use the silences as occasions, not for the condemnation or the defense of their author, but for listening to the texts in a way that takes them "beyond" themselves.

This listening takes place within the fundamental context that Bonhoeffer's texts themselves assume – the context of God's responsible silence, God's listening to God's own Word and therein to the whole of created reality. It is this context that relates the text to its reader and to the other voices to which she attends, and which makes non-arbitrary "new" ways of speaking and hearing possible. I treat the central silences I identify within the texts I read as signs of God's responsible silence. I consider, therefore, that they cannot adequately be "filled" by restatements of doctrines or of ethical claims, nor by biographical or bibliographic details. Nor, importantly, can they be "filled" by combining the author's thought with that of others. The response to these silences is, rather, creative reflection that takes seriously the text's own claim to be "grounded" in a reality that cannot fully be brought to speech.[26] Reading theological texts within the context of God's listening calls for a kind of "faithful" listening not limited to the accurate reproduction of the author's voice. I attempt, in this book, not only to theorize this faithful listening, but to experiment with its practice.

Overview of Contents

The first chapter concentrates on listening to feminist thinkers – including feminist theologians – as they put forward analyses and critiques of the many ways in which women have been silenced in theology and in other areas of discourse; and to an analysis and critique from within Christian theology of the many ways in which God has been silenced in the modern world. Both of these accounts of silencing, as I read them, tend to make the assumption that agency in communication rests wholly or mainly with the speaker – in other words, that silence cannot be rightly or usefully thought of as communicative activity. In feminist thought, however, this assumption is problematized, with the recognition of women's complicity in their own "silencing," and of the acts of silencing of which feminist discourse has itself been guilty. There is a recognition

---

[26]   The mode of reading used here is similar in general approach and presuppositions, though not in the details of the technique, to the "pragmatic" reading described by Peter Ochs and applied in his work to the writings of Peirce: Peter Ochs, *Peirce, Pragmatism and the Logic of Scripture* (Cambridge: Cambridge University Press, 1998). It relies on careful attention to the text's "plain sense" but is not limited to an exposition thereof. It identifies problems in the "plain sense" as invitations to a *pragmatic* rereading, the possibility of which relies ultimately on a "common ground" between text and reader, and which does not claim to provide a final or definitive "clarification" of the text.

that, if this kind of oppressive silencing is to end, the communicative situation must be fundamentally transformed; and some attempts to imagine
that transformation involve the rethinking of what silence means.

The feminist theologian Nelle Morton is well known for her concept
of "hearing into speech," which she develops theologically with the
counter-intuitive claim that the "first cause is hearing," and the questions
that pervade her writing: "Who hears? Who is heard?". In the second
chapter, I look at Morton's thought alongside the philosophy of Gemma
Corradi Fiumara, whose approach to the ethics of communication gives
priority to listening, and analyze the questions "Who hears? Who is
heard?" as they denote two forms of silence – the silence of the listener,
and the "silence of unknowability" signifying the freedom of the one who
is listened to. Questions then arise about the theological development of
such readings of silence. How can God be affirmed as the source and aim
of a changed ethics of communication, without re-imposing powerful
divine speech in a way that negates the aims of feminist thought?

Reading Morton's questions as theological – as questions about God as
the one "who hears" and "who is heard" – the third chapter outlines the
basic framework of my response to these problems, through a discussion
of Bonhoeffer's theology of the resurrection. The key categories of
Bonhoeffer's thought on which my reading is based are set out: the resurrection as that which determines the asking and answering of the "Who?"
question in relation to Christ; closely linked with this, the resurrection as
the "place to stand," the hidden basis for action and reflection from which a
response to the world is possible; and the interpretation of ethical life in
terms of the "relation between reality and realization." I argue that this set
of categories enables us to speak about God's silence of unknowability – the
resurrection as a "hidden" reality – and God's silence as a listener's silence –
the resurrection as reality being "realized," as God hears God's own Word
and thereby hears the world into new possibilities.

In each of the subsequent chapters, further reflection on the naming
of God as one who hears – and hence on the "reality" of the resurrection for God and for the world in relation to God – is closely bound up
with the analysis of particular practices of communication, thinking
through an ethics of communication alongside the development of the
theology. In the fourth chapter, I begin my consideration of what it would
mean for a communicative situation to be transformed in the light of the
resurrection as God's hearing of God's own Word. The resurrection does
not mean that the powerful Word of God reduces all other words to
silence, but rather that the whole situation of speaking, silence, and listening must be reconfigured Christologically.

Feminist critiques of Christian theology's acts of "silencing" have focused on the characterization of humanity as silent or passive vis-à-vis the powerful Word of God. The fifth chapter suggests how a theology of divine hearing – of the world together with the divine Word – can respond to this critique, and can shift the focus of an ethic of communication toward an emphasis on the capacity for listening. Analyzing specific texts of Bonhoeffer's theology, I argue that his work points to a deep concern for a contemporary communicative situation in which there is "too much talk" and not enough silence, in which the capacity for listening and discernment has been lost, and in which the recognition of the resurrection as "place to stand" and as divine act of hearing provides the possible basis for a recovery of that capacity.

The sixth chapter examines practices of communication – to which silence is fundamental – in which this "reconfiguration" might be seen. I consider Bonhoeffer's lectures on "spiritual care," in which the mediation of communication in Christ – the resurrection as common "place to stand" – is a central idea. This Christological mediation of communication establishes, first, the "unknowability" of the other – the impossibility either of exercising control over her or of subjecting oneself entirely to her words. Practices of silence, described in the lectures on spiritual care, signify and enact this unknowability.

Responsible silence as Christians practice it – in relationships of "spiritual care" and elsewhere – does not, however, merely signify and enact unknowability. More importantly, people can learn to "hear with God's ears," and hence to be drawn into God's act of hearing with love. The keeping of silence can make any given practice of communication open to transformations, which are not anticipated in advance but which can reflect the innerworldly realization of divine reality. Two aspects of such transformation in and through practices of communication are the learning of ethical discernment and the emergence of friendship. Taking these seriously in the context of thinking about "hearing with God's ears," I suggest, both relies on and enriches an understanding of the resurrection as reality *for God* – God's self-determination as love.

Both the idea of the "unknowability" of the other and the question of what it means to "hear with God's ears" are developed further in the seventh chapter. Here, I use the idea of "knowing by hearing" as part of a response to contemporary debates on the question of privacy. The aspect of personal "unknowability" – which prevents the person from being "silenced" by reduction to a fully comprehensible object of knowledge – is a point of contact with the modern concern for privacy. However, the terms in which the concern for privacy is couched – which require knowledge to be understood as controllable and defensible property, and which even affect some recent accounts of divine omniscience – are called into question by the Christological understanding of God's "hearing knowledge" developed in this thesis. "Hearing knowledge" is inseparable from relationships of responsibility and love, and from the formation of persons over time in relation to others. I am not rejecting the importance of privacy and reserve for the ethics of communication; in fact, the concern for privacy is linked ultimately to the concern, voiced repeatedly throughout my discussion, to say something about the reality of God in Godself.

The concluding chapter suggests further possible implications of this account of "God's responsible silence." Some of these relate to theology's own ethics of communication – for responses to acts of silencing, for biblical interpretation and for the reading of theological texts. Beyond this, however, I attempt to open up consideration of the wider consequences of an ethics of communication that takes "responsible silence" seriously.

Openings are, not accidentally, a theme of the conclusion. One of my key claims about practices of communication is that both writers and readers, speakers and hearers, should seek to hold utterances and texts open for further acts of hearing – an openness that does not preclude, but rather relies on, present commitment to specific claims and contexts, in the universal but also specific context of God's act of hearing. I have sought to do justice to, and to maintain, the openness of the texts I read. For the future openness of my own text, I am dependent on others.

Chapter One

ASSESSING SILENCE

Introduction

Wovon man nicht sprechen kann, darüber muss man schweigen. (Ludwig
Wittgenstein, *Tractatus Logico-Philosophicus*[1])

The technology of silence
The rituals, etiquette

the blurring of terms
silence not absence

of words or music or even
raw sounds

Silence can be a plan
rigorously executed

the blueprint to a life

It is a presence
it has a history   a form

Do not confuse it
with any kind of absence
(Adrienne Rich, "Cartographies of silence"[2])

---

[1] Ludwig Wittgenstein, *Tractatus Logico-Philosophicus*, trans. D. F. Pears and B. F. McGuinness
(London: Routledge, 1961), p. 150. See also ibid., p. 2. "Whereof we cannot speak, that we
must *pass over* in silence" is a slight overtranslation of Wittgenstein's sentence (part of the
problem being the lack of a good English equivalent of *schweigen*). I use it in what follows
because the resonance it brings out in the original phrase is particularly relevant to the subject
at hand – while recognizing that the original is open to other interpretations.
[2] "Cartographies of silence," in Adrienne Rich, *The Dream of a Common Language: Poems
1974–1977* (New York: W. W. Norton & Company, 1978), p. 17.

How do we know what it is that cannot be spoken about and must therefore be passed over in silence? Wittgenstein's famous sentence appears at
both the beginning and the end of his *Tractatus Logico-Philosophicus*. He
announces the discovery of the "whereof we cannot speak" as his project,
and marks its completion after the limitations of the speakable have been
thoroughly explored and defined – through language.[3] We might say that
the silence at the end of the book has been defined by the words that
precede it. The sentence that initially appears as a truism – of course we
must be silent about the "whereof we cannot speak" – has acquired
definite content, even if that content is by definition indescribable. The
fact that the sentence is so often quoted in a wide variety of contexts
draws attention to the transferability of the concept of the "whereof we
cannot speak," how it can be redetermined in different discourses – how
silence can come to mean, or refer to, many different things. As it stands,
the aphorism places a non-specified subject (*man*, "one") over against an
equally unspecified – and apparently impersonal – object (*wovon, darüber,*
"that which"). It is not an injunction to anyone in particular about
anything in particular – it is a general statement about the limits of
speech, rather as Dauenhauer aims at a general account of "silence, the
phenomenon."

The extract from Adrienne Rich's poem brings us back into the particular social contexts in which silence occurs and is maintained – "the technology of silence/the rituals, etiquette." The apparent ahistoricality of the
"man" in Wittgenstein's aphorism is challenged by such a rereading; already
the reader is forced to ask who "we" are who cannot speak of this or that.
The question about that "whereof we cannot speak" is not just a question
about what is, as such, incapable of being conveyed in language; it is a question about that whereof *we* in a particular situation or discursive context
"cannot speak," and how we maintain its unspeakability.

Rich's poem, then, indicates the complexity of the silence that is kept
concerning that "whereof we cannot speak." Silence has its "technology,"
the set of techniques by which it is achieved; but this is a communicative
and social technology, consisting of "rituals" and "etiquette." Silence has
"history" and "form;" so this description refers not to silence in general,
but to some silence in particular, which in its specificity is not to be confused with "any kind of absence."

The second verse quoted above points to the more specific concern of
Rich's poem, and indeed of much of her work. With the claim that
"silence can be a plan," the question immediately arises, "Whose plan?"

---

[3]   See Wittgenstein, *Tractatus*, p. 2: *"Die Grenze wird . . . nur in der Sprache gezogen werden."*

The challenge to the impersonality of Wittgenstein's *man* becomes sharper, as the possibility is raised that the consignment of something to the "whereof we cannot speak" is an act involving violence and allowing the assignation of responsibility.[4] "Rigorously executed" reinforces the suspicion that this is a plan to impose silence, a plan that both carries out and conceals violence *(who* might have been "executed" in the "execution" of this plan of silence?). The "technology" of silence becomes the means whereby the violent silencing is maintained.

The rituals and etiquette are structured to ensure that something remains unsaid. However, at the same time, they maintain the silence *as* a particular silence – giving it "a presence . . . a history, a form." Whether or not the silence can be referred back to some original act ("a plan/ rigorously executed"), the silence itself becomes a "presence" through the rituals of concealment.[5] The apparatus of secrecy in a totalitarian state, or the multiple layers of lies required to conceal an initial minor act of concealment, are familiar instances in the political sphere of the massive material "presence" and "form" of silences. The first two parts of Rich's poem consider this presence of silence in the lie that structures a conversation, a relationship or a whole life:

A conversation begins
with a lie . . .

A conversation has other laws
recharges itself with its own

false energy . . .

The loneliness of the liar
living in the formal network of the lie

twisting the dials to drown the terror
beneath the unsaid word[6]

The question, "Whose plan is this silence?" or "Who has determined what it is whereof we cannot speak?" raises the further question, "Who

[4] See also the foreword to Adrienne Rich, *Of Lies, Secrets and Silence: Selected Prose 1966–1978* (London: Virago, 1980), pp. 9–18.
[5] The uncovering of such acts of silencing through the "presences" of silence they create is one common description of the task of critical or suspicious reading, feminist or otherwise. See for a concise statement and discussion of the understanding of "silence" implied by this, Jack Bilmas, "Constituting Silence: Life in the World of Total Meaning" *Semiotica* 98, 1–2 (1994).
[6] "Cartographies of Silence," 1 and 2.

keeps silent?" Rich's claim that silence can be "the blueprint to a life" suggests that a discourse's limits can be defined such that not only possible subject matter, but also possible speakers are excluded.[7] The "history" and "technology" of silence can prevent a given speaker or group of speakers from entering a discourse or a conversation. For these silenced subjects to speak would require the disruption or destruction of "rituals" and "etiquette," and the rethinking or abandonment of the ways of life that depend on this particular "form" of silence. Yet the very fact that a continued practice of silencing occurs means that the "silence" of the excluded does not disappear into "absence." To be recognized as silent a person or group must be present. Were there nothing "whereof we cannot speak," there would be no need to mark, reinforce or debate the limits of possible speech.

To say that silence is "not absence" is to recall, not only the possibility of future speech from the one who is silent, but the fact that the "silenced" have their own history – and possibly their own speech, which is currently unheard. Defining silence as "absence" is part of the pretence by which silencing is maintained – the pretence that there is nothing there to be heard. The silencing of potential speakers perpetuates a lie.

Why does this form of silencing matter? Rich's poem points to two interconnected aspects of the experience of the silenced. On the one hand, silence becomes "the blueprint for a life;" being silenced is being unable to determine oneself as a speaker and thus to identify oneself by speaking. It is having one's life shaped by the silence imposed by another. On the other hand, silence is confused with "absence;" being silenced is being unrecognizable and unable to demand recognition within a social world ("the rituals, etiquette").[8] Both of these are contained in the suggestion that to be silenced is to be depersonalized. The silence in Rich's poem is an "it," from which a possible "who" emerges gradually and ambiguously.

Rich is describing the silencing of lesbian women, the restriction of their lives by lies and secrets; but the basic dynamics of silencing to which her work points can be recognized in numerous contexts. In fact, it has been argued that modernity has seen the greatest possible act of silencing – the silencing of God.

---

[7] Rich's work, both poetry and prose, analyzes the silencing of lesbian women both as objects of discourse and as speakers. The denial of the very existence of lesbian women is in Rich's understanding part of the process by which all women are silenced. See Rich, *Of Lies, Secrets and Silence*, pp. 9–18.

[8] As we shall see, certain forms of silencing deprive their "objects" of the former (the power to be a speaker) but not of the latter (recognition).

The Silencing of God

Although it has often been suggested that God is silent, or that "silence" can appropriately refer to God, it is also the case that the "silence of God" as experienced in any historical context will have a specific "history" and "form." Today, then, to speak of the "silence of God" is most often to refer to the prevalence of atheism, and of modes of discourse that apparently presuppose atheism. If this silence of God ceased even to appear as silence – if the word "God" or the possibility of a word from God were no longer thinkable – the silence of God would cease to have "a history, a form." This is not yet entirely the case. The silence of God is a "presence;" it is still thought necessary to deny that God speaks. The silence of God has a "form" – for example, as the impossibility of authoritative/authorial speech.[9] More significantly, the silence of God has a "history." Its origins in certain specifically modern experiences of the world have been traced and discussed.[10] God is silent because our speech and thought proceeds without hearing a word from or about God. Many have spoken of the "silence of God" in the context of the twentieth century's experience of unassimilable and incomprehensible horror.[11]

One further claim, with which I shall be concerned here, about the history and form of the late modern or postmodern silence of God is that it is the product of theological acts of silencing. The history and form of God's silence can, according to the analysis I shall now consider, be traced within the history of theology, particularly in modernity – within the ways of talking about God that have reduced God to silence. The rules of speech about God, and the theological "etiquette" that reinforces them, have silenced God. Like Rich's descriptions, the attack on the silencing of God argues that silencing is a lie – resting ultimately on the lie that claims self-sufficiency for human thought and action.

---

[9] As most famously in the work of Roland Barthes – see Roland Barthes, "The Death of the Author," trans. Richard Howard, in Sallie Sears, ed., *The Discontinuous Universe: Selected Writings in Contemporary Consciousness* (New York: Basic, 1972). See also Giorgio Agamben, *Language and Death: The Place of Negativity*, trans. Karen Pinkus and Michael Hart (Minneapolis: University of Minnesota Press, 1991).

[10] Perhaps most influentially by Walter Ong – see Walter Ong, *The Presence of the Word: Some Prolegomena for Cultural and Religious History* (New Haven: Yale University Press, 1967).

[11] As in the work of Elie Wiesel – see Elie Wiesel, *Night (& Dawn; the Accident; Three Tales)*, trans. Stella Rodway (London: Robson, 1974), esp. pp. 42, 73–6. See also André Neher, "Shaddai: The God of the Broken Arch," in Alvin H. Rosenfeld & Irving Greenberg, eds., *Confronting the Holocaust: The Impact of Elie Wiesel* (Bloomington: Indiana University Press, 1978).

Analyzing God's Silence

> Compared to atheistic thoughtlessness, this is the much greater danger . . .
> that God will be talked to death, that he is silenced by the very words that
> seek to talk about him. Both . . . the dumb and the garrulous silencing
> of God are the result of the fact that we no longer dare to think God.
> (Eberhard Jüngel, *God as the Mystery of the World*[12])

At the beginning of his work on *God as the Mystery of the World*, Eberhard Jüngel sets out what he takes to be the key problem for contemporary theology – the problem of the silencing of God. This silencing is, Jüngel claims, performed both in atheism – the "dumb silencing" of God – and in theology – the "garrulous silencing" of God. In fact, he will later argue, theology's "garrulous silencing" of God is at least partly responsible for the "dumb silencing" of God in modern atheism. A kind of God-talk that effectively silences God has made it possible for subsequent thought simply to ignore the question of God.[13]

Jüngel's critique of the modern "silencing of God" follows Karl Barth, and twentieth-century theology that reflects on and develops Barth's work, in interpreting the turn to the human subject in theology as a refusal to admit the possibility of God's speech. What is at stake is the freedom of God to speak for Godself, or, more precisely, to speak Godself as the basis for all possible speech about God. Not "daring to think God" is not daring to think God *as* God, that is, as the self-identifying subject of theological discourse, the one whose freedom to speak and become known in the world is in no way constrained by the limitations of human knowledge, thought, or speech; whose speech, indeed, is the "condition of possibility" for human knowledge, thought and speech (p. 227).

---

[12]   Eberhard Jüngel, *God as the Mystery of the World: On the Foundation of the Theology of the Crucified One in the Dispute between Theism and Atheism*, trans. Darrell L. Guder (Grand Rapids: Eerdmans, 1983) p. vii. Subsequent references appear in parentheses in the text.

[13]   This is not intended to be a full overview of Jüngel's complex argument in *God as the Mystery of the World*. For fuller discussion, particularly of the understanding of speech and word that underlies the work, see Ingolf Dalferth, "God and the Mystery of Words," *Journal of the American Academy of Religion*, 60 (1992); Roland Spjuth, *Creation, Contingency and Divine Presence in the Theologies of Thomas F. Torrance and Eberhard Jüngel* (Lund: Lund University Press, 1995), pp. 41–6; Roland Daniel Zimany, *Vehicle for God: The Metaphorical Theology of Eberhard Jüngel* (Macon: Mercer University Press, 1991); John Webster, *Eberhard Jüngel: An Introduction to His Theology* (Cambridge: Cambridge University Press, 1986); John Webster, ed., *The Possibilities of Theology: Studies in the Theology of Eberhard Jüngel in His Sixtieth Year* (Edinburgh: T. & T. Clark, 1994).

But why speak of the *silencing* of God in this connection? What specific aspects of the critique of previous theology and the engagement with modern atheism are named when the silencing of God is denounced? Jüngel locates his discussion of the silencing of God in a chapter on "The Speakability of God," and specifies the problem by referring to the theological use of the conclusion of *Tractatus Logico-Philosophicus* – "Whereof we cannot speak, thereof we must be silent" (p. 250ff.). The *Tractatus* quotation suggests an understanding of silence as being "beyond words" and pertaining to that which is "beyond words." Speech reaches a limit, and whatever lies beyond the limit is consigned to silence. However the limits of possible speech are defined, silence is beyond them.

For Jüngel, what is at issue here is the definition of God's mystery. The use of the quotation from the *Tractatus* (or its theological equivalents) would, he argues, define God's mystery only negatively – as the *inex*-pressible, the *un*knowable, the *un*thinkable. This would in turn render all talk of God "*inauthentic* talk," failing to correspond to the reality of God in any way. It would have defined God as the "whereof we cannot speak" – and thereby, importantly, as something that cannot speak to *us*, the object at the limit of speech that cannot become the speaking subject.

Defining God's mystery negatively, Jüngel suggests, would leave four possibilities open for talk about God:

> *a*) It is possible to *remain silent* about God and in that silence to *affirm* him, since he is totally unthinkable and therefore unspeakable . . .
> *b*) It is possible to *speak* of God as the one who is totally unthinkable and therefore unspeakable, and in speaking to *negate* him . . .
> *c*) It is possible to *remain silent* about God as one who is totally unthinkable and therefore unspeakable, and in remaining silent to *negate* him . . .
> *d*) It is possible to speak of God as one who is not unthinkable in every regard and thus is somehow speakable, and in speaking thus to affirm him . . . *non ut illud diceretur, sed non* [sic] *taceretur omnino.*[14] (p. 252)

Jüngel's judgment on these four possibilities – which he links respectively to mysticism,[15] to atheism, to a point "beyond atheism" where the question of God no longer arises, and to "theism, deism, and . . . the meta-

---

[14] Augustine of Hippo, *De Trinitate* 5 : 9 has *ne taceretur* – "Not in order to say something, but in order not to be silent."
[15] This attribution is omitted from the third edition, which is the only one translated into English. See Eberhard Jüngel, *Gott als Geheimnis der Welt: zur Begründung der Theologie des Gekreuzigten im Streit zwischen Theismus und Atheismus*, 2nd edn. (Tübingen: Mohr, 1977), p. 343.

physical tradition" – is uncompromising. "The Christian faith, if it understands itself properly, can only protest against each of these possibilities as well as against any combination of them" (p. 252).

What exactly is the object of "Christian" protest here? We can identify two forms of the "silencing of God" arising out of the negative understanding of mystery that Jüngel delineates. One is the "dumb silencing" of God – God is simply excluded from discourse, and even God's "unspeakability" is not marked in speech. In assigning this (his option *c*) to a "point beyond theism and atheism" and speaking of it in the subjunctive mood,[16] Jüngel indicates that this point has not in fact been reached. God's silence continues, as I suggested above, to be a presence, to have a history and a form.

For this reason, the "garrulous silencing" of God is, as we learned in the introduction, the most urgent problem for Jüngel. How is God spoken of in such a way as to silence God? Two different forms of "garrulous silencing," with their corresponding "technology" and "etiquette," arise in Jüngel's first and fourth possibilities, above – those he assigns to "mysticism" and "theism, deism and the metaphysical tradition." In "mysticism" (his option *a*), speech, even theological speech, thematizes God *as* unspeakable, and hence silences God. In "theism"(his option *d*), more subtly, theological speech thematizes God in such a way as to imply and enact God's incapacity to speak for Godself.

The "garrulous silencing" of God permits the word "God" to be used – it may indeed have a great deal to say about God – but does so within a framework that excludes God as a speaker. God is rendered mute by the philosophical move that defines God as "unthinkable and therefore unspeakable." While this approach recognizes, and seeks to thematize, the difference between God and the world, it suggests that that difference can appear only through the self-silencing of language. This, however, requires – so Jüngel claims – the constitution of language and the thinkable as a self-contained and self-sustaining whole, which defines whatever lies outside it as the "whereof we cannot speak" (p. 251).

The consequence of Jüngel's analysis of the "negative conception of mystery," within his work, is the almost complete rejection of the apophatic tradition in Christian theology, as fundamentally opposed to that form of theological discourse within which "God is permitted to speak." Defining God as mystery in the negative sense opens the possibility of a

---

[16] In the German edition: "*Eine solche Verarbeitung der Gottesfrage wäre dasjenige Jenseits von Mystik*" (Jüngel, *Gott als Gehemnis*, p. 344). Note that in the introduction (p. 3) Jüngel apparently attributes this dumb silencing of God to *academic* discourse.

discourse that proceeds without the need for a word from or about God; and it makes God into one who could not in any case speak such a word. "The strictest reference to God as mystery would then have to be a finger placed to the lips . . . well known as an expression of Buddhist piety, but could well serve as the last gesticulation of European metaphysics" (p. 251). Silencing God is "depersonalizing" God – defining God as one who cannot identify Godself through speech, and refusing to acknowledge God's speech as significant.

Jüngel's proposed response to the silencing of God is a theological reaffirmation of God as the one who constitutes the world by speaking, and of theology as a "speaking after" God's primary speech. Philosophical-theological attempts to limit God's speech and speakability are rejected in favour of God's self-definition *through* speech *as* the one who speaks. The affirmation that God speaks is the primary affirmation of theology, because the event of God's speech is the event that makes theology possible.

Jüngel understands the addressing word as that which constitutes the hearer's relation both to the word and to the world. God's word is the primary "address," in relation to which humanity is "'*hearer* of the word,' who cannot do anything at all as long as he is listening, and then on the basis of his hearing he can act out of the *newly gained freedom*" (p. 309, emphasis original). But what is communicated in God's word is *God*, who "comes" to the world in God's act of utterance. Both God's "coming to the world" and God's granting of freedom are associated with the biblical identification of God as love; but love in turn is regarded as inherently self-communicative, oriented towards utterance.[17]

The key point to note about this response to the silencing of God is that it requires not only an account of who God is, but also an account of what speech is and how it works. For Jüngel, God's speech is like all speech in its basic character. Understandings of the world-constituting power of speech, and of the character of speech as interpersonal "address," are adapted from recent linguistic philosophy and used to analyze and

---

[17] See p. 261: "To grasp God as love, this certainly means to grasp God as self-communication . . . God is no more degraded or reduced in his being through his communicability than is a lover deprived of his power through his self-communicating love. All theological concern of this kind . . . fails to see that God is not envious." p. 298: "Love possesses the power of speech: *caritas capax verbi.*" God's self-determination as love, central to Jüngel's work, will also be significant in my later discussion (see in particular chapter 6). I shall question, however, the association between love and speech, here taken as self-evident.

critique the silencing of God.[18] My later discussion will raise questions both about the association between love and speech, and about the philosophical framework within which this response to the "silencing of God" is developed.

Commentary

What do we learn about the process of silencing from Jüngel's account of the silencing of God? First, the silencing of God is, according to this analysis, a lie; God is not silent, but speaks. In fact, on this account, it is by speaking that God *as God* enters discourse concerning God; God must be recognized as the primary speaking subject, or talk about God becomes systematic falsehood.

Second, the "garrulous" silencing of God is attributed principally to the theology that developed from particularly modern concerns about the limits of human knowledge, and from attempts to specify the limits of discourse that we associate most readily with modernity. It is, by definition, twentieth-century theology that makes use of Wittgenstein's concept of the "whereof we cannot speak;" and its use is read as the culmination of modern attempts to make human discourse self-contained and self-defining. The silencing of God is, then, on this account, the consequence of a discourse that claims the power to determine both what admits being spoken of and what is allowed to speak, and that is incapable of admitting the possibility of interruption from outside its self-imposed limits.

Third, the proposed "solution" is the recognition that God *does* speak Godself to the world, and, in the light of this, a return to "obedient hearing" as the primary human activity in relation to God's communication. Theology should become a discourse that acknowledges its prior dependence on an act of hearing, and that attempts to "speak after" what it hears. The sphere in which "garrulous silencing" occurred is to undergo conversion, a conversion shaped and determined by the activity of the speaker it has previously silenced.

---

[18] Jüngel's concept of the "addressing word" is discussed further in chapter 4. For rather different attempts to overcome the "silencing of God" by re-examining the concept of divine speech, see Kevin Vanhoozer, *Is There a Meaning in This Text? The Bible, the Reader and the Morality of Literary Knowledge* (Leicester: Apollos, 1998); Francis Watson, *Text and Truth: Redefining Biblical Theology* (Edinburgh: T. & T. Clark, 1997), and for a more complex understanding of the speech-act that follows a similar basic pattern, Nicholas Wolterstorff, *Divine Discourse: Philosophical Reflections on the Claim That God Speaks* (Cambridge: Cambridge University Press, 1995).

The challenge Jüngel's analysis, and the approach it represents, offers to any Christian "theology of the silence of God" is whether it can avoid a violent silencing of God through "technology," "rituals," and theological "etiquette." Picking up Rich's words again, the risk in any attempt to read the silence of God positively is the "blurring of terms" that leads us to think God as only an "absence."

Does this criticism really apply to all attempts at developing genuinely theological accounts of the silence of God? It is possible, as Jüngel does, to tell the story of the silence of God in a way that links the apophatic tradition and monasticism, on the one hand, with modern atheism on the other. In his account, the "mystical theology" of Pseudo-Dionysius and others begins a tradition of "metaphysics" that passes through Descartes and ends somewhere after Wittgenstein. But it might already be apparent that the Wittgensteinian dictum – which is, after all, not explicitly referred in its context to any theological tradition – does not obviously capture the intention of the negative theology of Pseudo-Dionysius or John of Damascus, of the monastic disciplines of silence, or even of Schleiermacher's critique of anthropomorphism.

For these thinkers, to recognize God as "beyond" all finite words and concepts is precisely to guard against the kind of hubris of discourse of which Jüngel accuses certain traditions. *Apophasis* is what allows speech – about God or about the world – to be recalled to its source and limit in God. The incomprehensibility of God is a characteristic of God's essence and not of human thought or speech. God's "silence" is how God determines Godself to be; it is not just what any human discourse attempts to impose on God, nor just the mark of a deficiency or lack in God.[19]

What Jüngel rejects in the course of his discussion, then, may on a more careful listening hold out the possibility that the emphasis on God's *speech*, in considering how God "comes to" the world and grounds its practices of communication, is itself open to challenge. God's freedom from determination by the limits of discourse, and the act by which God relates Godself to the world, can, within the traditions Jüngel rejects, be thought otherwise than in terms of God's speech and speakability. This in turn suggests that there may be possible responses to the "silencing of God" that leave scope for a more positive reading of the communicative function of silence.

---

[19] Thus the recognition that "God is not envious," discussed above, is precisely what underlies the praise of God's ineffability in John of Damascus; the self-sufficiency of God, unthinkable except as the self-sufficiency of trinitarian life, pertains to God's incomprehensibility. See John of Damascus, *An Exact Exposition of the Orthodox Faith*, Nicene and Post-Nicene Fathers, second series, vol. 9 (Edinburgh: T. & T. Clark), Book 1, chapter 1.

To see why such a reading might be particularly important in contemporary theology, I turn now to the consideration of another critique of silencing, which is very similar in form to the critique of the silencing of God.

The Silencing of Women

Analyses of silence

"Silence" has been a significant trope in feminist thought since its early days – feminist theology being no exception. The critique of the silencing of women – its "technology, rituals, and etiquette" – is well developed, as is the debate about the means by which this silence can be overcome.

The analysis of the silencing of women discovers, as in Jüngel's analysis of the silencing of God, both a "dumb" and a "garrulous" silencing.[20] The "dumb" silencing occurs where women are simply ignored within the philosophical, political, or theological discourse dominated by men. The theoretical aspects of this silencing include the construction of the universal subject as male, and the exclusion of concerns specific to women (however understood) from public consideration. Clearly these theoretical positions have their counterparts in social and institutional "technologies" – the processes by which women are prevented from speaking. The absence of "women," in the definitions of humanity used in these public conversations, is mirrored by the absence of women's voices from the conversations themselves.

In Christian theology, prominent concerns pertaining to the "dumb silencing" of women have included the predominance of male imagery for God, the use of "man" and masculine pronouns in liturgy and theological texts that purportedly refer to humanity as a whole (both reflect-

---

[20] On all the forms of silencing discussed in this section, see further Rebecca Chopp, *The Power to Speak: Feminism, Language, God* (New York: Crossroad, 1989), pp. 24–30. Chopp's work is particularly important for the argument advanced here, in that she recognizes that feminist theology calls, not only for a different pattern of access to communication, but for a different theological understanding of what communication is or can be. She approaches this task through a reinterpretation of the key concept of "proclamation," interpreting feminist theology as a form of "proclamation" that is at the same time "emancipatory transformation." In an analysis of "proclamation," however, she finds it necessary to refer to the activity of listening as its prerequisite (p. 52).

ing the construction of the "universal subject" as male),[21] and the marginalization or virtual invisibility of women in biblical interpretation and the writing of Church history.[22] The social and institutional process of silencing has been even more obvious as a target of critique – the perceived "silencing" of significant women during or after their lifetimes,[23] and the continuing contestation of the right of women to preach.[24]

Critiques of the silencing of women sometimes, however, start from the paradoxical fact that women *do* appear in theological discourse – as mute objects of enquiry. Women are subjected to a "garrulous silencing" as well as a "dumb silencing;" and the garrulous silencing is considerably harder to overcome than the simple fact of exclusion. Again, as in Jüngel's discussion, we can make a distinction between two forms of this garrulous silencing. On the one hand, women are constructed within a particular discourse as silent. Women's "mysteriousness," their "closeness to nature," their "place in the home," are aspects of the portrayal of women that contribute to their exclusion as speaking subjects.[25]

Within theology, these and other attributes accentuated by Romanticism are combined with the biblical and traditional injunctions to silence and obedience, to produce a complex portrayal of the woman who is most truly a woman insofar as she remains silent.[26] Luce Irigaray's words concerning psychoanalysis could equally have been said of theology – and,

---

[21] On both of these see Letty M. Russell, *Human Liberation in a Feminist Perspective: A Theology* (Philadelphia: Westminster, 1974), pp. 93–103.
[22] See Elizabeth Schüssler Fiorenza, *In Memory of Her: A Feminist Theological Reconstruction of Christian Origins*, 2nd edn. (London: SCM, 1994); Russell, *Human Liberation*, pp. 80–9.
[23] For an example of the feminist "rediscovery" of such women in Christian history, see Mary T. Malone, *Women and Christianity*, vol. 1 (Blackrock, Co. Dublin: Columba, 2000).
[24] For a detailed analysis of debates relating to the latter, see Anne E. Carr, *Transforming Grace* (San Francisco: Harper & Row, 1990), pp. 21–59. See also Nelle Morton, *The Journey Is Home* (Boston: Beacon, 1985), p. 40. A different example of the institutional "silencing" of women – through failures in pastoral care – is analyzed in Riet Bons-Storm, *The Incredible Woman: Listening to Women's Silences in Pastoral Care and Counselling* (Nashville: Abingdon, 1996).
[25] For summary discussions of this, see Serene Jones, *Feminist Theory and Christian Theology: Cartographies of Grace* (Minneapolis: Fortress, 2000), pp. 25–31. Rosi Braidotti, *Patterns of Dissonance: A Study of Women in Contemporary Philosophy*, trans. Elizabeth Guild (Cambridge: Polity, 1991), pp. 123–32.
[26] For discussion of important recent examples of this, see Carr, *Transforming Grace*, pp. 50–1. See also on specific examples Rachel Muers, "The Mute Cannot Keep Silent: Barth, Von Balthasar and Irigaray on the Construction of Women's Silence," in Susan Frank Parsons, ed., *Challenging Women's Orthodoxies in the Context of Faith* (Aldershot: Ashgate, 2000).

indeed, are developed in her discussions of Christianity: "[Woman's life] is assigned within a discourse that excludes, and by its very "essence," the possibility that it might speak for itself." [27]

In certain cases, women's silence is apparently defined as the necessary condition for theological or ecclesiastical discourse itself; women are the hearers that theological speech requires as its necessary counterpart. Consider, for example, Kierkegaard's address to "you, O woman" in *For Self-Examination*:

> Let me describe for you such a woman, a hearer of the Word who does not forget the Word . . . she does not speak in the congregation, she is silent; neither does she talk about religion at home – she is silent . . . If, in observing the present state of the world and life in general . . . someone asked me "What do you think should be done?" I would answer, ". . . the very first thing that must be done is: create silence. God's Word cannot be heard, and if in order to be heard in the hullabaloo it must be shouted deafeningly with noisy instruments, then it is not God's Word; create silence!" . . . And that a woman can do.[28]

There is no explicit reference here to the question of who *does* speak in the congregation, who is authorized to be a speaker of the Word, or indeed who is in a position to ask, concerning the present state of the world, "what should be done?" In addressing these observations to "you, O woman," the author assumes and reinforces the assignation of this role to men; and he makes this explicit by informing any "woman" present that her primary task is to "create silence."

Silencing women does not, however, depend on explicitly defining them as silent. The garrulous silencing of women, feminist thinkers have recognized, can occur when women are silenced simply by being talked about. Virginia Woolf's famous description of a researcher's foray into the British Library to investigate the question of "women and fiction" is an account of how this form of silencing was experienced, in particular, after

---

[27] Irigaray's whole analysis of the silencing of women in both philosophy and Christianity is extremely significant. See Luce Irigaray, *Marine Lover of Friedrich Nietzsche*, trans. Gillian C. Gill (New York: Columbia University Press, 1991), especially the "Epistle to the Last Christians;" and her critique of Fiorenza's project for its failure to tackle this "garrulous silencing" (Luce Irigaray, "Equal to Whom?," *differences*, 1, 2 (1989)). For a detailed analysis of this theme in her work, see Michelle Boulos Walker, "Silence and Reason: Women's Voice in Philosophy," *Australasian Journal of Philosophy*, 71, 4 (1993).

[28] Søren Kierkegaard, *For Self-Examination*, trans. Walter Lowrie (Oxford: Oxford University Press, 1941), pp. 46–7. See for a more recent example Hans Urs von Balthasar, *New Elucidations*, trans. Mary Sherry (San Francisco: Ignatius, 1986), pp. 189–97.

the explosion of writing on the "Woman Question" from the late nine-teenth century:

> Have you any notion how many books are written about women in the course of one year? Have you any notion how many are written by men? Are you aware that you are, perhaps, the most discussed animal in the uni-verse? . . . Merely to read the titles suggested innumerable schoolmasters, innumerable clergymen mounting their platforms and pulpits and holding forth with a loquacity which far exceeded the hour usually allotted to such discourse on this one subject. It was a most strange phenomenon; and apparently . . . one confined to the male sex. Women do not write books about men.[29]

Woolf's account suggests that the delimitation of woman as an object of study often appears to exclude from the outset the subject-position of a "speaking woman" – the woman who could "write books about men." Having been determined as the spoken about, the written about, the "question," or the "problem," women have also been determined as those who cannot speak, write, set questions, or raise problems – determined, that is, as objects rather than possible subjects of this discourse.

Proposed responses to the silencing of women

How, in feminist theory, is the silence of women broken? Obviously the initial response will be very different in form or assumptions from the responses to the silencing of God, outlined above. Here as there, it is claimed that the act of silencing is based on, or perpetuates, a falsehood; the objects of silencing are in fact speakers. In the case of feminist thought, however, this claim is articulated from the position of the "object of silenc-ing," as she becomes or shows herself to be a "subject of speech." It is, at least in the first instance, the silenced themselves who perform the cri-tique of silencing, and, precisely in doing so, demonstrate that they can be speakers.[30]

[29] Virginia Woolf, *A Room of One's Own* (London: Penguin, 1945), pp. 27–8.
[30] For fuller taxonomies of feminist approaches from a historical perspective, on the basis of which the following overview is developed, see Alison M. Jaggar, *Feminist Politics and Human Nature* (Brighton: Harvester, 1983); Rosemarie Putnam Tong, *Feminist Thought: A More Comprehensive Introduction* (Oxford: Westview, 1998). For the contemporary debates, see Selya Benhabib, ed., *Feminist Contentions: A Philosophical Exchange* (London: Routledge, 1995).

How does this work? The demand that women be recognized as speakers was already prominent in the first movements described as "feminist." One set of feminist arguments[31] has been based on minimizing or denying innate differences, as far as participation in public life or rational debate are concerned, between women and men. From this perspective, if women's silence were to be broken – by removing impediments to their equal participation in any given forum of discussion or decision-making – all members of the community could take part in a democratic "conversation," itself neutral and universally accessible.

The education and empowerment of women, in the liberal feminist project, is intended to enable them to fulfill their responsibilities in this sphere – to be able to speak and be heard among other rational speakers. The goal is to demonstrate that women are and have always been possible speaking subjects within any conversation presently taking place. In some cases, the "speech" of women might be presented as an end in itself – a necessity either for the health of the public sphere or for the verification of its claim to universality.[32] In other cases the power of women to speak is linked with their power to demand justice – improvements in material conditions or the power of self-determination more generally. Silence, read as the exclusion of women from the public sphere, both is itself oppression and allows material oppression to remain concealed.

A recent rearticulation of this position can be seen in feminist appropriations of the communicative ethics of Jürgen Habermas, himself either praised or stigmatized for rearticulating a form of liberal humanism.[33]

---

[31] Referred to as "liberal feminism" in Jaggar, *Feminist Politics*, pp. 27–50; Tong, *Feminist Thought*, pp. 10–44. See also Rosemary Radford Ruether, *Sexism and God-Talk* (London: SCM, 1983), p. 43. The term is associated in these works both with fin-de-siècle feminism and with that line of thought in "second wave" feminism that draws on liberal philosophical and political ideas. Daphne Hampson, particularly in her earlier work – Daphne Hampson, *Theology and Feminism* (Oxford: Blackwell, 1990) – is perhaps the clearest example of a feminist theologian who begins from this perspective. As her critics have noted, her objections to Christianity, albeit feminist in their articulation, are on a continuum with more widespread "liberal" objections. Janet Martin Soskice, "Response," *Swallowing a Fishbone? Feminist Theologians Debate Christianity*, ed. Daphne Hampson (London: SPCK, 1996), pp. 125–8.

[32] On this aspect of the liberal feminist project, see Jaggar, *Feminist Politics*, p. 39.

[33] Selya Benhabib is probably the most influential feminist reader of Habermas; see Selya Benhabib, *Situating the Self: Gender, Community and Postmodernism in Contemporary Ethics* (Cambridge: Polity, 1992). Various issues in the feminist appropriation of Habermas are debated in Johanna Meehan, ed., *Feminists Read Habermas: Gendering the Subject of Discourse* (London: Routledge, 1995). See also Iris M. Young, *Justice and the Politics of Difference* (Princeton: Princeton University Press, 1990), pp. 106–7. While I have here associated Habermas with "liberal" philosophy, it is important to note theological appropriations of

Commitment to the speech situation in which all participants have equal opportunity to demand the "discursive justification" – the giving of public reasons – for any claims made, and in which truth, appropriacy, and sincerity are recognized by all as the basic norms that structure dialogic interaction, seems to many feminist thinkers entirely coherent with their aims.

However, the perceived need, within this recent "liberal" feminism, to ask questions about the gendered particularity of the participants in discourse, points to a basic problem with the whole idea that women who begin to speak where they were previously silenced are simply joining a neutral or equalizing conversation.[34] An alternative feminist approach, which likewise has a long history,[35] begins from the assumption of women's distinctiveness, biologically or otherwise determined. Women's participation in speech then becomes a matter, not merely of equal recognition for basically equivalent speaking subjects, but of the articulation of something distinctive – perhaps through the appeal to a distinctive realm of "women's experience."

Clearly this difference may imply a different way of speaking – in Carol Gilligan's terms, a "different voice."[36] The question has arisen as to whether the rules of the conversation are established to exclude women's speech, not merely through the construction of women as silent, but through the suppression of ways of speaking particularly associated with women. The perceived need to seek out separate institutional, practical, and theoretical spaces, within which the "voice" of women can be raised, arises from the analysis of the exclusion of women from mainstream

---

his thought that stress its eschatological tendency and, in doing so, distance it from "liberalism" on many interpretations of the term. See Nicholas Adams, "Imagining God's Reign: Ideal Speech and Our Common Future," PhD, University of Cambridge, 1997.

[34] See on this Jodi Dean, "Discourse in Different Voices" *Feminists Read Habermas* ed. Johanna Meehan (London: Routledge, 1995); and Benhabib, *Situating the Self,* pp. 9–13.

[35] Various interlocking terms are used to designate feminist theory that takes this approach – of which the best-known theological representative, again a self-described "post-Christian," is Mary Daly (Mary Daly, *Beyond God the Father: Towards a Philosophy of Women's Liberation* (London: Women's Press, 1986)). Ruether, *Sexism and God-Talk,* p. 44, refers to "romantic feminism" and "difference feminism." Jaggar uses the term "radical feminism" (Jaggar, *Feminist Politics,* pp. 83–122), where Tong specifies those adopting an essentialist position as "radical-cultural" feminists (Tong, *Feminist Thought,* pp. 47–8). See also the discussion of "feminist essentialism" in Jones, *Feminist Theory and Christian Theology,* pp. 24–31. In recent years, as Jones' discussion indicates, the debate over "essentialism" in Anglo-American feminism has been dominated by issues in the reception and interpretation of French feminist theorists such as Helene Cixous and Luce Irigaray.

[36] Carol Gilligan, *In a Different Voice: Psychological Theory and Women's Development,* 2nd edn. (Cambridge: Harvard University Press, 1993).

discourse. If it turns out that the exclusion of women is built into the very structure (again, institutional, practical, or theoretical) of discourse, the possibility of women's speech can only arise in a location "outside" that structure.

The tension between these two approaches to "breaking the silence" has shaped many of the most important debates in feminist thought – and reflections of it can be found at all levels of discussion of feminist politics. Stay in this situation still shaped by sexist assumptions and try to bring about change from within, or leave and try to construct something different? Welcome women's progress in traditionally male institutions, or regret the support it gives to structures that are hopelessly patriarchal?[37]

It is argued, on the one hand, that a focus on the distinctiveness of "speaking" (or theorizing, or acting ethically) "as a woman" reinforces the exclusion of women from those fora within which the power of speech is properly exercised. It creates a discourse that others can only hear as silence.[38] A voice speaking in ways that do not meet the normal criteria for admissible speech will be excluded from the outset. On the other hand, the attempt to speak with an "equal" voice can, it is claimed, serve simply to perpetuate the silencing of women's distinctive voices; the only women who are heard are those who speak like men.[39]

The assumptions about speech and silence that shape this debate are, however, open to further challenges that fundamentally alter its parameters.

How to break the silence?

Both the feminist demand for justice or equality and the feminist affirmation of difference are based on the claim that the silencing of women is falsehood. Does this mean that women's speech – whether the speech of fully rational subjects of a common discourse, or of "different voices" – is "already there," waiting to be released into the public sphere from

---

[37]   And, as the male chief executive asks the female worker in a cartoon by Jackie Fleming: "Which do you want, equality or maternity leave?"

[38]   See Walker, "Silence and Reason," on the problems of Irigaray's attempt to speak "outside" philosophy.

[39]   See Victoria Lee Erikson, *Where Silence Speaks: Feminism, Social Theory and Religion* (Minneapolis: Fortress, 1993), p. 197: "People without speech are those people . . . who seek to speak to the masculine sacred machine in a language it recognizes . . . others, who resist being captured . . . form what the machine hears as silence. But they can hear themselves."

which it has been excluded? Feminist analysis suggests that this would be a problematic assumption to make.

Accounting for women's silencing involves describing the linguistic and discursive processes – the "rituals, etiquette" – by which that silencing has been effected. The more significant these processes are understood to be, however, the more difficult it becomes to see how the silence can be broken. If our identities, including our gender identities, are formed through speaking and being spoken to, the silencing of women is part of what makes them who they are – and what determines how they "speak." The language within which women have attempted to speak is the same language that silenced them.[40] In Rich's words, silence in this case is not merely "a plan/rigorously executed" but "the blueprint for a life."

An analysis of the process of silencing, then, leads to the disturbing recognition of women's complicity in that process. This is intensified and complicated by criticisms of the early feminist movement from those whom *it* silenced. Perhaps the greatest challenge to the whole idea of "feminism" has been the recognition that in its earlier forms the movement suppressed, by its own complex "technology" and "rituals," the differences among women. A single "different voice" that claims to be the voice of women as such performs a silencing just as violent as those involved in the maintenance of a universal, supposedly gender-neutral subject. Lesbian women, Black women, "uneducated" women, and non-feminist women had been further silenced by a voice that claimed to speak for them; and feminist theologians had been just as much part of this silencing process as had theorists who made no theological claims.[41]

Where can the analysis and critique of women's silencing go, beyond the recognition that the critics themselves have been complicit both in their own silencing and that of others?

---

[40] Extended discussions of the complicity of the silenced in their own silencing, which relate this process to doctrines of sin, are in Alistair McFadyen, *Bound to Sin? Abuse, Holocaust and the Christian Doctrine of Sin* (Cambridge: Cambridge University Press, 2000) (see especially pp. 57–79 on the sexual abuse of children, and pp. 139–66 on feminist articulations of the sin of "sloth" as characteristic of women in patriarchy); Jones, *Feminist Theory and Christian Theology*, pp. 116–19.

[41] See Susan Brooks Thistlethwaite, *Sex, Race and God: Christian Feminism in Black and White* (London: Chapman, 1990); Mary McClintock Fulkerson, *Changing the Subject: Women's Discourses and Feminist Theology* (Minneapolis: Fortress, 1994). The work of bell hooks is particularly important in identifying the ways in which talk of "the Other" or "difference" in feminist theory can itself be used to silence white-dominated feminism's own "Other." See bell hooks, "Choosing the Margin as a Space of Radical Openness" in Ann Garry and Marilyn Pearsall, eds., *Women, Knowledge and Reality* (London: Routledge, 1996).

One significant move has been towards an emphasis on feminist theories and texts as strategic. If all women's speaking in the present is shaped
by the discourses that silence women, the "different voice" is something
to be hoped for rather than identified as a present and accessible reality.
That hope gives rise to a task or project, in the shape of practices intended
to allow the "different voice" to emerge. Theories of women's nature or
women's language are read as provisional articulations of a possibility that
still lies in the future, and as strategic moves towards its realization.[42] If
there is going to be new or different speech, it has to be learned.

Insofar as the possibility of a "different voice," or the space within
which it can be heard or articulated,[43] is described in feminist theory, the
descriptions are often future-oriented, "utopian," written as dreams or
hopes; they set out not what *is* being said, but where and how something
could be said. Precisely because, not only the exclusion of women as speaking subjects, but the history and form of women's silence, has been determined within a patriarchal framework, the nature of the "different voice"
cannot be predicted. Perhaps, as Luce Irigaray's work suggests, sexual difference itself should be understood as a future promise rather than a
present reality; we do not yet know, culturally, what it would mean for
there to be women who were not constructed as the mirror-image of
men.[44] Recent feminist epistemologies emphasize how early feminist work
provides insights into the partiality of all knowledge – and thus transcends
its own limitations, undermining by implication all claims to speak "for"
or "of" women.[45]

---

[42] Jones' discussion of "strategic essentialism" (Jones, *Feminist Theory and Christian
Theology*, pp. 42–8, 51–5) indicates the congeniality of this approach, in the eyes of many
feminist theologians, for Christian theology. For Jones, the feminist theological appropriation of strategic essentialism (which could apply to various forms of "strategic" feminist
practice) is "rooted decisively in a theological vision of an already/not-yet future."

[43] Clearly the language of "space" here is itself problematic, insofar as it implies that a
stable subject position is a prerequisite for the possibility of speech. Judith Butler and others
arguing from her Foucauldian premises would reject the implication that there could be
any source of resistance to a discourse not produced by the discourse itself. As I explain at
more length below (chapter 2), I am retaining the concept of a subject or agent – a "Who"
– in communicative acts, but am privileging understandings of communicative agency that
do not make this "subject" sovereign or self-sufficient.

[44] For this reading of Irigaray, put forward to counter the early interpretation of her as
an "essentialist," see Elizabeth Grosz, *Sexual Subversions: Three French Feminists* (Sydney:
Allen & Unwin, 1989); Margaret Whitford, "Irigaray, Utopia and the Death Drive," in
Carolyn Burke, ed., *Engaging with Irigaray: Feminist Philosophy and Modern European Thought*
(New York: Columbia University Press, 1994).

[45] As discussed in Elizabeth Karmack Minnich, *Transforming Knowledge* (Philadelphia:
Temple University Press, 1990), pp. 147–75.

Feminist writing does not only describe the strategies that might begin the process of learning, or creating space for, a different way of speaking; it exemplifies these strategies in different ways. Sometimes the move is stylistic – styles that emphasize incompleteness, perhaps calling the reader to participate in the "completion" of the text, as Michèle Le Doeuff does in the introduction to her "Essay concerning Women, Philosophy, etc.": "The aim of an introduction is . . . to make contact with whoever is going to read and ask for that person's tolerance and goodwill, in other words for voluntary help . . . Texts are written in anxious intersubjectivity."[46]

Sometimes the imaginative construction or reconstruction of "female" societies, religions, or philosophies is used, not as a claim about how things are, but as a challenge to the projected self-evidence of dominant voices.[47] Feminist science-fiction novels, or accounts of matriarchal religions or societies, are used not simply as programatic statements or pieces of "objective" history. They work to challenge the reader's assumptions about what is necessary or possible, and hence to create the space in which more different ways of being or speaking can be imagined. In opposition to discursive practices that seek to define the limits of speech (*Wovon man nicht sprechen kann* . . .), these approaches to reading, writing, and speaking seek to stretch existing limits. That "whereof we cannot speak" becomes, in effect, that "whereof we cannot speak *yet*." Not just the content, but the rules and patterns of speech, are being challenged.

The critiques of early feminism, that highlight its tendency to exclude or minimize the diversity of women's lives and experiences, also highlight a failure to "change the rules." Breaking the silence, it has been claimed, produced either the substitution of one monologue for another, or a cacophony of competing voices within which there was no guarantee that any of the new voices will be heard – and within which the defeat of some of the voices was inevitable.[48] Feminism, at least in its Western academic contexts, learned from the critiques described above about the need to examine its own "technology of silence . . . rituals, etiquette."

---

[46] Michèle Le Doeuff, *Hipparchia's Choice*, trans. Trista Selous (Oxford: Blackwell, 1989), p. 47.

[47] See for an important analysis of recent feminist writing in these terms Susan Sargisson, *Contemporary Feminist Utopianism* (London: Routledge, 1996). Sargisson argues that feminist writing (including the work of Cixous and Irigaray as well as various examples of feminist fiction) both inhabits and extends the category of "utopia" by forming visions of alternative cultural or political spaces that are themselves "imperfect" or hold a range of possibilities in tension.

[48] On feminist theology's own acts of silencing, see especially Angela West, *Deadly Innocence: Feminism and the Mythology of Sin* (London: Cassell, 1995).

Silencing, then, within feminist thought as well as outside it, has to be analyzed from a position of complicity. The demands of justice and of the recognition of "different voices" have to be seen from this perspective. Practices of communication, and the assumptions about speech and silence they carry, need to be subjected to critical interrogation – but with an awareness of one's own location within those practices of communication.

In contemporary feminist texts, then, the end of silencing emerges as a hope that shapes a process – the process of the critique of a given communicative situation and its assumptions, and of the experimental reconfiguration of that situation. The process demands and furthers the "conversion" of those who participate in it; its consequences are not fully predictable, and its conditions not open to specification. It is on these terms that conflicting demands, such as those of "justice for all" and "the affirmation of difference" must be worked out.

Theologians concerned with the feminist project find, in these moves, indications of eschatological thinking. Feminism calls for thought about the *telos* of human existence, as that which emerges out of a future not within the control of those who now look toward it, but as that which nonetheless demands ethical commitment and action in the present.[49] Feminist thought about the silencing of women puts to theology the question of the relationship between ethics and eschatology – of the relationship between the sense of movement into an open future which is in some sense "given," and the action demanded now. In response, theologians can put to feminist writers the question of the basis of hope; what are the conditions of possibility for the kind of future-oriented communicative action advocated and practiced in feminist writing? Even the deliberate avoidance of closure in communication will already, by the way it is enacted, imply normative claims about the source or nature of the "more" to which it remains open.[50]

---

[49]   It is noteworthy that Butler and Irigaray, as two significant representatives of different "strategic" approaches to the theorizing of gender difference (behind which lie, of course, subtly different accounts of "silencing'), have both attracted interest from theologians precisely on the grounds of their implicit eschatologies. On Irigaray, Fergus Kerr, *Immortal Longings* (London: SPCK, 1997); Grosz, *Sexual Subversions*, pp. 140–72; Tina Beattie, "Carnal Love and Spiritual Imagination: Can Luce Irigaray and John Paul II Come Together?," in Jon Davies and Gerard Loughlin, eds., *Sex These Days: Essays on Theology, Sexuality and Society* (Sheffield: Sheffield Academic Press, 1997). On Butler, see Sarah Coakley, "The Eschatological Body: Gender, Transformation and God," *Modern Theology* 16, 1 (2000).

[50]   Thus texts such as Jones' that explicitly demand completion and critique from the reader's exploration of feminism and Christianity (Jones, *Feminist Theory and Christian Theology*, pp. viii–ix) accord a certain primacy to narrated experience as source of

A theology that takes the feminist critique seriously needs to give an account of the basis on which the new ethic of communication, which this analysis of silencing seems to require, is put forward – and about the grounds for believing that its intention can be realized. This is the point at which the problem of the silencing of God – and the proposed solutions – intersects again with the multiple problems of the silencing of women and other "voices" – and the proposed solutions.

The Silencing of God and the Silencing of Women: Theological Issues

The power of speech

The similarities between the analyses of the "silencing of God" and of the "silencing of women" provide a useful starting-point for considering the specific challenges to theological understandings of communication that arise from feminist thought, and vice versa. I have suggested that the "dumb silencing" of God in modern atheism and the "garrulous silencing" perceived in certain theological approaches are mirrored in a "dumb" and a "garrulous" silencing of women. In both cases the silencing is perpetrated by a self-proclaimed single "voice of reason" that claims to determine its own scope and exclude whatever lay beyond it from coming to speech.

The approaches to speech and silencing discussed above share a basic assumption, so trivial that it barely needs to be mentioned: speech is powerful. I began with a consideration of the power to impose silence by speaking – silence being associated with exclusion, with the denial of freedom, and with powerlessness. Silence, as I have been discussing it, is the antithesis of the exercise of power, passive where speech is active; being silenced is having something done *to* one, and one resists it in the first instance by speaking.

The association of speech with activity and silence with passivity does not depend on any specific philosophical account of the nature of agency

---

emancipatory truth. The use of imagery related to the female body in Cixous and Irigaray, and the exploration of *ecriture feminine*, implies by contrast a future way of "speaking" not compatible with existing genres such as narrative. Preliminary sketches of communicative environments within which women's speaking might be possible – such as Fiorenza's "ekklesia of wo/men" – likewise make implicit normative claims about the nature of future speech.

in speech, or of the fundamental purpose of speech. Strongly intentionalist models such as those implied in discussions of divine "authorship" of scripture; expressivist models that might support an account of women's speech as the voicing of "different experience;" the world-disclosing capacity of language that the hermeneutic appropriated by Jüngel requires; or speech's function of coordinating action in a shared world, as described by Habermas and others – all of them, as we have seen, can fit with an account of silence as "inactive." So far, the only way we have seen to respond to the injunction in Rich's poem, "Do not confuse [silence]/with any kind of absence" is to identify the "silenced" as a potential or actual speaker.

In the discussions of both the silencing of God and the silencing of women, however, a reshaping of the communicative environment was called for, to allow the excluded speech to be heard. Jüngel's response to the silencing of God involved the redescription of the theologian, or more generally of humanity in relation to God, as the hearer of God's speech. I noted, above, that this approach still works on the model of "powerful speech and passive silence." On the other hand, the various strategies advocated and practiced in feminist writing, for allowing different voices to emerge, appear to mark out a discursive position that belongs neither to the silenced nor to the powerful speakers; a position from which the end of oppressive silencing is a hope and a task, rather than a demand corresponding to a present reality. Does this imply a form of communicative activity not exercised primarily through speaking – perhaps, even, a responsible or active silence; and how would this activity relate to God's action?

God's communication and our communication

With these questions in mind, I now turn to a consideration of the theological issues arising from the analysis of the silencing of women, in relation to the earlier analysis of the silencing of God.

The obvious point should perhaps be made first. Christian theology, and not only feminist theology, has long recognized the condition of enforced silencing as contrary to the redemption promised and enacted in Christ. Liberation from oppressive silencing is part of the good news.[51]

---

[51] In commentaries on Luke's Gospel, theologians from the patristic period onwards have linked the muteness of Zechariah with the "silence of the prophets" before John the Baptist. Speech was impossible before, but now through the coming of the incarnate Word and

The dumb spirits are cast out and the voiceless are given back their speech; if the disciples become mute, the stones themselves will lose their muteness and cry out.[52] Christian feminist theology, from its earliest years, has belatedly claimed this promise of the Gospel for women. Attention has been drawn repeatedly to the muting of women within the Churches and within academic theology. In recent years attention to liberation theology, Black theology, Jewish responses to earlier Christian theology, and other recognizably "different voices" has forced the Western theological academy – including, as we have seen, academic feminist theology – to acknowledge and repent of such acts of silencing. Our question is not whether acts of oppressive silencing – other than the "silencing of God" – should be a concern for theology, but rather how this concern should be carried forward.[53]

The particular responsibility for feminist theology, suggested by the discussion above, is to maintain the memory – and awareness of the continuing possibility – of being silenced while being aware of one's own acts of silencing others. I suggested, above, that the end of silencing was regarded in feminist thought as a hope rather than a given fact, and that the need to give an account of this hope was the starting point for theological engagement with the issue. I now suggest, on the basis of the discussion so far, some requirements for an adequate theological account of the hope for an end to silencing.

A theological ethics of communication will require an account of God's free, prevenient, and loving action as the basis for human communication. This requirement arises both from the critique of the "silencing of God" and from the eschatological orientation of feminist reflection on communication, explored at the end of the previous section. However, that account must, to take full account of the feminist critique, include a more

---

through the Holy Spirit which gives the power of speech, creation has been given back its voice. (See on this Raoul Mortley, *From Word to Silence*, vol. 2, 2 vols. (Bonn: Hanstein, 1986), pp. 63–5.)

[52] Mk 9:17ff. & pars; Lk 19:40.

[53] Clearly it would be unsatisfactory – thus a common argument against all forms of "liberation theology" runs – to make this the sole *criterion* for theology. "The morally unquenchable longing that the murderer should not triumph over his innocent victim . . . has something to do with God only on the presupposition of God. To construct a God for that is unworthy of God." (Jüngel, *God as the Mystery*, p. 343, n. 45). To put the question in terms of *silencing*, however, is to draw attention to the fact that the "construction" (and hence the silencing) of God by overconfident human speech is not the only possible failure of theology. Theology itself can become complicit in the triumph of the murderer over the victim, and to ignore this is no less "unworthy of God."

complex view of God's communicative action than the model of "powerful speech" appears to allow.

The attempt to restore to theology its acknowledgment of God as a
speaker sits ill with many aspects, not only of feminist thought in general,
but of feminist theology. What is the silence of God, after all, it might
be claimed, but the long-awaited silence of the voice of mystifying male
authority, that had itself silenced the voices of women, and of countless
others who can now speak from the margins?

Even for theological appropriations of the feminist critique, it might
be claimed that what is needed is not a return to understanding humanity as "hearers of the Word" – which has, after all, been a gendered
category. To reaffirm God as a speaker would be to reaffirm a model of
divine action and authority associated with patriarchy. Do we not require,
rather – thus the possible challenge from feminist theology – the reaffirmation of the human capacity to name God in many ways according to
the plurality of human circumstances, stories, and desires?[54] The silence of
God becomes the precondition for the liberation of human speech about
God.[55]

The content and limitations of speech about God is determined, on
this model, not by a depersonalized and monological "reason" but by
many historically situated "voices." But this, from the point of view of
Jüngel and the approach he represents, perpetuates the "garrulous silencing" of God. This account of how liberation from silencing takes place
in theological discourse can look like another version of "speaking about
God by speaking about humanity in a loud voice" – or in several loud
voices. It appears to require or imply a God who, or which, is less than
personal – who has no capacity for communicative action. Moreover, the
implication that the speech of God competes with human speech is theologically problematic. Whatever the account of divine speech introduced

---

[54]   Thus, in different ways, Sallie McFague, *Models of God: Theology for an Ecological Nuclear
Age* (London: SPCK, 1987); Grace Jantzen, *Becoming Divine: Towards a Feminist Philosophy
of Religion* (Manchester: Manchester University Press, 1998); Paula Cooey, *Religious Imagination and the Body: A Feminist Analysis* (Oxford: Oxford University Press, 1994). For the
latter two thinkers in particular, the re-naming or re-imagining of God becomes a key
aspect of feminist "strategy" – naming God is both itself part of women's "speaking in a
different voice" and one of the acts that makes such speaking possible. See also Luce
Irigaray, "Divine Women?," in Garry and Pearsall, eds., *Women, Knowledge and Reality*.
[55]   A particularly clear example of this is Isabel Carter Heyward, *The Redemption of God*
(Lanham: University Press of America, 1982), pp. 96–100, who uses Elie Wiesel's pronouncements on God's silence as prolegomena to her defense of a theology of divine imma-
nence (and hence of a plurality of names for God arising out of the struggle for "right
relation").

to break God's silence, it must not – and in most cases does not – make God a power among powers in the world. For Jüngel, as we have seen, the world-constituting character of divine speech means that it is the basis of all creaturely freedom – including the freedom to speak a response to God.

So – we cannot attach weight to the simple claim that the recognition of God as primary speaker per se denies the plurality or the freedom of human speech. We can, however, further refine the feminist challenge to the theology of divine speech, to put questions that carry more weight. Feminist thought in general, and theology in particular, has, as we have seen, placed great importance on recognizing, and speaking in, one's "own voice." Liberation is from the condition in which one cannot speak (in a voice that does not reproduce the voices that silence one's own). The struggle to "find a voice" – however this process of "finding" is conceptualized – in turn forces one to recognize that voice's partiality, alongside the partiality of the quasi-monological voices that silenced it.

For feminist theology, to repristinate the idea of an authoritative primary speech of God that constitutes the hearer and the world is to raise the question: who is given authority to "speak after" this primary speech? Whose discourse does it authorize, and whose does it exclude? The suspicion arises that theology claiming to "speak after" God is attempting to conceal the theologian's voice, and hence to conceal the silencing of other voices by claiming to speak for all.[56] It does not indicate how to develop a theological ethic of communication that accepts responsibility for the hearing or silencing of different voices. It does not allow a theological account to be given of the hope for liberation from silencing and the practices that enact and sustain that hope. More generally, it does not in itself allow a theological challenge to the assumption that activity in communication is associated with speech, and silence with passivity.

"[Silence] is a presence/it has a history a form/Do not confuse it/with any kind of absence." I suggested in an earlier section that the challenge of the apophatic tradition to the theology of the speech of God might be the recognition that our understandings of speech and silence are themselves limited. Do we need to understand silence – the silence of God or human silence – as chosen or enforced inactivity? Is there, perhaps, a "form" of silence that enables us better to understand our responsibility

---

[56] See on this Mary Grey, *The Wisdom of Fools? Seeking Revelation for Today* (London: SPCK, 1993), pp. 26–7; "the Christian tradition needs to reflect on the sociological status of 'Word' as such and its connection with power and status. The question is, who proclaims the word and who decides on its content?".

for the recognition – or our complicity in the silencing – of different voices? The next chapter will look, first within feminist theology itself, and then more broadly in the "philosophy of listening," in the attempt to uncover such a form of silence and show its possible importance for theology.

Chapter Two

WHO HEARS?

The subject, or first cause . . . is hearing and not speaking. The redemptive factor is hearing. Who hears? Who is heard? (Nelle Morton, *The Journey is Home*[1])

I have suggested that an understanding of communication that attributes all activity to speakers, and hence is capable of understanding silence only as "absence," leaves the silenced one with no choice but to enter a battle of competing voices and to become complicit in the silencing of others. In this chapter, I begin the search for a way of understanding God's activity in communication that would risk silencing neither God nor humanity, and that would allow the development of a new theological ethics of communication. The claim introduced here, to be developed and tested in succeeding chapters, is that listening can rightly be spoken of as active, creative, politically and ethically significant, in some respects thinkable as *prior* to speech within a communicative relationship – and, as we practice and experience it, a reflection of the communicative activity of God.

I begin by following a clue to this effect within one of the most frequently cited works of Christian feminist theology – Nelle Morton's *The Journey is Home*. Morton's work is one of a very few theological attestations of the importance, and of the difficulty, of thinking about hearing and hearers, listening and listeners – of thinking how hearing can be a "first cause" and a "redemptive factor," how it can be attributed to a "subject," and how our understanding of communicative existence might have to be changed if it were taken seriously.

As Morton seems to have realized, there exist very few philosophical discussions that can help to shed light on the phenomenon of hearing as "redemptive factor." One is the work of Gemma Corradi Fiumara, who, drawing on psychoanalytic practice and on knowledge of both the content and the methods of twentieth-century philosophy, invites further exploration into the "other side of language," the neglected communicative

[1] Nelle Morton, *The Journey is Home* (Boston: Beacon Press, 1985), p. 41.

capacity on which so much relies. I use Fiumara's work to expand on Morton's insight into "hearing to speech" – and to establish the theological and ethical challenge that it presents.

One central concern that emerges from my reading of both these thinkers concerns the "personalizing" of silence – how silence can be identified and spoken of as personal action, in order to acknowledge its particular "presence, history, and form." This is clearly important, not only (as suggested in my introduction) for the thinking of silence within ethics, but also if we are to understand silence, as discussed in the next chapter, as the activity of a God affirmed as personal.

God's Silence as "Hearing to speech"

Aphorisms:
– Hearing to speech is political
– Hearing to speech is never one-sided. Once a person is heard to speech, she becomes a hearing person.
– Speaking first to be heard is power-over. Hearing to bring forth speech is empowering. (Nelle Morton, *The Journey is Home*[2])

One of the common descriptions for attempts, within feminist theology, to find new patterns of communication is "hearing one another to speech." Introduced by Nelle Morton in *The Journey is Home*, the expression refers in the first instance to what happened in the consciousness-raising groups characteristic of the feminist movement of the 1970s.

In the essay that explains her coinage of, and reflection on, the phrase, Morton describes how women in these groups were *enabled* to tell their stories and describe their experiences by the prior and continuing presence of the listening group. As Morton saw it, the speech that emerged as a result of the "hearing to speech" was genuinely new; stories and insights were articulated in ways that the women in question had not previously found to be possible. This speech was only able to come about in the context of a "depth hearing." Women described being "heard to their own stories," being heard "all the way down" to the point at which utterance became possible. The whole process drew Morton to speculate about what could have been involved in "a hearing that is more than acute listening. A hearing that is a direct transitive verb, that evokes speech – new speech that has never been spoken before."[3]

---

[2]   Morton, *The Journey is Home*, p. 210.
[3]   Morton, *The Journey is Home*, p. 205.

Morton's own theology, as she understands it, is the result of "hearing to speech." The words and ideas she articulates were made possible by the people who heard *her* to speech, without whom her passionate and prophetic articulation of the injustices suffered by women in the churches could not have emerged. The tendency of her later readers has been to treat "hearing to speech" as referring to the method of feminist theology, and indeed of feminist practice more generally. Thus, where Morton's phrase is quoted, it is almost invariably in the context of a response to the question – implied or expressed – "How should feminists do theology?"[4]

What is less often discussed is the deeper theological significance of Morton's reflections on "hearing to speech." A study of *The Journey is Home* suggests that Morton is at least as much concerned with the possibility that *God* "hears us to speech" as with the imperative that we should learn to hear each other to speech. More is at stake for her than a shift in ecclesial and other institutional practices of "doing theology." She announces a corresponding and implied shift in our understanding of God in God's relation to the world – and, crucially, to human communicative activity. Thus, alongside an account of the practice of the consciousness-raising groups, we find theological suggestions. "God as a great hearing one, one who has heard us to speech" (p. 60); "a prior great Listening Ear . . . an ear that hears without interruption down through our defences, cliché-filled language, pretensions . . . until we experience at the lowest point of our lives that we are sustained" (p. 55). There are allusions to a biblical basis for this theological reconfiguration of listening and word in the story of Pentecost (p. 209).

Of particular interest for our discussion is the rethinking of the *silence* of God in the light of the experience of being "heard to speech."

[There are some] theologians who claim that God is sometimes silent, hidden or withdrawn . . . and that we must wait patiently until "He" deigns to speak again. A more realistic alternative . . . would see God as the hearing one, hearing us to our own responsible word. That kind of hearing would be prior to the theologians' own words.[5]

---

[4] See for example Mary Grey, *Redeeming the Dream: Feminism, Redemption and Christian Tradition* (London: SPCK, 1989), p. 158; Isabel Carter Heyward, *The Redemption of God* (Lanham: University Press of America, 1982), p. 219. On feminist "hearing to speech" more generally, see Marilyn Frye, "The Possibility of Feminist Theory" in *Women, Knowledge and Reality*, eds. Ann Garry and Marilyn Pearsall (New York: Routledge, 1996), pp. 34–47; and note her conclusion (p. 45) that the capacity to *speak* in different voices (by which she means primarily, voices that do not reproduce patterns of communicative domination) "is . . . related to what voices one hears and responds to."

[5] Morton, *The Journey Is Home*. Subsequent references are in parentheses in the text.

In this reflection, embedded in her discussion of the practice of the consciousness-raising groups, Morton contrasts two ways of thinking about
the silence of God, and correlates them with two ways of thinking what
it means for God to act in communication. Theologians who say that God
is "sometimes silent, hidden, or withdrawn" and that the appropriate
response is to "wait patiently until 'He' deigns to speak again" are assum-
ing that the way in which God relates to the world communicatively is
through speech. On this model, God's silence can only be interpreted as
a "withdrawal," a breaking-off of communication.

In rejecting this model and putting forward a different interpretation
of God's silence, Morton calls into question the dichotomy established in
Jüngel's critique of the silencing of God, which I discussed in the
previous chapter: the dichotomy between the theology that declares that
God (has been defined such that God) *will not* speak, and the theology
that acknowledges that God *will* speak and we must "wait patiently." She
shifts the emphasis away from the question of God's speech, which allows
silence to be defined only as "unspeakability" or violent silencing, and
toward other ways of understanding God's act. She rejects the "hidden"
God who allows our speech to be self-contained and self-sufficient, but
she perceives in God's silence a "presence" and "form" that cannot be
"confused with any sort of absence." What, she asks, if silence were part
of the way God relates most closely to the world – so that silence is not
only "withdrawal," but integral to God's action? Would it be possible to
understand "God as the hearing one?"

It is important to note that Morton, in describing God as the "hearing
one," is still talking about a God who makes communication between God
and humanity possible and who shapes how it occurs. There is no equation of God with the world process; God is clearly "before we are" and
"giving us what we are." What is remarkable and counter-intuitive, in this
account of divine communication, is that God is prevenient as the one
who *hears*; God exercises a "kind of hearing [that] would be prior to the
theologian's own words." The "prevenience" of God's silence has as its
intention "hearing us to our own responsible word."

This priority of hearing, Morton suggests, "resists analysis;" to
speak about it would need "another and a different logic" (p. 128).
Nonetheless, she can record that "hearing to speech" does happen, and
that as a theologian she can only understand it as a correspondence to
God's own activity. As Dauenhauer asks about the phenomenon of silence
and its ontological significance – what must the world and human
existence be like for silence to be possible and meaningful? – Morton
asks about the phenomenon of hearing to speech and its theological

significance – what must God be like for "hearing to speech" to be possible and meaningful?

Such an enquiry might indeed need a rather unusual "logic" of communication – if, as the last chapter suggested, the assumption that speech must have the priority in all accounts of communicative activity is so widespread. Very few philosophers of language take listening seriously; but one who does can offer some ways of conceptualizing what Morton describes. Gemma Corradi Fiumara's *The Other Side of Language*, subtitled "A Philosophy of Listening," comes from a similar perspective to the work of Dauenhauer; but the close attention to listening produces, as we shall see, a rather different account of the phenomenon of silence.

Philosophy of Listening: "The Other Side of Language"

Silence, power, and activity in the "philosophy of listening"

silence is radically different . . . from an expressive inability or stuporous state of imposed muteness. (Gemma Corradi Fiumara, *The Other Side of Language*[6])

Fiumara undertakes the analysis of the Western *logos* – by which she means a set of communicative practices, the philosophy that underlies them, and the culture to which they correspond. Her claim, as outlined in her early chapters, is that the *logos* we inhabit is "halved;" we know how to speak but have forgotten how to listen.[7] A lack of philosophical interest in listening as a practice and process both derives from and reinforces a communicative environment in which listening is not practiced. The suggestion is not merely that we need to learn *about* listening, but that we need to learn *to* listen.[8] The culture Fiumara describes is one in which, as we shall see later, the possibilities for creative thought, for fruitful

---

[6] Gemma Corradi Fiumara, *The Other Side of Language: A Philosophy of Listening*, trans. Charles Lambert (London: Routledge, 1990), p. 99. Subsequent references are in parentheses in the text.

[7] See her p. 2. Compare Rebecca Chopp, *The Power to Speak: Feminism, Language, God* (New York: Crossroad, 1989), p. 27: "the Word that excludes women has itself been depleted, emptied, made an idol."

[8] "We" are variously philosophers, psychoanalysts, politicians, and, most importantly, people resisting the division of the world into such confined fields of expertise – which, as we shall see, is itself a function of the non-listening *logos*.

coexistence, and for adequate response to the needs of each other and of the world, are reduced or excluded by the failure of listening.[9] Listening is understood, as it is in Morton's work, as an activity that brings about effects in the world – and as an activity on which truthful or creative speech and thought relies.

In her advocacy of a rediscovery of listening, Fiumara draws, among others, on Heidegger, Wittgenstein, Gadamer, and a rereading of Plato's dialogs. Many of her descriptions of listening and its possible consequences also recognizably reflect psychoanalytic practice. Like the feminist writers who refuse to give a systematic account of the meaning of "women's speech" or of sexual difference, Fiumara deliberately avoids attempting to put forward a comprehensive theory of listening. Such a move would simply repeat the monological pattern of philosophical discourse; a single "theory of listening" would be a contradiction in terms. The missing half of the *logos* is not the mirror-image of the half that is present; that is precisely the understanding of "otherness" that the monological culture has sought to maintain, as can be seen in the representation of woman as man's "other." Fiumara's practice of "listening to philosophical tradition" is an attempt to uncover hints and indications of suppressed possibilities, but not of a suppressed alternative meta-theory.[10]

One of Fiumara's central concerns is, then, the problem of silencing. The "halving" of the *logos* itself implies the "silencing" of listening – the importance of this area of communicative activity has been systematically ignored or suppressed. Its suppression, in turn, produces other acts of silencing. As Fiumara reads it, the discourse produced by the Western *logos* is unable or unwilling to "hear" anything that falls outside its prior understanding of the rational or the comprehensible.

A closely connected tendency is the inability or unwillingness to perceive the *totality* of reality. The non-listening culture divides itself into separate discourses, which are free from the desire or obligation to listen to others and thus to develop an integrated understanding. Fiumara recognizes, then, the phenomenon of silencing as it occurs in a communica-

---

[9]   Another discussion of the fragmentation of contemporary discourse (particularly, professional/academic discourse) as the sign of a failure of listening is Anne-Janine Morey, "The Literary Physician," in *In Good Company: Essays in Honour of Robert Detweiler,* eds. David Jasper and Mark Ledbetter (Atlanta: Scholars Press, 1994). See in particular her discussion of the gendering of listening (pp. 194–5) and of the loss of the divine listener (p. 183, pp. 195–7.) Morey sees psychoanalysis as the contemporary – and in many ways problematic – replacement for confidence in "a supreme active listener."

[10]   In this she resembles Irigaray – see chapter 1 – and lays herself open to similarly "essentialist" readings.

tive environment dominated by competing monologs.[11] Both the "dumb silencing" that passes over whatever does not fit the terms of the discourse, and the "garrulous silencing" that prevents the object of knowledge from speaking for itself, are apparent as features of the philosophical culture she rejects.

The Wittgensteinian dictum, *Wovon man nicht sprechen kann, darüber muss man schweigen*, is described by Fiumara as "a somewhat circumscribed philosophical statement . . . quite at variance with the maieutic silence of the person who listens in order to allow something apparently inexpressible to emerge" (p. 98). What is missing from Wittgenstein's statement, on Fiumara's analysis, is the possibility of *keeping* silent, listening to "that of which we cannot speak." She thus rereads the sentence, and in the process reverses its most obvious meaning, the one on which its uses and abuses in theology have mainly depended: "only when we know how to be silent will that of which we cannot speak begin to tell us something" (p. 99).

In this work, then, as in the group practice Morton describes, the "whereof we cannot speak" is redescribed as that "whereof we cannot speak *yet*" – and the listener's silence is what enables its transition into speech.

This reversal depends on a contrast, central to Fiumara's work, between the "power" of speech and the "strength" of listening. The "powerful" and "productive" discourse seeks to expand its territory through the silencing of others and the ever-closer determination and definition of objects of knowledge. "It is . . . a language rooted in a delusion of omnipotence" (p. 57). The claim here is that academic and popular discourses as currently constructed both rely on and reinforce an understanding of power as sovereign control, and as the capacity to eliminate – that is, perhaps, to silence – anything that resists that control. "One can even say that the logos that knows how to speak but not how to listen represents the model of power in its primordial form" (p. 54).[12]

---

[11] For a complementary analysis (from a feminist perspective) of the adversarial character of modern "reasoning," see Janice Moulton, "A Paradigm of Philosophy: The Adversary Method," in Garry and Pearsall, eds., *Women, Knowledge and Reality*, pp. 11–25.

[12] One of Fiumara's implied criticisms of the postmodern thinkers on whom she draws for her analysis of "thought-as-power" is their acceptance of the inevitability of this form of "power." Her description of the false dilemma in which contemporary philosophy finds itself suggests this: "Either we move conceptually according to western logical and dialectical methods . . . or . . . compete in the . . . propensity to unmask, demythify, desacralise and deconstruct: either a procedure that exults in its own abilities or a pantoclastic, suicidal trend" (p. 65). Both the modern ideal of the hegemony of "western logical and

Fiumara locates the suppression of *listening*, in a discursive environment oriented toward power, in her discussion of the "problem of benumbment." Benumbment is the condition of defensiveness produced by exposure to warring discourses. It is a refusal to listen or be listened to, as a means of defending one's own discursive space against the predatory invasion of other discourses. Fiumara identifies it as a strategy practiced by those who recognize the power of the prevailing culture to "make them hear" and, in resistance to it, deliberately inhibit their capacity for listening.[13] Benumbment becomes an attractive option because hearing, within the "non-listening *logos*," is a condition imposed by the "power" of discourse on those who are, for whatever reason, unable to participate actively in speech; it is "an antiphilosophical acceptance of an invasive message" (p. 23). In a culture that cannot listen, hearing tends only toward imitation and hence to the reinforcement of the monologue.[14] Benumbment is the attitude of those who refuse to take part in communication in the forms which the monological culture makes possible.

In itself, as a strategy of mere resistance, benumbment leads only to the continued loss of the possibility of non-coercive speech or listening. Deliberate inhibition of one's capacity for listening is a fearful response to the threat of power, that itself does nothing to overcome the failures of the prevalent culture of discourse; stopping one's own ears will not stop the noise. By drawing attention to the condition of hearers in a monological discourse, however, the analysis of benumbment opens the way for a discussion of an alternative mode of "agency" in communication – the "strength of listening" (p. 57). Listening's "strength" lies precisely in those attributes that in a power-based communicative culture are identified with weakness – just as listening itself is defined as an activity of the "weak."

Fiumara offers a fascinating list of adjectives for the mode of thought that displays strength precisely in its supposed weakness: "mild, moderate, modest, available, vulnerable, welcoming, patient, contained, tolerant,

---

dialectical methods" and the "postmodern" attempt to destroy that hegemony accept the same basic understanding of the nature of philosophical and political discourse – the powerful speaker is the one who does not or need not listen.

[13] "It is almost as though the individual tacitly said to himself, 'I am trying to find a way of not thinking because I no longer want to think the thoughts of others' " (p. 82).

[14] "The interactive modes that are commonly envisaged, in fact, are either that of 'listening' and falling victim to a possessive and exclusivist discourse that binds the 'hearer,' or alternatively, 'listening' in order to be able to rebut" (p. 83).

conciliating, receptive, pitiful (with reference to *pietas*), humble (with reference to *humus*)" (p. 69). Elsewhere we find: "the qualities of attention, tenacity, patience, respect, resilience, rigour and farsightedness . . . constitute a way of relating that is based upon strength" (p. 71). The *logos* that either listens or exposes itself to listening risks a "defeat" – in the conflictual terms of current discourse – but it is precisely that defeat that enables the emergence of new forms of thinking. Listening is by its nature a risk-taking, but it displays its strength precisely in its capacity to accept risk. Understanding listening as an activity allows Fiumara to consider how silencing is overcome – not by a reassignment of forces on the battlefield of discourse, nor by continued "benumbment" and fragmentation as a defensive strategy.

The differentiation between "power" and "strength" is intended to allow the activity of listening to be thought. Fiumara is prepared to speak of this activity, implicitly and explicitly, as causal in character (although not according to "the deterministic principle of [linear] cause and effect"). Speech can occur *because of* the listener: "we commonly say, for instance, that the adult listens because the child begins to speak. By transforming and broadening our conception of causality we could then justifiably affirm that the child begins to speak because the adult listens" (p. 118).

What Morton describes as "hearing into speech" is recognized, and discussed in terms of the inadequacies of linear/sequential causality for explaining complex phenomena. The linear perception of "speech causing listening" is not simply reversed; listening that "causes" speech is only possible within an open dialogic field that relates listener and speaker reciprocally to one another.[15] Thus, the relationship between speaker and listener is asymmetric, but not to the extent that either remains unaffected by the act of listening. The listener acts by allowing herself to be acted upon, taking a risk for the sake both of the interlocutor and of whatever is going to be said – which is not necessarily known "before" the act of listening. Creativity and novelty are not a matter of the single voice asserting its power, as cause in a non-reciprocal relation to its effect, but rather emerge within a field of asymmetric but reciprocal action.

What is the activity of the listener, or of the one who "knows how to be silent," as Fiumara understands it? Fiumara begins her analysis of

---

[15] Fiumara apparently wants to present the causality of listening as somehow "natural" here; but the *creative* capacity she attributes to listening elsewhere remains unexplained, if indeed in her terms it could ever be "explained" without reducing it.

listening with an etymological exercise, drawn from Heidegger, in which *logos/legein* is "traced back" to "laying" or "letting-lie." Reality (both the *logos* and what it excludes) needs to be "gathered" in thought. Against the desire forcibly to assimilate – and to exclude whatever refuses assimilation – Fiumara calls for the "gathering" of apparent contradictions and a readiness for "coexistence with the incomprehensible." Silence is reinterpreted as allowing the "object of knowledge" to speak for itself. The "irrational" – intuition, bodily experience, the unassimilated "anomaly" or "singularity" – is not passed over, but is attended to in a listening silence. Where Heidegger's account of *Gelassenheit* focuses on attention to an "originary" silence, Fiumara is more concerned with attention to the particular silences of whatever appears incomprehensible or irrational.

From the perspective of the listener, the recognition of difference implied in allowing "that of which we cannot speak" to be heard also implies the patience to allow the various "unspeakable" things to become integrated, with each other and with established frameworks of knowledge. The "powerful" discourse assumes that assimilation and incommensurability are the only two options when confronted with something new or different – either this is something we *can* speak about, or it is something to be "passed over." The unity of the world-that-can-be-listened-to is not theorized, but is the hope that underlies any act of listening.

Part of the importance of keeping silent here lies in the interruption of one's own speech. Deliberately falling silent is sacrificing one's own "power" for the sake of whatever would otherwise be forcibly silenced; but it does not represent a cessation of interest or activity. A further implication of this, suggested above, is that to fall silent is to expose oneself to risk, by ceasing to control the discursive space. The most important risk taken in listening, however, is not the risk of being "defeated" by some more powerful speaker, but the risk, shared with the one who is listened to, of allowing unpredictable creativity. The listener's silence requires willingness to "make space" for the new, the unexpected, and the undeveloped thought.. Listening is repeatedly described as that which permits "transmutation" or "transformation," the emergence of genuine novelty or creativity – from the "gathering" and integration of previously separated discourses and ideas, and the interruption of monologs. What emerges as a result of listening cannot be predicted on the basis of what is "said." In a final chapter, Fiumara discusses the possibility, in dialog, of both the listener and the one who is "heard into speech" – and, it is even suggested, the world they inhabit – being changed through listening.

Hope in the "philosophy of listening"

What is Fiumara trying to do in describing the possibilities of listening?

The philosophy of listening as I have described it is necessarily open-ended, experimental, utopian in the sense of a desire to imagine possibilities beyond those that are immanent in the present as we see it. Fiumara often writes in the form of hints, suggestions, and self-consciously counter-intuitive claims – a listening rationality is something we have not experienced and hence cannot "understand." This is a style that arises naturally from the subject matter. Listening as Fiumara portrays it is a risk, refusing to assume the power to control its own effects and final consequences.

In a sense, then, the philosophy of listening is advocating and practicing eschatological thinking. The listener acts for the sake of a future "healing," the nature of which is radically unknowable. The end of silencing, and the growth of the "strength of listening," is a hope, which every particular act of listening both relies on and proleptically enacts. The activity of listening rests in each case on the hope for the possible integration of fragmented discourses or objects of knowledge. The various "predictions" about the political, social, and (perhaps most importantly) ecological consequences of a rediscovery of listening are offered as suggestions or dreams – which themselves invite the process of integrative, critical, and transformative listening. Close connections are made, as may already be apparent, between the listener's silence and the "eschatological" orientation of listening. The keeping of silence is what allows unexpected or unexplored possibilities to emerge; it is also what allows the listener herself to be changed.

But what account can really be given of the hope of and for a rediscovery of listening? Fiumara's use of the vocabulary of "capacity" and "potential" treads a fine line between biological determinism (listening belongs to our essential nature) and the idea that we have control over the direction of social and cultural evolution (we can choose to become listeners). Listening has to be presented as a possibility even within the non-listening discourse – the transformations effected through it are transformations *of* what is already "given" to the listener. The philosophical etymologies, and the retellings of human evolutionary history, are attempts to locate the capacity of listening in some "forgotten" region of human existence to which we can still have access. All of this might be challenged in a theological attempt to appropriate the "philosophy of listening."

Theological questions arising[16]

Fiumara's work does not concern itself explicitly with theology, although the adoption of theologically loaded terms is occasionally striking. The only explicit, if cursory, reference to theology describes the language of the contemporary *logos* as "the sort of language that 'competes with the gods', that confronts the creative power of the 'divine word' and that, in any case, does not need to listen" (p. 57). We can surmise from this passing reference that, in common with other secular-philosophical critics of the Enlightenment, she regards theology, as it is generally undertaken, as part of the problem. Theology participates in the "halving of the *logos;*" it speaks and hardly listens.[17] We have seen that theological critics of the silencing of God, while condemning the human *logos* for "competing with God," argue that an understanding of God as a speaker need not imply "competition" with human discourse. The problem – as again we noted earlier – is the difficulty in developing an adequate account of the hope for an end to silencing on the basis of an exclusive concentration on the primacy of divine speech.

Fiumara's work, especially read in conjunction with the challenge presented by Morton and other feminist theologians, poses a genuine challenge to theology – to think through the significance of the activity of listening. If the philosophy of listening enables us to understand more about "hearing to speech," it potentially enables us to consider how *God* "hears to speech." If it allows us to understand how human silence can be active in listening, it could also point to the rereading of God's silence as a listener's silence.

---

[16]   The only extended discussion of Fiumara's work in Christian theology is in Mary Grey, *The Wisdom of Fools?: Seeking Revelation for Today* (London: SPCK, 1993); Grey uses the "philosophy of listening" to develop a critique of *logos*-centered theologies of revelation. Her discussion, however, while giving extended and broad-ranging consideration to practices of human listening, pays little attention to the representation of God as a listener. Reflection on the ethics of communication is not accompanied by an interrogation of the predominant understanding of God's communication. The final suggestion that God (in the figure of divine *wisdom*) is "the one who listens to unheard cries" is significant but scarcely elaborated in what has gone before.

[17]   Compare Michèle Le Doeuff, *Hipparchia's Choice*, trans. Trista Selous (Oxford: Blackwell, 1989), p. 20, where the claim is made that the appeal to religion rests on the prior silencing of philosophy; or Habermas' contention (which, interestingly, appears to be leveled more at Heidegger than at theology per se) that theology is inherently inimical to dialog – Jürgen Habermas, "Transcendence from within, Transcendence in This World," in *Habermas, Modernity and Public Theology*, eds. Don S. Browning and Francis Schüssler Fiorenza (New York: Crossroad, 1992), p. 226.

In subsequent chapters, I shall be referring to Fiumara's work in a theological context to develop suggestions for an ethic of communication that takes seriously the activity of listening. I read her, then, as a contemporary teacher of wisdom – one who seeks to describe and develop the "hearing mind" as a prerequisite for individual and social well-being.[18] The theological appropriation of this wisdom teaching will, however, raise various questions concerning the wider framework within which it is presented, and hence also concerning its limitations as "wisdom."

My discussion of the silencing of God and the silencing of women emphasized the problem of depersonalization – the extent to which the "whereof we cannot speak" is excluded from personal categories. In Fiumara's work, the use she makes of Heidegger raises concerns in this area. In the wider context of contemporary philosophy, Heidegger is the thinker to whom reference is made most often in attempts to refocus attention on the role of silence and listening in communication; he presents, in his later philosophy, an account of active silence, receptivity to that which communicates itself, as the basis for the possibility of speech.[19]

The problem with Heidegger's account, as has frequently been noted by his critics, is his failure to specify the "object" of listening in a way that permits it to be related to the problems of ethics and politics. His examples – like those of Dauenhauer, who follows him closely – predominantly suggest an esthetic account of silence.[20] Fiumara's work, while

---

[18] Wisdom encompasses the recognition and understanding of particulars, the integration of knowledge, the discernment of value, and the formation of right response, all of which have been identified as aspects of listening well. What Solomon asks for and receives from God is a "hearing mind" (1 Kings 3 : 9), the basis both of his ability to "discern good and evil" (ibid.) and execute justice (3 : 28), and (by implication, though the "hearing mind" is not specifically mentioned here) of his knowledge of the natural world and his creation of proverbs and songs (4:29ff.). See on this R. W. L. Moberly, "Solomon and Job: Divine Wisdom in Human Life," in *Where Shall Wisdom Be Found? Wisdom in the Bible, the Church and the Contemporary World*, ed. Stephen C. Barton (Edinburgh: T. & T. Clark, 1999), pp. 4–5, where Solomon's "hearing mind" is equated with "ability actively to engage with the reality of what people say" and (importantly for my subsequent discussion) with "responsive obedience to God."

[19] For discussions of the theme of "listening" in Heidegger, see Robert Mugerauer, *Heidegger's Language and Thinking* (Atlantic Highlands: Humanities Press, 1988); Joseph J. Kochelmans, ed., *On Heidegger and Language* (Evanston: Northwest University Press, 1972). For other appropriations of Heidegger for "philosophies of listening," see David Levin, *The Listening Self: Personal Growth, Social Change and the Closure of Metaphysics* (London: Routledge, 1989); Peter Wilberg, *Being and Listening: Counselling, Psychoanalysis and the Heideggerian Philosophy of Listening* (London: Third Ear, 1998); Bernard Dauenhauer, *Silence: the Phenomenon and its Ontological Significance* (Bloomington: Indiana University Press, 1980).

[20] See for a discussion and overview of scholarship on this topic, Stephen K. White, *Political Theory and Postmodernism* (Cambridge: Cambridge University Press, 1991). On the links

focusing her "philosophy of listening" closely to problems in ethics, may in the end merit similar criticisms. There is a lack of specificity about the "whereof we cannot speak" even after it begins to tell us something; is it a philosophical text, an aspect of ourselves, an object of scientific study – or a partner in conversation? Within Fiumara's text it is clearly all of these, and yet there is still a question about how listening to the thing "whereof we cannot speak," listening to a person and "listening to the *logos*"[21] are related.

The problem about not asking *what* is being listened to – or more importantly, as in Morton's questions, "*Who* is heard?" – is, as I suggested in the analysis of phenomenologies of silence, that the answer to this question affects the ethical status of listening. If an abstracted *logos*, somehow the source or ground of all communication and akin to the Heideggerian "originary silence," becomes the main object of listening, the "philosophy of listening" could become either another and more subtle strategy for the mastery of the world – overcoming identifiable problems, furthering our own evolution – or a depoliticized esthetic philosophy that prescinds from the problems of world-affecting action. Listening can become a set of "techniques" the application of which remains within the control of the listener and the outcomes of which are predictable; or, listening can become an avoidance of responsibility for the activity involved in understanding or entering dialog. (When a political party announces a public "listening exercise," for example, the suspicion is usually that one or both of these is happening.)

Fiumara's constant return to the problems of dialog, of hearing *other people*, is an attempt to resist this possibility; and it suggests the need for further reflection on the question of "who is heard." The act of listening to another, we might suggest, implies not only "attention" or receptivity but also recognition – the knowledge of the other as "like oneself," related to oneself neither simply as an object of curiosity or care nor as the absolutely ungraspable source of authoritative address. Noticeable in Fiumara's work is the relative lack of attention to the situation of being heard – in contrast to Morton's claim that those who learn "hearing to speech" are themselves always already heard. Morton's theological framework, it would seem, allows her to recognize a complex pattern of reciprocity in hearing, which in turn means that she can retain the

---

between Heidegger's non-specified object of "listening" and his support for Nazism, see Berel Lang, *Heidegger's Silence* (London: Athlone, 1996).

[21] p. 3 – Fiumara follows Heidegger in her use of the Heraclitean fragment "When you have listened, not to me but to the . . . *Logos*, it is wise to agree that all things are one."

centrality of persons, silenced or speaking, to her understanding of communication – and that she can assert clearly that "hearing to speech is political."

The "philosophy of listening," then, calls for a closer consideration of the "Who?" questions with which this chapter began – who is silent, as a listener or as a potential speaker? Another complex of questions arising from the discussion of Fiumara's "eschatology," above, concerns the presentation of the philosophy of listening as the solution to an identifiable contemporary problem. The theologian reading Fiumara should ask about the place in her work of the failure of listening, the fragility of her own project, and the fact that some unheard voices are altogether irrecoverable. As I have noted, the work as it stands relies on a basic optimism, both about the human capacity for listening and about the capacity of the "whereof we cannot speak" to enter communication. The task of the recovery of silenced voices, as undertaken (for example) by some of the feminist scholars discussed above, must, if done honestly, involve the acknowledgment of irrecoverable loss – loss both of the "whereof we cannot speak" and of the capacity for hearing it, formed as we are by the "technology" of silence within which even the listeners exist.

At the same time, the emphasis on species and individual "survival" as the goal of the rediscovered philosophy of listening[22] raises the question of whether, if the problem has been underestimated, the possibilities of the "solution" are themselves understated. The relationship of listening to another, we might assume a priori, is not necessarily or paradigmatically therapeutic. A full account of "listening" will have to speak about relationships of mutual enjoyment, of friendship and of love – activities of listening that go beyond the desire for "survival" and bespeak a possibility of abundant life.

All of these issues point in different ways to the possibility of a theological rereading of Fiumara's central concept of the "halved *logos*." What would it mean to consider these challenges to the ethics of communication Christologically? Has Christological reflection, in its interaction with philosophies and popular understandings of language, itself been "halved" or diminished by an emphasis on speaking at the expense of listening? Fiumara's analysis raises the possibility that we have to consider, not the diminishing of theology to a discourse that "does speak but hardly listens," but the diminishing within it of the God of Jesus Christ to one who

---

[22] See the final paragraph, pp. 197–8, with its description of a situation of "extreme danger" and the claim that the existing patterns of communication are "no longer suitable for co-existence or even for survival."

"does speak but hardly listens."[23] At the same time, the demand that the
communicative situation be redescribed Christologically sharpens the
question about the identity of the *logos*. If the *logos* is the "*Logos* made
flesh," both "being heard" and "hearing" acquire an irreducible personal
reference, and it is in relation to this that the further questions concerning the relationship of ethics and eschatology have to be considered.

Before considering (in the next chapter) what it means for the speaking and listening *logos* to be "*Logos* made flesh," then, we need to look
more closely at what it means for "being heard" and "hearing" to be
attributed to persons, and associated with questions about what it means
to be a personal subject. Taking up again Morton's questions, with an
emphasis on the first word – "*Who* hears? *Who* is heard?" – I turn to the
philosophy of Paul Ricoeur, as it enters dialog with Levinas and others,
to elucidate further the importance of hearing and being heard for our
understanding of personhood.

"Who Hears? Who is Heard?"

The poem that introduced the previous chapter described silence as having
"a presence/ . . . a history a form." I suggested there that the form of
silence cannot or need not be understood simply as the "form" of a speech
unuttered or unheard. In fact, in the discussion of silencing that began
the chapter, I identified and differentiated "silences" not so much by the
unuttered speech they represented as by the possible *speakers* whose silences
they were – the "silence of God" and the "silence of women." Particularly in the discussion of feminist theology, it became clear that the
problem of "finding a voice" was intimately connected with problems of
identity; claims by some women to "speak for" women in general were
contested by others, who developed self-definitions over against the discourse that claimed to incorporate them. Morton's questions "Who hears?
Who is heard?" on the one hand point back to the identification of
women as a silenced group (women are not heard) and on the other hand
put a question about the activity of hearing – crucially, as a question about
the identity of the hearer. One of the key issues in the theological appropriation of a "philosophy of listening" on the lines indicated in Fiumara's
work would be the possibility or otherwise of rereading it to make the
question "Who is heard?" more central.

---

[23] See Morton, *The Journey Is Home*, p. 54: "Could it be that *logos* deified reduces communication to a one-way relationship – that of *speaking* . . .?"

The approach to the "Who?" question is, however, problematic. Debates over the nature of identity, subjecthood, and other associated concepts are central to the contemporary feminist debate. The intricacies of that debate need not concern us here, but its basic contours are well known. On the one hand, there is the call to reject the notion of the "subject" as agent of speech or action, as the product of a masculinist world view; on the other hand, there is the claim that a strong notion of subjecthood is essential to the project of women's liberation.[24] My focus on Morton's questions might appear to ally me with the latter position. It is important to note, however, that the focus is the *questions*. I make use, in what follows, of Paul Ricoeur's analysis of the "aporiae of self-hood" in *Oneself as Another*,[25] an analysis that centers initially on the capacity, or incapacity, of contemporary philosophies to ask and answer "Who?" questions. By setting out the problem in this way, Ricoeur is making the modest claim that the "Who?" questions are in some respect irreducible – without presupposing the structure of their answers. I am suggesting, similarly, that the questions "Who hears? Who is heard?" point to significant problems to which an ethics of communication must attend. They are considered here simply *as* problems, to be developed further in what follows.

I turn first, then, to the question "Who is heard?" It is clear that "hearing to speech," as described by Morton and others, begins with the recognition of a possible speaker, that is, of someone who is silent; this was one of the issues on which I suggested that there were questions to be put to Fiumara's "philosophy of listening." The act of hearing to speech presupposes trust in the possibility of an agency to which speech can be ascribed. I claimed in the previous chapter that the temporal structure of a listening silence was that of "awaiting future speech." I would now suggest that this activity of awaiting requires the prior recognition of the future *speaker*. To distinguish between silences, as I have done, in the first instance by ascribing them to "subjects" – the silence of God, the silencing of women – implies the recognition that there is *someone* who keeps silent or is consigned to silence.

The problem of "garrulous silencing," however, indicates the possibility that certain ways of ascribing silence make the silence unbreakable. To

---

[24] The debate is well represented in Selya Benhabib, ed., *Feminist Contentions: A Philosophical Exchange* (London: Routledge, 1995), with Judith Butler on the one hand and Benhabib on the other presenting the two approaches.

[25] Paul Ricoeur, *Oneself as Another*, trans. Kathleen Blamey (Chicago: University of Chicago Press, 1992).

define someone or some group implicitly or explicitly *as* a "silent" object of enquiry is to exclude from the start the participation of the object in the discourse that defines it. The ascription of silence for which feminist theology calls is the recognition of the silenced as agents, as the potential or actual inaugurators of action that is not stably determinable from the actions of others upon them.[26]

For the purpose of this discussion, I shall designate this aspect of the personal "presence, history and form" of silence – this way of asking and answering the question "Who is silent?" – the silence of *unknowability*.[27] Consideration of this aspect of the "Who?" question threatens, as the previous chapter has already suggested, to involve me in the complex debate over the ethical relationship between, on the one hand, the recognition of irreducible difference, and on the other hand the enacting of (at least formal) equality. Clearly the critique of silencing, and the attempt to hear the silenced, involves both the acknowledgment of the irreducible otherness of the other – as one who has been silenced – and the acknowledgment that that silencing represents injustice.[28] "Hearing to speech," the practice of feminist groups, as Morton describes it, may appear as an interpersonal occurrence determined by what Ricoeur terms "solicitude" (the relation to the particular other as irreplaceable);[29] but it is located in a

[26]   None of this is to deny the problematization in feminist thought, discussed in chapter 1, first of "women's experience" as a pure source of (theological or other) speech, and second of feminism's own construction of the "women" out of whose silence it is supposed to speak.

[27]   Although the focus here is on the identification and critique of violent silencing, it should also be noted, from phenomenological and conversation-analytical accounts of silence, that certain *deliberate* acts of keeping silent have a similar "structure," in that they enact (and in these cases call attention to) the impenetrability of the person *qua* agent. See Don Ihde, *Listening and Voice: A Phenomenology of Sound* (Athens: Ohio University Press, 1976), p. 184, on silence under interrogation.

[28]   For a sensitive account of the difficulties of negotiating these two aspects of "breaking the silence," see the introduction to Edith Wyschogrod, *An Ethics of Remembering: History, Heterology and the Nameless Others* (Chicago: University of Chicago Press, 1998), pp. xi–xvii. Wyschogrod locates the work of the "heterological historian" – the historian who seeks to uncover previously untold stories – between the "imperative," the unconditional demand of the silenced that she become their advocate, and the "indicative," the historian's drive to discover and present "the facts."

[29]   The relation of solicitude as Ricoeur describes it is characterized by "reversibility, non-substitutability and similitude" (with the third arising as "the fruit of exchange between esteem for oneself and solicitude for others"). (Ricouer, *Oneself as Another*, pp. 192–3). I emphasize the second aspect – non-substitutability or irreplaceability – at this point because it is the one Ricoeur draws from Levinas' uncompromising insistence on the priority of the *other*. This is represented (by Levinas and his commentators) as the priority of the *speaker* (or the one from whom the "injunction" comes) in relation to which the "I," the hearer, is "passive beyond passivity."

context of political activism to which the desire for justice is central. If listening begins with the recognition of the claim of the other upon me – the claim of the other not to be "silenced," either by being ignored or by being treated as a mute object of comprehension – it goes beyond the acknowledgment of that claim.[30]

In listening to someone, one also listens to discourse that locates her in a shared world; the act of listening intends the other as a participant in the making and discernment of meaning in this shared world. To understand this, we have to look more closely at the activity of listening and the person who undertakes it – integrating what is said into established patterns of understanding, making judgments about its importance, and shaping a response to both the speaker and the world thus interpreted. This is the second sense, identified in the previous chapter, in which "silence has a presence . . . a history a form." We do need to ask "Who hears?" as well as "Who is heard?"

Central to the "philosophy of listening" is the claim that the capacity to listen well is not to be taken for granted. What can we say about the self that has this capacity? Accounts of the genesis of the self that make it rely on the prior condition of "being addressed" or "being spoken to" seem to give at most a derivative significance to the capacity for the discerning reception of the other's speech. Morton's and Fiumara's claims invite us, by contrast, to understand the activity of listening, and the listener as acting self, as central to the thinking and practice of communication.

Emmanuel Levinas could be taken as an example of a thinker who gives absolute priority, in his account of the self, to the other's claim on "me" – the self arises first in the accusative, as one who is the object of the other's demand. In *Totality and Infinity* Levinas can speak of a prior condition of self-absorption, the possession of self and world as a "totality" which is shattered by the irruption of the other's "infinite" demand; the face of the other person is what brings about the self as responsible and capable of ethical response. The "listening to the *logos*" that did not mark this irruption of the ethical claim would, it seems, for Levinas, have nothing in common with "exposure" to the face and voice of the other.

Does this give us the basis for a full account of the ethical relation of listening? Ricoeur's refusal, in *Oneself as Another*, to follow Levinas in

---

[30] As Robert Gibbs, for example, demonstrates in his use of Habermas' "ideal speech situation" in conjunction with Levinas' "ethics as first philosophy." Robert Gibbs, *Why Ethics?* (Princeton: Princeton University Press, 2000).

referring all otherness to the absolute prior claim of the other person[31] can, I suggest, be read as a claim that the formation of listeners is a precondition for the possibility of ethical communication. He argues, for example, that "the theme of exteriority [i.e. in Levinas] does not reach the end of its trajectory, namely awakening a responsible response to the other's call, except by presupposing a capacity of reception, of discrimination, and of recognition."[32]

In the first section of *Oneself as Another*, Ricoeur has considered speech and speech-acts as fundamental to the self – and has indicated that speech-acts already suggest "the specific passivity of the self affected by the other than self"[33] through the necessary presence of the listener. He now relates this "specific passivity" in turn to an act of listening not reducible to the condition of "being addressed." To be able to hear the other already requires "a reflexive structure," which Ricoeur claims is "better defined by its power of reconsidering pre-existing objectifications" than by the "initial separation" by which Levinas marks the sharp distinction between self-absorption and responsibility.[34]

Without presupposing any particular origin for the capacity for listening – without forcing us, for example, to regard it as a biological or psychological given – Ricoeur here raises the question "Who hears?" as fundamental to the understanding of the self in communication. The political significance of this move has already been indicated in the discussion of Fiumara, above – it is the capacity of "reception, of discernment, and of recognition" that enables the hearer to move beyond the alternatives of unquestioning submission to the powerful voice, on the one hand, and self-imposed "benumbment" on the other. Unless we have some idea of the listener as making judgments about what she hears or whom she responds to, there is no reason to suppose that listening per se is a good thing.

In considering "hearing to speech," I have identified two forms of silence – the silence of "unknowability" and the silence of the listener – corresponding to the questions "Who is heard?" and "Who hears?"[35] The

[31] For feminist interrogations of which, see Morny Joy, "Levinas: Alterity, the Feminine and Women," *Studies in Religion*, 22, 4 (1993), 463–85, esp. pp. 483–4.

[32] Ricoeur, *Oneself as Another*, p. 339.

[33] Ibid., p. 329.

[34] Ibid., p. 339.

[35] The gender aspect of these two forms of silence should be noted at this stage, to be discussed further in subsequent chapters. Morton's questions "Who hears? Who is heard?" invite – both in terms of the practice of her church-community, and more broadly in terms of cultural specification of gender roles – the answers "women" and "men" respectively.

legitimacy of both these questions can clearly be contested. While neither requires the prior positing of an isolated self, the very attempt to put and answer the question "Who?" would be challenged by those – feminist thinkers and others – who reject the language of selfhood and subjectivity as recalling an unacceptable ideal of sovereign self-sufficiency.

One provisional response to such challenges would be to point out that I have drawn the two questions of "selfhood" from a relation – "hearing to speech" – and the two forms of "silence" they identify have been considered in each case as silence toward and for another. At this stage, no attempt has been made to think them apart from the relation that presupposes both. This can be taken further; the unacceptable ideal of sovereign self-sufficiency is the ideal of a self that speaks without dependence on a hearer or a dialog partner. A debate about the "subject" constructed in these terms cannot recognize the question "Who hears?" at all; sovereignty, self-sufficiency, being the unique origin of one's actions, are categories that make no sense when the "action" under consideration is the act of hearing.

All of this relies, however, on the assumption that something like "hearing to speech" is possible. Morton's suggestions that God could be regarded as the "hearing one" are based on the experience, as she understands it, that hearing to speech *does* happen. Reflection on her accounts of the activity of hearing to speech, however, gives rise to questions about the conditions of possibility for its occurrence. I mean here, not only the practical or empirical conditions of possibility, but the ontological conditions, the being of the one "who hears" and "who is heard;" and not only the ontological conditions, but the ways in which the practical and empirical conditions reflect them. I cannot hear you to speech unless there is more to you than the discourses that have silenced you or have reduced your speech to untruthfulness, that is, more than can presently be experienced or named; but "hearing to speech" makes a difference to the world, can itself be experienced or named, gives rise to new forms of speech or communicative relationship. In speaking about the theological ethics of communication, we will need to be able to give an account of both of these.

The previous chapter began to raise questions about the account of hope that underlies any theological talk about silence, and this discussion

---

Correspondingly, the silence of unknowability looks like masculine "reserve" (the "strong silent man" as contrasted with the weak talkative woman; see on this Jonathan Rutherford, *Men's Silences: Predicaments in Masculinity* (London: Routledge, 1992)) and the silence of the listener looks like feminine "receptivity."

has reinforced the need to respond to those questions. Listening as we have described it is itself already a hopeful activity. We have to ask about the basis for the listener's hope that new speech is possible; on what grounds can the other be recognized and affirmed as a possible speaker? Beyond this, we have to ask about the capacity for listening, its sources and development, and the grounds on which it may be hoped that this capacity can re-emerge.

Within Christian theology, as I have already suggested, the answers to these questions would be expected to be Christological in form. Feminist thinkers who are not Christian theologians are, however, unlikely to be convinced prima facie that an "account of hope" developed on such terms would do anything other than deprive women of the hard-won hope that they might now be able to speak with a voice not determined by patriarchal structures. The challenge for the next two chapters will be to put forward a Christological account of God's listening silence that does not betray the hope discovered by those who have been heard to speech.

Chapter Three

RESURRECTION SILENCE

It is not for us to prophesy the day (though the day will come) when
people will once more be called so to utter the word of God that the
world will be changed and renewed by it. It will be a new language...
Until then, the Christian cause will be a silent and hidden affair. (Dietrich
Bonhoeffer, *Letters and Papers from Prison*[1])

"Who is God?"

"Encounter with Jesus Christ"[2]

Considerations of the silence of God, no less than the "breaking of
silence" in feminist theology, are determined by a "presence, history, and
form" to which questions of identity and the ascription of action are
central. The claim that "God is silent," in other words, invites the
question "Who is the God who is silent?" As I have already noted, the
characterization of God as one who speaks has often been taken as central
to the recognition of God as personal or as subject of free action, and
resistance to the "silencing" of God identifies that silencing as the "depersonalization" of God. My discussion so far has raised the question of
whether the naming of God as speaker provides the only or the best
framework within which God's communicative action in relation to the
world could be understood. Answering that question in the negative will
require closer consideration of the personal "presence, history, and form"
of the silence of God.

How should a discussion of the silence of God, as the silence of one
"who is heard," and "who hears," be developed further? It would seem
reasonable to suggest that, if a *Christian* theology of the silence of God is

---

[1] Dietrich Bonhoeffer, *Letters and Papers from Prison*, ed. Eberhard Bethge, trans.
Reginald Fuller et al. (London: SCM 1971), p. 300; *Widerstand und Ergebung: Briefe und
Aufzeichnungen aus der Haft*, DBW 8, p. 436.
[2] *Letters and Papers*, p. 381; DBW 8, p. 558.

possible, it will be the "presence, history, and form" of Christ that determines what can be said about the silence of God and its relation to human
silences. But would such a "theology of the silence of God" ever be able
to respond adequately to the concerns of feminist thinkers? Shaping the
silence of God according to a word of revelation already spoken – a word,
moreover, that is heard from and as a male figure – is bound to be suspect
in the terms of the critiques outlined in the previous chapter. In effect,
the suspicion must be that the use of Christology in an account of divine
silence amounts to the reimposition of an authoritative male voice. When
the chosen conversation partner in the Christological analysis of divine
silence is a man – and a man, his extensive use by feminist theologians
notwithstanding, without feminist sympathies – the suspicion must be
redoubled.

I intend to outline here, through a reading of Dietrich Bonhoeffer's
theology that attends both to his words and his silences, a Christological
interpretation of the silence of God that loses none of the force of the
ethical critique of silencing that has been discussed so far. The basic belief
that underlies such a project is that the Gospel of Jesus Christ includes
liberation from silencing, from "dumb spirits," and from communicative
structures that reproduce falsehood, and that a true presentation of it will
likewise tend toward that liberation. What feminist and other critiques of
Christianity reveal clearly, however, is that this belief cannot merely be
asserted. Anyone who examines theological and ecclesial history can find
ample evidence to discredit it, and to suggest that, rather, the Christian
Gospel can only be sustained through oppressive practices of communication. This is the question that Nelle Morton's work puts to Christian
theology – is it possible to understand and speak of God's communicative
action in a way that does not perform some further act of silencing?

The silence of Christ, as I noted in the introduction, has been a
subsidiary but significant theme of theological reflection throughout
Christian history, and I trace it here in Bonhoeffer's thought. Central to
my argument is the idea that the *resurrection* both is (uncontroversially) the
focus of the asking and answering of the "Who?" question with regard
to the God of Jesus Christ, and (more controversially) can be read in terms
of an intensified silence of God. The resurrection silence is, to refer back
to the discussion in the last chapter, a silence of unknowability – the risen
Christ is not available to comprehensive analysis, has no defined set of
innerworldly characteristics, cannot be reduced to a collection of words,
is irreducibly a *who*. The risen one is known – is the one "who is heard"
– in the particular ways in which the reality of the resurrection is made
present within history – without annulling the complexity of history or

human responsibility within it. This "silence of unknowability" can be thought through using the categories of Bonhoeffer's *Ethics* – thinking historical existence as "penultimate" in relation to the resurrection as the "ultimate" toward which it is oriented.

I shall also suggest, however, that the silence of God as thought from the resurrection is the silence of a listener; that the resurrection is God's hearing of God's own Word, and the point from which God's hearing of the whole of creation can be understood. This is the point at which the discussion must move beyond a narrowly Christocentric focus – and beyond the explicit content of Bonhoeffer's work – to think about the resurrection as event *for God*. As we shall see in the next chapter, this dimension of the theological thinking of the resurrection is extremely important when we come to consider what it means for people to "hear the Word of God" – and if we want to understand how that act of hearing is itself part of their transformation into the image of God.

Why begin with Bonhoeffer for a theological response to the questions "Who hears? Who is heard?" The initial attraction is his consistent atten- tion to "Who?" questions in theology – and the ways in which he con- nects these, both to fundamental theological issues and to ethics. When Bonhoeffer asked the question "Who is God?" in a book outline that forms part of his correspondence with Eberhard Bethge from Tegel prison, he refused the answers that came from an "abstract belief in God, in his omnipotence etc.", and turned instead to the "encounter with Jesus Christ," with "God in human form".[3] The question "Who is God?" becomes the question of Christology – "Who are you?", asked of Christ and, as we shall see, reflected back on the one who asks it.[4] The answer to this Christological "Who?" question, as it emerges in Bonhoeffer's work, is given in the threefold designation of Christ as the incarnate one, the crucified one, and the resurrected one – a designation that will provide the structure for the discussion that follows.

In all the varied interpretations of Bonhoeffer, there is widespread agreement on the centrality of Christology, and more specifically the determination of Christ as the incarnate, crucified, and resurrected one, for all aspects of his thought. A reading of Bonhoeffer's Christology

---

[3] *Letters and Papers*, p. 381; *DBW* 8, p. 558.
[4] As, most importantly, in the introduction to the lectures on Christology: *Berlin, 1932–1933, DBW* 12, pp. 280–9, *Lectures on Christology*, trans. Edwin Robertson (London: Fount, 1978) (hereafter *Christology*), pp. 27–37. More extensive discussion of the *Christology* introduction and its more direct implications for the ethics of speech and listening follow in chapter 4.

requires an understanding of how these three terms together express who Jesus Christ is.[5] Furthermore, in the *Christology* lectures, the incarnate, crucified, and resurrected Christ is also identified as the center of human existence, nature, and history;[6] and, in other works, in similar terms as "the real one"[7] and "the truth," and the one who *stands for* all.[8] The three-fold determination of the identity of Christ implies a corresponding deter-mination of the world in relation to God. The answer to the "Who?" question, addressed to Christ, necessitates the extension of the threefold structure to the theological reading of the whole of reality. This will prove particularly important for our understanding of the relation between Christology and ethics.

Scholarly interest in the theme of silence in Bonhoeffer's work has tended to focus on certain passages in his *Letters and Papers from Prison* in which he appears to advocate a "discipline of the secret" for the Church.[9] While there have been innumerable attempts to resolve issues in the inter-pretation of Bonhoeffer's later work by reference to earlier writings, there has been relatively little comprehensive discussion of the theme of silence in Bonhoeffer's work as a whole.[10] This is not entirely surprising. The

[5] See the "Outline for a book," *DBW* 8, p. 558, *Letters and Papers*, p. 381: ". . . partici-pation in this being of Jesus (incarnation, cross and resurrection)."

[6] *DBW* 12, pp. 307–11.

[7] A pervasive theme in the *Ethics*, first introduced in the section on "Christ, Reality and the Good" (*Ethik, DBW* 6, pp. 31–61).

[8] See *DBW* 12, p. 306; *DBW* 6, pp. 249–50.

[9] Bonhoeffer first uses the term in lectures at Finkenwalde, describing the practice of the early Church (*Illegale Theologenausbildung: Finkenwalde 1935–1937, DBW* 14, pp. 549–51); the subsequent and more famous references are in the prison letters (*DBW* 8, pp. 405–6, 415; *Letters and Papers*, pp. 281, 286). For an overview of interpretation, see Andreas Pangritz, *Dietrich Bonhoeffers Forderung einer Arkansdisziplin* (Cologne: Pahl-Rugenstein, 1988), chapter 1. See for other discussions of "silence" in Bonhoeffer, Renate Bethge, "'Elite' and 'Silence' in Dietrich Bonhoeffer's Person and Thoughts," in John D. Godsey and Geffrey B. Kelly, eds., *Ethical Responsibility: Bonhoeffer's Legacy to the Churches* (Lewiston: Edwin Mellon, 1981); Albert Altenähr, *Dietrich Bonhoeffer – Lehrer des Gebets: Grundlagen für eine Theologie des Gebets bei Dietrich Bonhoeffer* (Würzburg: Echter Verlag, 1976), pp. 160–5; Frits de Lange, *Waiting for the Word: Dietrich Bonhoeffer on Speaking About God*, trans. Martin N. Walton (Grand Rapids: Eerdmans, 2000); Kenneth Surin, *The Turnings of Darkness and Light* (Cambridge: Cambridge University Press, 1989), pp. 180–200.

[10] The role of mystery in Bonhoeffer's thought has been considered rather more widely. Discussed in Ernst Feil, *The Theology of Dietrich Bonhoeffer*, trans. Martin Rumscheidt (Philadelphia: Fortress, 1985), it is the focus of Hans-Jürgen Abromeit, *Das Geheimnis Christi: Dietrich Bonhoeffers Erfanhrungsbezogene Theologie* (Neukirchen: Neukirchner Verlag, 1991). Abromeit concludes that Bonhoeffer's *Christology* – and hence both his theology and his anthropology – centers on ethical *Erfanhrung*, lived experience, as the *locus* of the knowl-edge of Christ. In choosing (unlike Abromeit) to focus on the resurrection, I identify a particular "material" Christological connection between mystery and *Erfanhrung*, and thus

scattered and cursory nature of Bonhoeffer's pronouncements on silence, together with the general difficulty of talking about silence in a differentiated way, means that analyses have tended to conflate uses that are not obviously identical.[11] It is not the main intention of this chapter to provide a comprehensive overview of the theme in Bonhoeffer; but the distinctions between "silences," developed already and in what follows, are also useful for the analysis of his work.

It should, of course, be noted that when we look at Bonhoeffer's theology we see a theology developed in the context of the Nazi state – that is, the context that came, in late twentieth-century Europe, to symbolize the distortion of all aspects of human social life, including the distortion of communication. Bonhoeffer's life, as a leader in the Confessing Church that resisted the Nazi government's attempt to control Church life and worship, and subsequently as a participant in the conspiracy to assassinate Hitler, is well known, and frequently recounted in connection with studies of his theology. As I read Bonhoeffer's theology here, I consider it as a response to the situation of distorted communication that he faced – while asking how it can speak to a situation not unrelated, though far less extreme.

Bonhoeffer's work has been appropriated in the years after his death, on the one hand, by those seeking a theological critique of political and ecclesial "silencing." Feminist theologians have drawn on his later work, with its perceived critiques of prevailing models of divine power, and its emphasis on the ethical. Slogans from the *Letters and Papers from Prison* – "religionless Christianity," life "*etsi deus non daretur*," the "world come of age" – are used to defend a theology in which the silence of God is the source of human freedom and responsibility,[12] allowing the world to "speak for itself," without the imposition of divinely authorized speech.

---

also to indicate (for further elaboration in subsequent chapters) a clearer link between human practices of speech and silence and the *Erfahrung* in which Christ is known. It should be noted that, while Abromeit places his main discussion of "mystery" before the section on "material Christology" – treating "mystery" as a formal or methodological feature of Bonhoeffer's *Christology* – I deliberately link discussion of silence and mystery with "material" Christology and eschatology, chiefly with the resurrection.

[11] For example, it is by no means obvious that the "qualified silence" of the Church in *Sanctorum Communio* is the same as the *disciplina arcana*, as the editors of *DBWE* 1 (p. 251, n. 382) seem to assume.

[12] See William Hamilton, "Dietrich Bonhoeffer," in Thomas J. J. Altizer and William Hamilton, eds., *Radical Theology and the Death of God* (London: Penguin, 1968), pp. 112–23; Dorothee Sölle, *Christ the Representative: An Essay in Theology after the Death of God*, trans. David Lewis (London: SCM, 1967), pp. 150–2.

On the other hand, Bonhoeffer's work has been used by those who reaffirm the prevenient action of God and the centrality of the Word of God in Christian theology.[13] For these interpreters, Bonhoeffer's theology does not affirm, but rather helps to defeat, modernity's attempt to consign God to silence.

It will be apparent from the discussion in the first two chapters that I do not believe either of these positions is sustainable as the basis for a theological ethics of communication. The former does not explain why the silence of God in the world gives rise to anything beyond a collection of competing human monologues; and the latter simply retains the "top-down" model of communication that produces patterns of silencing. I would also claim, and shall be demonstrating here at greater length, that neither of these positions is based on an adequate reading of Bonhoeffer's thought. In order to develop a more satisfactory reading, and one that will enable a different theological understanding of communication, we must first attend to the central "silences" in Bonhoeffer's theology – the silences of Christ – as they shape his theology and ethical thought.

Three silences of Christ

The framing of answers to the question "Who is God?" around the affirmation of Jesus Christ as the incarnate, crucified, and resurrected one is central to Bonhoeffer's theology.[14] What does the threefold identification of the presence, history, and form of Christ say about the presence, history, and form of God's silence? One of the characteristic features of Bonhoeffer's Christology is an emphasis on the Christological *incognito* – the unknowability of Christ in the world. The question "Who is God?," in Bonhoeffer's theology, brings us to this *incognito* inseparably associated with a particular personal history. I begin, then, with a discussion of Bonhoeffer's presentation of the silence of Christ as the "silence of

[13] See, for example, Jüngel's use of Bonhoeffer's description of existence *etsi deus non daretur* to develop the idea that God is *"more* than necessary" – Eberhard Jüngel, *God as the Mystery of the World: On the Foundation of the Theology of the Crucified One in the Dispute between Theism and Atheism*, trans. Darrell L. Guder (Grand Rapids: Eerdmans, 1983), pp. 24–5, discussed in David F. Ford, *Self and Salvation: Being Transformed* (Cambridge: Cambridge University Press, 1999), pp. 55–6.

[14] Abromeit traces the beginning of the threefold structure of Bonhoeffer's Christology to the presentation on dialectical theology given in America in 1931, and believes that it receives an "ever-increasing significance" in Bonhoeffer's work from that point onwards. Abromeit, *Geheimnis Christi,* pp. 229–30.

unknowability" discussed above. What does it mean for the incarnate, crucified, and resurrected one to be the one "who is heard?"

Famously, Bonhoeffer suggests in the *Letters and Papers* that God allows Godself "to be pushed out of the world onto the cross." This claim provides a useful starting point for consideration of the Christological *incognito*. Although, as I noted above, the *Letters and Papers* have been the focus of attempts to develop this aspect of Bonhoeffer's thought, the theme of the weakness and hiddenness of Christ in the world is not new in these letters. Christ appears in Bonhoeffer's writings as the "humiliated one," offering no unambiguous manifestations of power, speaking in a way that cannot enforce a hearing.[15] Here, then, the Christological *incognito* refers to the "taking on" of human nature, existing within the world (and its ambiguities and uncertainties) for the sake of the world – the incarnation "moment" in the Christological narrative, as described above.

The image of God "pushed out of the world onto the cross," on the one hand, points to the crucifixion as the culmination of the self-humiliation of Christ, the point of greatest weakness and complete hiddenness. On the other hand, it indicates another aspect of the *incognito* – the irreducibility of Christ to what is knowable, and hence to his transcendence of attempts to define or judge him, a radical freedom over against the world. God "pushed out of the world onto the Cross" is the one whom the world has refused to know, and who is set over against the world to condemn it. The paradox of the weakness of the incarnate Christ, as the place where the power of God is seen, reaches its greatest intensity in the crucifixion.[16]

To stop at the crucifixion, in our consideration of the silences of Christ, would be to leave the two aspects of the Christological *incognito* – the "taking on" of the world to affirm it, and the freedom over against the world to condemn it – unreconciled. The paradox of the cross – the weakness of God as the power of God – is reflected in the different interpretations of the silence of God, to which I have already referred. If there is nothing from God beyond the silence of the crucified Christ, the "death of God" is succeeded by a set of principles or projects for human self-making, without the possibility either of hearing a word from "outside"

---

[15] For the *incognito* and the "humiliation" of Christ, the *locus classicus* is the *Christology* lectures (see *DBW* 12, pp. 345–8); for the "weakness" of Christ as Word (besides the passages cited earlier), *DBW* 4, pp. 180–1, *DBWE* 4, pp. 173–4.; *London 1933–1935*, *DBW* 13, pp. 338–43, 409–13.

[16] For recent discussions of the tension between the "power" and the "weakness" of Christ in Bonhoeffer's thought, see Clifford J. Green, *Bonhoeffer: The Sociality of Christ and Humanity* (Missoula: Scholars Press, 1972); Lange, *Waiting for the Word*.

our self-contained discourse or of being heard by one who could confirm that discourse's claims to be concerned with truthfulness.

As we saw in the previous chapter, and noted in the introduction with reference to Bonhoeffer's work, this terminal silence can be read as opening up the possibility for human responsibility, through emancipation from the authoritative divine voice and those who claimed to speak or interpret it. We also saw, however, that the terminal silence of God leaves no grounds for the hope that silencing can be justly ended, or that the liberated speech of humanity will amount to anything more than a cacophony of competing voices. To see God "pushed out of the world onto the cross" is also to see the continuing violence of the world – including the violence of practices of silencing – held up to judgment.

As I have already claimed, the structure of Bonhoeffer's Christology requires that the cross is seen only in the light of the resurrection, and the identity of Christ known only because the risen Christ testifies to himself. Likewise, it requires that the resurrection "include" both incarnation and crucifixion. Without losing the significance of the emphasis on the incarnation and the crucifixion here, I present, in what follows, a reading of Bonhoeffer's theology in which the resurrection both intensifies and changes the Christological *incognito*.

The Silence of the Resurrection: Deepening the Christological *Incognito*

Overview

Of the three Christological "moments" discussed above – incarnation, crucifixion, and resurrection – we might expect the resurrection to be least associated with silence. Both internal and external critiques of Christian theologies have argued that an emphasis on the resurrection produces triumphalism, the premature foreclosure of "unfinished" histories and the refusal to recognize ineliminable *aporiae*.[17] The resurrection can be read as the point at which silence, including the silence of the Christological incognito, is decisively and irreversibly broken, after which

---

[17] For a recent example of external critique that, because of the proclamation of the resurrection, portrays Christianity as the religion of the unjustifiable triumph of word over silence, see André Neher, "Shaddai: The God of the Broken Arch," in Alvin H. Rosenfeld and Irving Greenberg, eds., *Confronting the Holocaust: The Impact of Elie Wiesel* (Bloomington: Indiana University Press, 1978), especially pp. 252–3.

no indeterminacy is possible — and, consequently, after which the single voice of Christian proclamation silences all other possible interpretations of the world, while itself refusing to maintain silence.

Placing the resurrection at the center of a theology of the silence of God seems, then, illogical at first. It seems especially illogical when we consider that Bonhoeffer, whose understanding of the "silence of Christ" I have been following so far, says relatively little about the resurrection. This has led some commentators to criticize what they see as his unbalanced emphasis on the powerlessness, the suffering, and the death of God.[18] Bonhoeffer put forward an extended critique of the *theologia gloriae* that offers "cheap grace" by proclaiming the resurrection without the crucifixion; and the passages from the *Letters and Papers*, already quoted, reinforce the impression that the resurrection is at no point seen to abrogate the significance of the crucifixion.[19]

I shall suggest that it is precisely because of the importance of the resurrection for Bonhoeffer that he says so little.

> It's . . . from the resurrection of Christ that a new and purifying wind can blow through our present world. *Here* is the answer to δος μοι που στω και κινησω την γην ["give me a place to stand and I shall move the earth"].[20]

In this quotation from the *Letters and Papers*, the image of the "place to stand" ("the answer to δος μοι που στω") should alert us from the start to the possibility that the most important reality might be that about which very little is said. The resurrection is the place *from which*, or on the basis of which, action and reflection occur, and as such is not itself necessarily an object of extended consideration.

The δος μοι που στω quotation points us, further, to two general features of Bonhoeffer's discussion, which will be reflected in what follows. First, the resurrection is interpreted as an event for the world and for humanity ("through *our present world* . . . the answer to δος μοι που στω").[21] Second, and more specifically, the resurrection is interpreted in

---

[18] See for example Martin Hohmann, *Die Korrelation vom Altem und Neuem Bund: Innerbiblische Korrelation statt Kontrastkorrelation* (Berlin: Evangelische Verlagsanstatt, 1978), pp. 156–7.

[19] *DBW* 4, pp. 29–43.

[20] *DBW* 8, pp. 68–9; *Letters and Papers*, p. 240.

[21] This can be clearly seen from the structure of the "Theological Letter on the Resurrection," in *Konspiration und Haft 1940–1945, DBW* 16, pp. 471–4, Bonhoeffer's most extended treatment of the topic. Two of the three main sections are headed

relation to both eschatology and ethics (the "*new* and purifying wind" and that which "moves the earth"). For both these aspects, as we shall see, the character of the resurrection as intensification of the Christological incognito is crucial.

Bonhoeffer's concentration on the *pro me* of the resurrection should not be taken as evidence of an exclusive interest in soteriology – in Christ "for us" to the exclusion of questions of Christ's being. That would risk losing sight of the "Who?" question and dissolving Christ into a collection of "benefits." In his remarks on method in Christology, Bonhoeffer asserts, contra Melanchthon (or his interpreters), the priority of Christology over soteriology, and thus the absolute priority of the "Who?" question. In the same lecture, however, the being of Christ is then defined as *pro me* or *pro nobis*, the "man for others." The soteriological interpretation of the resurrection is not separable from questions of the "personal structure of being" of Jesus Christ; likewise, as the discussion above implies, the *incognito* is a determination of that "structure of being" rather than a function of extrinsic relations.

What does the resurrection mean for the "personal structure of being" of Jesus Christ? In Bonhoeffer's work, the resurrection is seen, first, as the free act of God that brings about a "new thing." The reality it inaugurates is connected to what precedes it by no form of continuity that can be established from the perspective of that preceding reality.[22] In the *Christology* lectures the implications of this for the "historical" nature of the resurrection are made clear. The resurrection is not an event that can be proved from within a framework of historical causality; it is accessible only through the faith that is given by God. This is the first and obvious sense in which the resurrection maintains and deepens the Christological incognito.

---

respectively "The resurrection is God's Yes to us" and "The resurrection is God's Yes to creation." The first is "The resurrection is God's Yes to Christ and his atoning work," where the discussion focuses chiefly on the "atoning work."

[22] See *Creation and Fall* on the "void" that precedes creation, which is compared with the death of Christ. Just as creation arises out of no causal necessity, and therefore cannot be thought apart from the word that announces it, so "There is absolutely no transition, no continuum between the dead Christ and the resurrected Christ, but the freedom of God." (*Schöpfung und Fall, DBW* 3, p. 33; *Creation and Fall, DBWE* 3, p. 35). This discontinuity is expressed in ethical and historical terms in the earlier sections of the *Ethics*; the miracle that can save humanity from the void is " the . . . saving deed of God, that creates new life out of nothing – it is the resurrection of the dead." (*DBW* 6, p. 123, my trans.). The resurrection as *new creation* is a theme already apparent in the doctoral dissertations (the contrast between life "in Adam" and "in Christ").

The resurrection is also, however, as suggested above, a point that establishes continuity – the continuity of Jesus' identity, in incarnation and crucifixion, and in the new existence that the resurrection makes possible. At several points in Bonhoeffer's work we find reflection on the biblical insight that the resurrected body of Jesus is both *the same* and *not the same* as the body that was crucified (the grave is empty; but the disciples fail to recognize Jesus).[23] The resurrection is the basis, not only of the single identity of the incarnate, crucified, and resurrected one, but also of the continuing self-identification of Christ, and hence of the possibility of Christological speech and reflection.[24] To believe in the resurrection is to believe that the particular identification of Jesus Christ as the incarnate and crucified one is both inalienable and trustworthy. This in turn means, however, that the resurrection confirms the identity of Christ as the one who on the one hand can be known as the bearer of a particular "history" and "form," and on the other hand cannot be reduced to a fully comprehensible object of knowledge.[25]

The two aspects of the Christological incognito discussed above – the weakness of the one who "takes on" the condition of the world, and the radical difference from the world that appears in the crucifixion – remain central to the identification of the risen Christ. Indications of the implications of this can be found throughout Bonhoeffer's work. In *Sanctorum communio*, in which the concept of personal mystery (the basis of the "Who?" question) is first introduced, the resurrection is discussed primarily as that which makes the new existence of humanity in community possible. The incarnation enacts God's "taking on" of fallen humanity as a whole; the crucifixion reveals, and pronounces judgment on, the fundamental isolation of humanity "in Adam" separated from God and hence from the neighbor; the resurrection inaugurates the "paradoxical reality of a community-of-the-cross."[26] Likewise, in *Discipleship*, the "community at the foot of the cross" is the central theme, but the resurrection remains its humanly impossible condition of possibility. Here, as indicated above, Bonhoeffer's main concern is to ensure that the resurrection is not thought without reference to the crucifixion – that the *theologia gloriae* does not overcome the *theologia crucis*.[27] The triumph of

---

[23] *DBW* 12, p. 347; *DBW* 4, pp. 229–30, *DBWE* 4, pp. 215–16.
[24] This is one of the key points of the introduction to the *Christology* lectures, as mentioned above.
[25] *DBW* 12, pp. 374–8.
[26] *DBW* 1, p. 95; *DBWE* 1, p. 151.
[27] The specific paraenetic and polemical importance of this in his own context is clear; see the afterword to *DBW* 4, pp. 312–17, *DBWE* 4, pp. 294–9.

Christ, and hence the triumph of the Church and its proclamation, is always and only the triumph of the *crucified* one;[28] conformity to Christ means taking up the cross.[29]

I noted above that the *theologia crucis* in Bonhoeffer's later work as a specification of God's silence — the God "forced out of the world and onto the cross" — has often been taken as the basis for a theological emphasis on responsible action in the world. The discussion presented here of Bonhoeffer's interpretation of the resurrection demands a more nuanced restatement of that claim. The resurrection is, on this reading, what makes responsible life possible.[30] The implications of this, as seen in Bonhoeffer's later work, go beyond the formation of the "community at the foot of the cross." The resurrection, as we have seen, is the event that establishes the single identity and decisive significance of Jesus Christ as the reconciliation of God and humanity — and of the antithetical divine "words" of affirmation and judgment.[31]

Speaking of the resurrection in terms of reconciliation draws attention to its eschatological aspect — and the temporal determination of its unknowability. Indeed, Bonhoeffer's discussions of the resurrection frequently focus on its importance for our understanding of temporal existence, our relation to past and future. The resurrection is understood, as we have seen, as the free act of God that brings about a new creation as a radical "interruption" of existing reality; and it is also the only basis from which the coming of God's kingdom can be anticipated. It is what takes place "already in the midst of the old world . . . as a last sign of its end and of its future," but is at the same time both a "living reality" and the mark of "God's will for a new world."[32]

On the one hand, then, the resurrection is the future of the world; on the other hand, it is inalienably *present* to the world and determinative of its reality. The "futurity" of the resurrection is another aspect, for Bonhoeffer, of its resistance to systematization and hence its unknowability.[33] Particularly

[28] See especially *DBW* 4, p. 300, *DBWE* 4, p. 284.

[29] *DBW* 4, p. 84, *DBWE* 4, pp. 90–91.

[30] See on this Abromeit, *Geheimnis Christi*, pp. 353–6 – although these observations on the "completion" of Christology in Christian existence are not explicitly linked to the resurrection, a link which I would claim is required by the logic of Bonhoeffer's *Christology*.

[31] The importance of this for Christian attitudes to the world is perhaps most clearly expressed (before the *Ethics*) in a public lecture given in Potsdam in November 1932, on the theme "Thy Kingdom come" (*DBW* 12, pp. 270–8).

[32] Dietrich Bonhoeffer, *Ethics*, Eberhard Bethge, ed., trans. Neville Horton Smith (London: SCM, 1955), p. 91.

[33] On this, see Wolf Krötke, "Der begegnende Gott und der Glaube Zum theologischen Schwerpunkt der Christologievorlesung Dietrich Bonhoeffers," in Wolf Krötke and

in Bonhoeffer's earlier work, the future (*Zu-kunft*) is that which comes "from outside;" life "out of the future" (paradigmatically the life of the *child*) is life in dependence on what comes from beyond oneself.[34] Here the discontinuity of the resurrection – as free act of God and new creation – is emphasized.

At the same time, the future given to creation in the resurrection is its own future; the "old world" is affirmed in and through "God's will for a new world." God's "taking on" of created reality in the incarnation is confirmed. The resurrection is the "answer to δος μοι που στω," the given that cannot be disputed – which cannot be understood as a purely formal "που στω," since its givenness is the givenness of a particular personal history.[35]

What are the implications of this configuration of eschatology and ethics in the theology of the resurrection – what does it really mean to say that the resurrection is the "place to stand" that "makes responsible life possible?"

An early section of the *Ethics* deals with the concept of *Ethik als Gestaltung*, ethics as conformation with Christ. Conformation with Christ is here described in terms of conformity to the incarnate, crucified, and resurrected Christ – each narrative determination pointing toward a different aspect of being human before God.[36] "To be conformed with the incarnate one – that means to be a real human being . . . To be conformed with the crucified one – that means to be a human being judged by God . . . To be conformed with the resurrected one – that means to be a new human being before God."[37] Conformation with Christ is the restoration of what is properly human – which is the unique form of Christ.

For both the individual and the community, then, in Bonhoeffer's account, the resurrection is the ground of the promise of continuing transformation into the restored image of God.[38] In the important discussion

---

Albrecht Schönherr, eds., *Bonhoeffer-Studien* (Berlin: Evangelisches Verlag, 1985), p. 30; Robert Scharlemann, "Authenticity and Encounter: Bonhoeffer's Appropriation of Ontology," *Union Seminary Quarterly Review*, 46, 1–4 (1992).

[34] *Akt und Sein*, DBW 2, pp. 157–61, DBWE 2, pp. 157–61.

[35] On the significance of "the past" in Bonhoeffer's later writings, see Robert Holyer, "Toward an Eschatology of the Past," *Theology*, 89 (1986), and the comments on recapitulation, below (n. 103).

[36] See Stephen John Plant, "Uses of the Bible in the 'Ethics' of Dietrich Bonhoeffer," PhD, University of Cambridge, 1993, chapter 3, for comments on the narrative approach to *Gestaltung* in Bonhoeffer's work.

[37] *DBW* 6, pp. 81–2 (my trans.); see *Ethics*, pp. 18–19.

[38] "The brilliant light and the life of the risen one will already shine forth from the form of death of the crucified one in which we live . . . The transformation into the divine

in the *Ethics* that relates "conformation" to incarnation, Crucifixion, and resurrection, conformation with the resurrected Christ is described primarily in terms of hiddenness. "His secret remains hidden from the world . . . The new *Mensch* lives in the world like any other. Often there is little to distinguish him from the rest . . . Transfigured though he is in the form of the Risen One, here he bears only the sign of the cross and the judgment." (*Ethik* 82–3).

The emphasis on the unknowability of the resurrection form is important here because it indicates the impossibility of using Christology to create a new ethical system. The resurrection is the basis on which it can be asserted that the presence, history, and form of Christ are active in the world, not as impersonal historical influences but as the unique criterion and determinant of historical reality. As such, however, it is also what makes the reduction of particular situations to instances of general principles, and the reliance on one or another ethical formula, "irresponsible" and false.[39]

The effect of the intensification of the Christological *incognito* in the resurrection is, then, first, to establish the primacy of the concrete practice of "conformation" over the capacity to judge "conformation" in oneself or others.[40] It is easy to identify, in Bonhoeffer's work, practices and ways of life that can be described as life "conformed to Christ."[41] Even these, however, could be misunderstood as guidelines for a project of personal or institutional self-creation. The cross can be estheticized, or made the basis for an uncritical affirmation of the demands of particular "victims;" any given understanding of "conformity to Christ" is open to suspicion. I would argue that identifying the *resurrection* as the only "place to stand" destabilizes even these attempts at securing an ethical starting point. Even the Church, to which Bonhoeffer famously refers as *Christus als Gemeinde existierend*,[42] is itself not an unambiguous sign of the new reality.

---

image [*Ebenbild*] will become ever more profound, and the image [*Bild*] of Christ in us will continue to increase in clarity." (*DBW* 4, p. 302, *DBWE* 4, p. 286.)

[39] See the rejection of various "principled" ethical stands, *DBW* 6, pp. 64–6, *Ethics*, pp. 4–7.

[40] This is exemplified in the important passage on "doing" the will of God as the "irreconcilable opposite" of judging (oneself or the neighbor) – *DBW* 6, p. 316, *Ethics*, pp. 154–5.

[41] *Stellvertretung* and life "for others" being the most consistent themes – both in Bonhoeffer's work and in subsequent discussion of his ethics. Abromeit culminates his discussion (see n. 30 above) with a consideration of *Stellvertretung* as "being Christ for the other."

[42] *DBW* 1, p. 127; *DBWE* 1, p. 190.

Furthermore, as I shall consider at greater length below, the hiddenness of the "new *Mensch*" in Christ appears to secure the "silence of
unknowability," the possibility of asking and answering the question "Who
is heard?," without the need to posit a sovereign self-possessing subject.
The "personal structure of being" of the resurrected Christ, as the one
who can only be approached through the question "Who?," grounds the
"structure of being" of persons in Christ.

This still leaves unanswered, however, the question of whether the
mystery of the resurrection, which I have so far described in terms of the
intensification of the Christological *incognito*, has any significance beyond
the negative one – of perpetually calling into question the final validity
of any particular reading, or personal or communal "manifestation," of the
history of Christ.[43] In the sphere of ethics, the question is about the positive content of "responsible life" – both in terms of the self (what more
can be said about the asking and answering of the "Who?" question?) and
in terms of the structures and practices in which responsible existence
occurs. As with the feminist thinkers discussed in the previous chapter,
the adoption of strategies of critique, calling all closures of discourse into
question, does not seem adequate ethically or theologically without some
account of the reality that orders and moves the process of critique and
transformation. The question is then whether such an account can be
given without repeating the imposition of powerful speech, and the act
of violent silencing, against which the critique was directed in the first
instance.

Bonhoeffer claims in the earliest sections of the *Ethics* that in
Christian ethics the relations between "should be" and "is," idea and
realization, and so forth, are replaced by the relation between "reality
and realization, past and present, history and event (faith), or, to replace
the ambiguous concept with the unambiguous name of the thing itself:
Jesus Christ and the Holy Spirit."[44] Bonhoeffer here locates ethics in the
time during which the "reality" of the resurrection is not fully apparent,
but is nonetheless active, shaping its own "realization." The resurrection
is not only a "place to stand" but is the point from which "I can move
the earth;" and it is the place from which "a new and purifying wind can

---

[43] This negative significance of personal unknowability, in relation to the resurrection, is
considered in Rowan Williams' "Between the Cherubim: The empty tomb and the empty
throne" (Rowan Williams, *On Christian Theology* (Oxford: Blackwell, 2000), pp. 183–96).
Williams' particular concern is with the empty tomb narratives as a resource for "the patient
diagnosis of untruths," and especially the diagnosis of untruthful claims to exclusive
possession of Jesus' presence and authority.

[44] *DBW* 6, p. 34; *Ethics*, p. 57.

blow." The dynamic of the resurrection – the power of "God's will for a new world," the possibility of being "conformed to Christ" – is present in the world.

Can Bonhoeffer think this "relation between reality and realization" in a way that goes beyond the negative significance of the *incognito* – the Christological "silence of unknowability" – without performing another act of silencing? I shall argue in what follows that the conceptual structure he introduces to define the field of ethics promises to achieve this, but that the content he gives it is too restricted to answer the legitimate questions of his critics. I shall then seek to extend that content by considering the significance of the resurrection for the identification of God as a *hearer*, that is, by returning to the second form discussed above of the question "Who keeps silent?"

The ultimate and the penultimate

I have noted that the silence or hiddenness of God – the godlessness of the world – is closely associated, in Bonhoeffer's later work, with the summons to ethical responsibility. The world in which ethical life and action occurs is the "godless world," within which the word of God is *not heard*. The world within which responsibility is possible, it seems clear from the *Letters and Papers*, is the "world come of age" – the world that no longer expects a divine answer to the questions of its existence, the world in which God no longer speaks with an authority the world can recognize as decisive. Looking more closely at the theological framework within which Bonhoeffer sets out his view of the "godless world" helps us to see how assertions about God's silence do not necessarily give rise to an endless battle between competing human voices – and, at the same time, how assertions about the decisive significance of the resurrection do not necessarily result in the silencing of all other voices by a triumphalist Christian proclamation.[45]

The basis for Bonhoeffer's account of Christian ethics as responsible action in this "godless world" is the contrast between the ultimate and the penultimate, between the final reconciliation achieved in Christ and the situation of continuing conflict that is nonetheless shaped by the reality

---

[45] On this whole section, see Paul Janz, "Redeeming Modernity: Rationality, Justification and Penultimacy in the Theology of Dietrich Bonhoeffer," PhD, University of Cambridge, 2000, chapter 5.

of the resurrection.[46] The ultimate/penultimate structure emerges in its developed form only in Bonhoeffer's *Ethics*, but is central to the argument of that work. Bonhoeffer wants to retain the claim – which sounds so threatening from the perspective of the critic of Christian imperialism – that the history and form of Christ *are* the history and form of the world; what the world is is determined by who Christ is.[47] At the same time, he wants to do this in a way that demands attention to, and an ethical response to, the complexity and openness of the world.

The important section of the *Ethics* that introduces the ultimate/penultimate distinction begins with an analysis of "Justification as the last word."[48] The "last word" is ultimate in a twofold sense. First, it "implies the complete breaking off of everything that precedes it . . . it is therefore never the natural or necessary end of the way which has been pursued so far, but . . . God's own free word compelled by nothing" (pp. 81–2). Second, however, it is ultimate in the sense that "It is always preceded by something penultimate . . . that is to say, in a quite genuine sense by a span of time, at the end of which it stands." The "last word," therefore, is both the free act of God compelled by nothing that precedes it and in contradiction to all existing understandings of continuity, and the act of God that establishes the reality of what precedes it. These are, as we have seen, the terms in which Bonhoeffer elsewhere discusses the resurrection.

So what can be placed alongside this "last word?" The *penultimate* is the span of time defined by the relationship between the "reality" of this last word and its "realization." Bonhoeffer's initial specification of the penultimate is, quite simply, "everything that precedes the ultimate." Its designation as "penultimate" indicates that it has its own proper value, but only in the light of the ultimate toward which it points.[49]

---

[46] The replacement of a spatial with a temporal contrast is identified in James H. Burtness, "Als ob es Gott nicht gabe: Bonhoeffer, Barth und das lutherische *Finitum Capax Infiniti*," in Christian Gremmels, ed., *Bonhoeffer Und Luther* (Munich: Kaiser, 1983). I refer to it here as a "supplement" rather than a "replacement," because, although Bonhoeffer rejects "thinking in terms of spaces" (*Raumdenken*) as an overarching ethical approach, he does retain a limited significance for some innerworldly "spatial" contrasts, in particular between Church and government.

[47] *DBW* 6, p. 47; *Ethics*, p. 66.

[48] I have preserved the translation "ultimate and penultimate," customary in English-language commentary on Bonhoeffer, for *Letzten und Vorletzten*; but it should be noted that this threatens to turn *Letzten und Vorletzten* into technical terms, and to obscure some of their appearances in Bonhoeffer's work – as for example "the last word," here, or "the last secret," discussed in chapter 5.

[49] As Pangritz notes (pp. 437–8 n.50), the terminology of *Letzten und Vorletzten* is found in Karl Barth, *Das Wort Gottes und der Theologie* (Munich: Kaiser, 1929), p. 64, but with the emphasis on the discontinuity between the penultimate and the ultimate. It is

The apparently simple move of designating the whole sphere of natural, cultural, and ethical life, the world in which human decision and activity occurs, as penultimate has far-reaching implications. On the one hand, it allows Bonhoeffer to develop a "world-affirming" ethic that accords importance to innerworldly distinctions of value, secular goodness, "the mature "worldliness" of the thirteenth century," and the category of the "natural."[50] On the other hand, it ensures that, for example, the principles of "natural law," or humanistic judgments of goodness, cannot be granted unconditional validity.[51]

Within Bonhoeffer's discussion the penultimate is not simply "fallen creation" or existence "in Adam." To speak of the world in terms of the "penultimate" is to represent it as affirmed, judged, and redeemed in Christ – but also, and more importantly for our purposes, as the world that "prepares the way" for the ultimate, the world whose temporal existence is reoriented toward a future external to its immanent possibilities. The most obvious difference between understanding the world as "fallen creation" and understanding it as the "penultimate" lies in the relation to the future implied by each designation. Viewed as the created and fallen world, the only optimism permitted to it is the assertion that orderliness, and hence the possibility of continued life, will prevail over chaos.[52] It has no *telos* beyond its own continuation. As the "penultimate," on the other hand, it has a *different* future that is nonetheless *its own* future. To recognize the world as penultimate is to be prepared, not merely to seek to preserve the order of the world as it is given, but to look for a "better future" of *this* world.[53] At the same time, it is clear that the determination of the penultimate by the ultimate and not vice versa means that "working for a better future" cannot take the form of the realization of a comprehensive plan – even, of a "Christian" plan.

---

noteworthy nonetheless that Barth's use of the terms occurs in a discussion of the resurrection as "new creation."

[50]   Oliver O'Donovan, *Resurrection and Moral Order: An Outline for Evangelical Ethics* (Leicester: Inter-Varsity Press, 1986), is a more recent example (interestingly, with very little explicit reference to Bonhoeffer) of a "use" of the resurrection as the basis for ethics.

[51]   Whether this is successfully demonstrated in the sections of the *Ethics* dealing with "natural life" – often considered the weakest parts of the work – is open to debate.

[52]   This "entirely immanent optimism," hope for the preservation of "natural life" over against whatever tends to destroy it, is nonetheless significant – see *DBW* 6, p. 170, *Ethics*, p. 106.

[53]   See the discussion of "optimism" in "After Ten Years" – *DBW* 8, p. 36, *Letters and Papers*, p. 15.

The introduction of the "penultimate" as an ethical category, alongside the simultaneous rejection of world-affirming and world-denying ethical programs, may be considered one of Bonhoeffer's most important moves in theological ethics.[54] It appears to allow an ethics at once fully Christocentric and fully engaged with the complexities of historical decision-making. Despite this, subsequent debates over the development of his ethics indicate problems in their application. How is the path between the affirmation of given realities and the condemnation of the godless world really to be negotiated? Is Bonhoeffer a "situation ethicist" – and, if so, what guidelines are there for the analysis of any given situation?[55] Is the refusal to provide a principle for the reconciliation of the various ethical antitheses in fact a way of avoiding the most difficult questions?

Feminist commentators in particular have asked whether Bonhoeffer, in practice, ends up reaffirming social conservatism, by according too much weight to the recognition and affirmation of given social orders and providing so little indication of how Christian ethics challenges or transforms them. Thus, for example, Bonhoeffer identifies the basic structures of ethical life within the orders of preservation in terms of divine "mandates" – the orders in which "the commandment of God takes concrete form," including marriage and the family, Church, culture, and government.[56] He is happy to assert that the mandates require "relations of superiority and inferiority," which are in themselves not called into question.[57]

In terms of the questions posed in my first chapter, then, it is not clear, within Bonhoeffer's thought, how the various attempts to express and

---

[54] Recent appreciative discussions include Jan Liguš, "Dietrich Bonhoeffer: Ultimate, Penultimate and Their Impact," in *Bonhoeffer's Ethics: Old Europe and New Frontiers*, ed. Guy Carter (Kampen: Kok Pharos, 1991); Janz, "Redeeming Modernity;" Ford, *Self and Salvation*, chapter 10.

[55] For discussion of Bonhoeffer's work in relation to "situation ethics," see James T. Laney, "An Examination of Bonhoeffer's Ethical Contextualism," in *A Bonhoeffer Legacy: Essays Iin Understanding*, ed. A. J. Klassen (Grand Rapids: Eerdmans, 1981); James H. Burtness, *Shaping the Future: The Ethics of Bonhoeffer* (Philadelphia: Fortress, 1985), pp. 63–120.

[56] *DBW* 6, pp. 392–8, *Ethics*, pp. 252–8, where the mandates are identified as "church, marriage and the family, culture (*Kultur*) and government (*der Obrigkeit*)." *DBW* 6, p. 54, *Ethics*, p. 73, lists "work, marriage, government and church."

[57] Helga Kuhlmann, "Die Ethik Dietrich Bonhoeffers: Quelle oder Hemmschuh für Feministisch-Theologisch Ethik?," *Zeitschrift für Evangelische Ethik*, 37 (1993); Thomas Day, *Dietrich Bonhoeffer on Christian Community and Common Sense* (New York: Edwin Mellon, 1982). Here, again, the grounding of ethics in the reality of the resurrection appears to be given mainly a negative significance – as a control on the exercise of power. See especially *DBW* 6, pp. 395–6, *Ethics*, pp. 255–6.

enact hope for change within society or the churches can be assessed theologically. After all, the feminist critiques of silencing that I discussed in the previous chapter have much that would appear to fit them into Bonhoeffer's scheme. They are attentive to historical complexity; they do not attempt prematurely to speak a "last word" about God or humanity, or to implement a "Christian plan" in the face of the given facts; and, as I suggested, they resist self-justification by recognizing the complicity of the silenced in their own silencing. However, their challenge to the communicative and social orders, and hence their claim to announce or permit something new within the present world, is not explicable in Bonhoeffer's terms as outlined so far.

Clearly on one level the demand that Bonhoeffer's ethics yield principles for the assessment of any given ethical question is misguided, since, as my earlier discussion indicates, this is precisely what the silent "reality of the resurrection" excludes. Asked to show how the polarities of affirmation and condemnation are worked out in ethical action, Bonhoeffer offers not a principle but a summons to responsibility,[58] as response to the encounter with the living Christ[59] grounded in the resurrection. The possibility of responsible action depends on freedom from "principles" – whether the "principles" that reshape the world according to a predetermined pattern or the "principles" that unquestioningly preserve it in its present state. This freedom in turn enables obedient response to the command of God discerned in the given situation. As suggested above, "conformation to Christ" is not accessible as a theoretical possibility outside the lives and actions within which it takes place.

At the same time, the reference to "conformation" here points to a legitimate question. My discussion of the possibility of "optimism" offered by the concept of penultimacy, above, indicated a difference between the hope for the continued preservation of the natural order and the hope based on "God's will for a new world." Bonhoeffer's discussions of penultimacy seem to demand that he take into account the possibility of innerworldly novelty, change, or transformation – as a possibility that is itself inaugurated and accepted by God. Love of the penultimate "for its own sake" demands, as Bonhoeffer makes clear in the *Ethics*, not only the desire to preserve it according to the "orders" commanded by God, but

---

[58]   Recent discussions of Bonhoeffer's concept of responsibility include Burtness, *Shaping the Future*; Ann L. Nickson, *Bonhoeffer on Freedom: Courageously Grasping Reality* (London: Ashgate, 2002); and the collection of essays in Wayne Whitson Floyd and Charles Marsh, eds., *Theology and the Practice of Responsibility: Essays on Dietrich Bonhoeffer* (Valley Forge: Trinity Press, 1994).

[59]   *DBW* 12, p. 288; *DBW* 6, p. 254.

also an attention to, and development of, the capacity for transformation that it possesses precisely by virtue of its ordering toward the ultimate. We have, however, not yet seen – and Bonhoeffer does not make explicit – what understanding of the action of God in the time between "reality and realization" corresponds to the idea of penultimacy.[60]

Silence on a given topic does not, in Bonhoeffer's work especially, mean that no importance is accorded to it. In interpreting and applying his work in a different context it may, however, be necessary to explicate aspects of his "significant silences" that he left unthematized. In what follows, I do this through a closer attention to the "silence of the resurrection," in an attempt to draw Bonhoeffer's work beyond itself and into connection with contemporary concerns.

Rethinking the Mystery

As the first quotation used in my discussion of the concept makes clear, Bonhoeffer describes the "ultimate" in terms of a word – the "last word." By contrast, penultimacy, in his work, is associated with silence. So, for example, adopting the "penultimate" attitude is remaining silent in the face of unresolved conflict or inexplicable suffering, not trying to resolve it by speaking a decisive word.[61] Silence in the penultimate is here an expression of dependence on, and orientation toward, the free act of God understood as future. More than this, however, the penultimate is defined by implication as a time during which *God* is silent. In the previous section I put the question: what does the concept of penultimacy mean for the action of God in the "relationship between reality and realization?" In what follows, I put this question in terms of God's silence. What does the silence of God in the penultimate mean and do? The silence of unknowability, on which I have concentrated so far in my discussion of the resur-

---

[60] The lack of a developed pneumatology in Bonhoeffer's work should be noted here. Clearly he cannot rightly be accused of making pneumatology as such irrelevant, since the whole program of the *Ethics* is defined in terms of the relation "between Jesus Christ and the Holy Spirit." It is also clear that any development of pneumatology that would identify the Holy Spirit too closely either with a "spirit" of proclaimed human progress or (I would argue) with the spirit of a church-community would be detrimental to his project.

[61] Prefigurements of this theme can be found at various points in Bonhoeffer's work. In *Life Together*, silence is kept at the end of the day to recall that "the last word . . . belongs to God" (*DBW* 5, p. 68; *DBWE* 5, p. 85). In the *Ethics*, this silence is particularly associated with bereavement – "remaining silent as a sign that I share in the bereaved man's helplessness . . . and not speaking the biblical words of comfort" (*DBW* 6, p. 143; *Ethics*, p. 84).

rection, does not of itself enable the question of the "relation between reality and realization" to be resolved. Later in this chapter, I introduce to complement it a discussion of God's silence as the silence of a listener.

God's silence as patience

How might the action of God in relation to penultimate reality be described? One of Bonhoeffer's attempts to conceptualize this appears in the notes for the *Ethics*, in two fragments that associate created time with God's patience. One reads "Time: another expression for the patience of God, with the aim that humanity becomes God's own."[62]

What might be the significance of this reference to God's patience, recorded as it was in the context of Bonhoeffer's work on "penultimacy?" There are various reflections on patience, waiting, and associated ideas in Bonhoeffer's sermons and letters.[63] Some of these are concerned with the human act of "waiting on God," the waiting that acknowledges God's power to speak "the last word."[64] In a sermon for Advent in 1931, however, the human capacity to wait is given an explicit Christological significance. Those who wait on God are those who know that God has already waited for them.[65] The "theological letter" on the resurrection (possibly contemporaneous with the fragment for the *Ethics*) states "It is the grace of Jesus Christ, that he does not yet reveal himself to the world openly; for when that took place, that same moment would bring the end, and the judgment on unbelief."[66] Here the mystery of Christ,

---

[62] In the *Zettelnotizen für eine Ethik*, *DBW* 6, *Erganzungsband*, p. 55 (Zettel nr. 60), my trans. See also p. 54 (Zettel nr. 61), and the discussion of these fragments in William Jay Peck, "From Cain to the Death Camps: An Essay on Dietrich Bonhoeffer and Judaism," *Union Seminary Quarterly Review*, 28, 2 (1973).

[63] See especially the letter to the Finkenwalde brethren of 1938, *DBW* 15, pp. 81–4, and the associated notes *DBW* 15, pp. 336–42, on the understanding of patience in the New Testament.

[64] See for example *Ökumene, Universität, Pfarramt 1931–1932*, *DBW* 11, p. 362; and compare the sermon on Ps 62:2, *Barcelona, Berlin, Amerika*, *DBW* 10, p. 479–85. For full discussion of this theme, see Altenähr, *Lehrer des Gebets*, pp.160–3.; Lange, *Waiting for the Word*.

[65] *DBW* 11, p. 393. The reference here (as we would expect in an Advent sermon) is primarily to the incarnation, and hence to the fact that what is awaited has already been accomplished; the Christological *incognito* and the "waiting" that corresponds to it are not accorded eschatological significance. It is, however, significant that God is here characterized as the one who "waits for" humanity, and that God's act of "waiting" is the ground of the possibility of human waiting – waiting that transforms the one who waits.

[66] *DBW* 16, p. 474.

intensified in the resurrection and experienced in the time of the Church, is interpreted as "grace." The passage recalls one of the key texts for Christian discussion of God's patience – 2 Peter 3:8ff.: "With the Lord one day is like a thousand years, and a thousand years are like one day. The Lord is not slow about his promise, but is patient with you."

What is the significance of these references to patience in the light of the issues discussed here? From the earliest days of the Church it has been found necessary, at various times and places, to exhort Christians to patience – patience in the expectation of divine deliverance, in the face of the experience both of human evil and of God's silence.[67] Early exhortations to patience such as that of 2 Peter drew, not only on the contemporary philosophic ideal of patience, but also on the Hebrew Bible's representation of God as patient.[68] In 2 Peter and elsewhere – including in Bonhoeffer's Advent sermon – the patience of God grounds the patience of Christians, which is distinguished from other practices of patience by being thus grounded.[69] The assertion that God is patient can be interpreted as a way of rendering specific the central assertion that God is love – specific, that is, to the God who identifies God's self with and in Jesus Christ.[70] It specifies God's love as the will to give time to the beloved, and, in that giving of time, to continue in love.

This would suggest that the idea of divine patience should be relevant, both to the theological interpretation of the "Who?" questions discussed earlier, and to the question of the relationship between Ethics and eschatology. How might this work in the context of Bonhoeffer's theology? It is possible to interpret Bonhoeffer's claim that the mystery of Christ is "grace," or the call in 2 Peter to "regard the patience of the Lord as salvation," simply in terms of the withholding of the divine word of judgment. Bonhoeffer's description of the "ultimate" as the *word of justification* invites such an analysis. In the *Ethics* and other later writings, the

---

[67] For a discussion of the formation of the early Christian ideal of patience, see S. R. Garrett, "The Patience of Job and the Patience of Jesus," *Interpretation* 53, 3 (1999).

[68] See further on the uses of μακροθυμια and νπομονη in the New Testament and LXX, J. Horst, "Μακροθυμια trans. G. W. Bromiley, *Theological Dictionary of the New Testament*, ed. G. Kittel (Grand Rapids: Eerdmans, 1967), p. 384.

[69] For example, in Cyprian, "On the Advantage of Patience," trans. R. E. Wallis, *Ante-Nicene Fathers*, vol. 13 (Edinburgh: T. & T. Clark, 1869), pp. 22–3; Tertullian, "Of Patience," trans. S. Thelwall, *Ante-Nicene Fathers*, vol. 11 (Edinburgh: T. & T. Clark, 1869), pp. 206–7.

[70] This is the argument of Eberhard Jüngel, "Gottes Geduld – Geduld Der Liebe?," *Wertlose Wahrheit* (Munich: Kaiser, 1990). Jüngel goes on to describe God's patience in terms of God's act of speaking – which seems counter-intuitive but is necessitated by his overall approach to the description of divine action, as discussed in chapter 2.

concealment of the "word of justification" is the ground of the refusal to pass decisive judgment, on the basis of a prior understanding of "the law," either on others or on oneself. Judgment has in one sense already been passed (justification is a given reality in Christ) and is in another sense always "of the future" (justification is the ultimate); in either case, inner-worldly "knowledge of good and evil" expressed in acts of judgment is revealed as penultimate, belonging to the fallen world and without decisive significance. It will be apparent that the concept of free responsibility put forward here relies, on the one hand, on the given reality of justification and, on the other hand, on the "silence" of the word of justification in the penultimate.

The "word of justification" as the "last word," withheld in the penultimate, appears to provide a basis for the hope that the silence of unknowability has a real basis, that the question "Who is heard?" can be asked and answered. The unknowability of Christ, which as we saw is intensified rather than abrogated in the resurrection, corresponds to the unknowability of the person "in Christ." Justification, as God's ultimate word concerning the person, means that she cannot be reduced to an object of classificatory knowledge.

What is not given here is an account of the hope that the further question "Who hears?" can rightly be asked and answered. The assertion that it is impossible to pass definitive judgment on another, *or oneself*, leaves the question of the right exercise of judgment – the capacity for discernment and recognition – unanswered. More generally, to understand the penultimate silence, or God's patience, merely as the indefinite withholding of a particular (and in some sense already "known") word leaves the question of God's transforming activity in the penultimate unresolved.

The discussion of God's patience, above, implied another possible line of development. The suggestion was that God's patience is the specification of God's love as the will to grant time to creation – to establish and sustain it in its freedom.[71] In this description of the "patience of God" there are obvious similarities with the philosophies of listening considered in the previous chapter, and with the practice of hearing to speech. Listening can be described as the act of "giving time" to allow the other's own possibilities for new speech to emerge – possibilities that are themselves in some sense given in and through the act of listening. The

---

[71] And see also Barth's discussion of God's patience – Karl Barth, *Church Dogmatics 2/1: The Doctrine of God*, trans. T. Parker et al. (Edinburgh: T. & T. Clark, 1957), pp. 408–18, where the "gift of time" is the key theme. Barth writes that God's patience is the will and power to allow space and time to creaturely existence (p. 410).

idea that God is patient, or that God "waits for" creation could, it would seem, allow the silence of God that grants responsibility to the world to be understood as coterminous with God's salvific action.[72]

As yet, however, we have not seen how this claim could be developed. The resurrection has been shown to intensify and specify the *unknowability* of God, but the silence of God as salvific action – which I am here associating with the silence of the *listener* – has not been considered. I now move, therefore, to a consideration of God's silence as the silence of a listener – asking and answering, in relation to God, the question "Who hears?" In order to do this, I must in fact begin by considering more closely what it means to understand the resurrection as an event of and for God.

God's silence as hearing

The claims I have made so far in this chapter about the way in which the resurrection intensifies and specifies God's silence all appear to relate to God's silence "to us" – and to say nothing about the appropriateness or otherwise of attributing silence to God in Godself. I have, however, suggested here with regard to Christology, as in the introduction with regard to "silence," that this on its own is unsatisfactory. Can we point to the "silence of the resurrection" as an indication of who God is? And how can it be that to do so will open up the possibilities for a theological ethic of communication?

In all Bonhoeffer's key affirmations about the resurrection – the "place to stand," "God's will for a new world," "God's Yes to creation" – there is an implicit reference to and reliance on the fact that the resurrection is an event of and for God.[73] In the *Christology* lectures the exaltation of

---

[72] See further on this Rachel Muers, "Silence and the Patience of God," *Modern Theology* 17, 1 (2000). I am grateful to Catherine Pickstock for discussions on this topic. See also, for a discussion of the same theme in a very different context, Jeremy S. Begbie, *Theology, Music and Time* (Cambridge: Cambridge University Press, 2000), pp. 104–5.

[73] Likewise, the identification of the resurrection as both "future" and "past" *pro nobis* reflects its reality as eternal reality; but, as we noted earlier, the discussion of the resurrection is predominantly in relation to created/historical time.

What follows reflects my acceptance, in essence, of Charles Marsh's fundamental claim (Charles Marsh, *Reclaiming Dietrich Bonhoeffer: The Promise of His Theology* (Oxford: Oxford University Press, 1994) , p. ix and chapter 1) that the "secondary objectivity" of God's being *pro me*, with which Bonhoeffer explores, presupposes the "primary objectivity" of God's trinitarian identity (as explored, chiefly, in Barth's work). I want to claim, however, that the recognition and explication of aspects of this presupposed "primary objectivity"

Jesus is described, without further discussion, as the "ultimate mystery of the Trinity."[74] In the theological letter of 1940, Bonhoeffer refers to the resurrection as "God's Yes to Jesus Christ and his atoning work." He does not, here or elsewhere, discuss at any length the implication of this – that the resurrection is "God's Yes" to *God's own* work. To speak in these terms is to interpret the resurrection as God's act of self-faithfulness and self-recognition, grounded in God's eternal self-faithfulness. This in turn already defines the resurrection as a trinitarian event through which God's triune being is understood in relation to the world.

The language of acknowledgment and recognition is, as Bonhoeffer's essay on the subject recognizes, extremely significant for theological reflection on the resurrection. It is important here that the acknowledgment of Jesus and his work, and the judgment against those who condemned him – the "Yes" to which Bonhoeffer refers – is at the same time God's "self-acknowledgment," the vindication by God of God's own work.

'Self-acknowledgment" or self-vindication might, apart from the specification given in the event of the resurrection, be regarded as a purely formal property of the self-sufficient divine subject. Locating God's "self-acknowledgment" in the resurrection, however, makes it clear that the act of acknowledgment that confirms the divine freedom also specifies that freedom as the free work of love that reconciles God and creation. The resurrection as "God's Yes" is the fulfillment of this work, that confirms and completes God's self-faithfulness as faithfulness to the creation. Since this work is a work of love, however, its "fulfillment" requires and brings about the participation of the beloved in the work; and the resurrection is also understood as the basis of that participation.

This interpretation of the resurrection can be seen to follow Bonhoeffer's Christological structure; God's "taking on" or acceptance of creation, and God's judgment on creation, are brought together in the resurrection as the completion of God's work. The ground of their reconciliation, however, is the *unity of God* understood from the resurrection. This unity can be understood here as a unity of self-

---

may help us to resolve difficulties in Bonhoeffer's *ethical* thought. Marsh seems to assume, by contrast, that ethics are Bonhoeffer's strong point, and that the uncovering of primary objectivity only serves to explain how he reached what is essentially a satisfactory understanding of the ethical life.

[74] *DBW* 12, p. 342: the expression is "*letzte Geheimnis*," which will become significant in a different context in subsequent discussion (see chapter 7). For the association of the Trinity with "mystery" in Bonhoeffer's thought, see also *DBW* 13, p. 359–63.

acknowledgment, in and through which creation is acknowledged in its relation to God.[75]

Two strands in the New Testament presentation of the resurrection and its significance are particularly important in relation to this discussion. In *Acts*, the resurrection is God's overturning of the world's judgment on Jesus (2:24; 3:15; 4:10–11; 5:30). It vindicates Jesus' work as *God's work* (2:22–4; 10:38ff.) and exalts him (2:36; 5:30–1; cf. Phil 2:9–11) as the one appointed by God to judge the world (10:42; 17:41), and the one in whom God's "judgment" of forgiveness is already pronounced (5:31; 10:43). The resurrection is also God's completion of God's own purposes, in the fulfillment of God's promises (2:25ff.; 13:32ff.); but this "completion" does not exclude, but rather produces, the participation of humanity in the movement of "acknowledgment." The followers of Jesus become both those whom God hears and acknowledges (the answering of prayer – 4:24ff.; 10:4; 16:25ff.) and those who hear and praise God.

In the Fourth Gospel, the theme of the vindication of Jesus as the one who does God's work is also prominent; the Father is the one who "testifies" on Jesus' behalf (5:31ff.; 8:16f.) and who "always hears" him (11:42; see 9:31). This recognition "before the world," seen in my discussion as culminating in the resurrection, is in the Fourth Gospel clearly grounded in the reciprocal knowledge and love between Father and Son, knowledge and love that were "before the world was."[76] This mutual "recognition" is expressed in terms of *glory* possessed and given (17:1ff.). The followers of Jesus participate in this glorification (17:22ff.), and are themselves given glory (17:22).

The identification of this theme points us to the trinitarian implications of the identification of God as a listener. The specific character of God's "capacity for listening" – the way in which God recognizes, judges, and responds – is shown in the resurrection, and shown as definitive of who God is.[77] God's "hearing" of creation is grounded in God's hearing

---

[75] Note Barth's pairing of the "patience and wisdom of God" in his discussion of the divine attributes – Barth, *Church Dogmatics* 2/1, pp. 407–22. Barth's summary of the significance of attributing wisdom to God is simply that God *knows what God is doing* (and, hence, that God's patience is neither aimless nor capricious). The activity of the God who both has and is wisdom is characterized as "meaningful" (reasoned and ordered) and self consistent, and brings itself to completion. On the reading I have suggested, the resurrection can be seen as the event in which God in this sense "knows what God is doing."

[76] See especially Jn 17:5, 22ff.; 5:20; 8:54ff.; 10:14ff., 17.

[77] Considering the resurrection in these terms invites reflection on the traditional use of the *verbum internum* analogy to describe innertrinitarian relations. The Son as *verbum internum* is God's knowledge of God's self, in which God also knows all God's works.

of God's self.[78] To understand God as *in se* the "one who hears" is to say that the completeness of God's self-possession is a completeness that includes openness to what is not God. It is another way of articulating how God's lack of jealousy and God's generosity are grounded in who God is.

The language of glorification indicates, further, an aspect of listening that has not yet been considered. My discussion of the questions "Who hears?" and "Who is heard?," and the corresponding identification of the silence of "unknowability" and the silence of the listener, began from the relation implied in "hearing to speech." The irreducible otherness of the one "who is heard," which I identified as the ground of the possibility of new speech, and the activity of the one "who hears" in discernment and acknowledgment, have hitherto not been brought together. In the resurrection, however, I have suggested, God is both the one who hears and the one who is heard. The claim to which this gives rise is that God's perfect self-knowledge (as the one "who hears") does not mean that God does nothing "new" (as the one who "is heard"). God's self-acknowledgment is infinitely creative.[79]

I introduced the question "Who hears?" within the context of the activity of hearing to speech, which activity, as we saw, implied a capac-

---

The *verbum internum* suggests a possible ground for the claim that there is hearing "in God" – that God hears God's own Word.

The use of dialogic analogies for innertrinitarian relations is common enough, but it is more usual to relate innertrinitarian hearing to the Son's obedience. See Walter Kasper, The God of Jesus Christ (London: SCM, 1984), p. 290, for a summary of this position as articulated in recent Roman Catholic theology. I would argue that a corrective is required to the association of hearing with obedient receptivity, presupposed by these analogies.

[78] Bonhoeffer's interest in "the doctrine derived from Eph. 1:10 – that of the restoration of all things, ἀνακεφαλαιωσις, *recapitulatio* (Irenaeus)" – is of particular interest in this regard. (See *DBW* 1, pp. 196–7, *DBWE* 1, pp. 286–7; *DBW* 8, pp. 246–7, *Letters and Papers*, pp. 170–1.) Discussing attitudes to the past, he describes *recapitulatio* as "a magnificent conception, full of comfort. . . . " Marsh asks (*Reclaiming Dietrich Bonhoeffer*, p. 103) whether *recapitulatio* as Bonhoeffer uses it tends to a "Hegelian" elimination of the concrete distinction between God and humanity. I would argue that, with the holding together of both aspects of the Christological silence of God discussed here, this need not be the case.

[79] To put this rather differently, in terms that relate it back to the discussion of Fiumara in the previous chapter: the resurrection is not to be characterized as the solution to a problem. If it were thus characterized, the accusations of Christian triumphalism would be justified. At the same time, it is not less than the solution to a problem. See on this the discussion of resurrection in Creation and Fall (*DBW* 3, p. 33, *DBWE* 3, p. 35): "That Christ was dead was not the possibility of his resurrection, but rather its impossibility."

ity in the hearer for "discernment and recognition." "Recognition" is here recognition of the particular other as a "Who?," that is, as a personal other, whose freedom and capacity for new speech is affirmed in the act of listening. I have suggested that the completion of God's work in the resurrection implies "the participation of the beloved in the work." The resurrection is, then, the point from which people are determined as those whom God hears.

Being brought into the relation through which God enacts faithfulness to, and acknowledgment of, Godself and the world means, then, being given the promise of *being heard*. It must also, however, mean being enabled to participate in God's act of hearing – to discern the truth of the world and to respond accordingly, which in turn includes the capacity to hear others to speech. The gift of the Holy Spirit is the gift both of the promise that God will hear and of the "capacity for discernment and recognition" that accords with God's own act of discernment and recognition. The possibility of innerworldly transformation depends on both these gifts – being freed for responsible action before God, and being enabled to understand the complexity of penultimate reality.

This discussion suggests that the resurrection and its innerworldly "realization" may be relevant to the formation and re-formation of listening selves – the development of the capacity for attention, discernment, and judgment. I have already suggested, and shall consider in more detail in subsequent chapters, that this aspect of the ethical life receives relatively little attention in Bonhoeffer's work. An emphasis on the *pro nobis* of the resurrection (and indeed of Christology more generally) to the neglect of explicit consideration of its significance "for God," is mirrored in an emphasis on the "other-directed" aspects of the ethical life and a suspicion of theological interest in interiority.

The reasons for, and possible correctives to, this suspicion of interiority will be examined further in subsequent chapters, but one formal reason can be mentioned here. The capacity for discernment and judgment is associated in Bonhoeffer's work with the "ground under our feet," the unspoken or non-thematized formation of persons and communities that makes reasoning and action possible. It is significant that one of the characteristics of the "ground under our feet," in Bonhoeffer's work, is silence. The "ground" of a particular cultural tradition becomes thematizable only as an object of mourning, that is, only when it is no longer the unquestioned basis for judgment and response. We saw earlier that the resurrection can be the only "answer to δος μοι που στω" because its givenness cannot be abrogated. The idea of the "ground under our feet" helps the full significance of this statement to be understood. The re-surrection is the place from which right judgment and action become possible; and it remains so "for us" because it cannot be reduced to an object of reflection. In order to understand more fully what it means for it to be the place from which right judgment and action become possible, however, we have had to move away briefly from Bonhoeffer's focus on the *pro nobis*.

This in turn suggests, however, that when looking for and developing ways in which the formation of listening selves can be thought theologically, we should not forget the importance of the *silence* of the resurrection. It remains the case, as discussed earlier, that the resurrection intensifies the Christological *incognito*. In particular, it is important that the nature of conformity to Christ is perceived only in its realization in lives and actions. I shall consider in subsequent chapters how human participation in God's act of hearing – the capacity to "hear with God's ears" – might be discerned and described.

Summary and Conclusions

I began this chapter by suggesting that "hearing to speech" presupposes two "forms" of silence, to which correspond the questions "Who is heard?" and "Who hears?" The former question denotes the unknowability or freedom of the other who is recognized as a possible speaker; the latter, the capacity for listening exercised by the one who hears. Bonhoeffer's theology of the resurrection, as I have described it here, shows how the first of these questions is asked and answered with reference to Christ. The resurrection is the basis for the asking and answering of the "Who?" question in Christology. It also intensifies the Christological *incognito*, which has in Bonhoeffer's Christology a double significance – the affirmation and condemnation of the world, associated respectively with the incarnation and Crucifixion. The resurrection is the reconciliation of these antithetical divine "words," but the form of this reconciliation remains (in the sense of the first "Who?" question) unknowable.

The hiddenness of the resurrection is given positive significance for ethics through Bonhoeffer's concept of the "penultimate." Creation is oriented toward the "ultimate" – the final reconciliation achieved in the resurrection – but the time of the "penultimate," during which the ultimate reality is not yet realized, is accorded its own validity. The penultimate as the time of God's silence is the time during which responsible action becomes possible, characterized neither by uncritical affirmation of the world as it is nor by the radical reshaping of the world as a condemnation of present existence.

The account of penultimacy in Bonhoeffer's work seems to demand an account of God's free and redeeming action (the resurrection) as "active" in the continuing historical existence of creation as penultimate; more specifically, as active in the responsible life *etsi deus non daretur*. I have suggested, however, that such an account is lacking in what Bonhoeffer says explicitly on the subject. His "silence" concerning the resurrection as an event for and of God is directly linked to wider problems in understanding his ethical thought – on the activity of God in the penultimate, but also on the nature and possibility of the transformation of penultimate reality. I have suggested expanding Bonhoeffer's account of the resurrection by considering it in terms of the second "Who?" question suggested above – "Who hears?" Understanding the resurrection as the event in which God "hears" Godself and creation suggests, first, that the silence of God in the penultimate can be understood as a silence of *hearing* (as discussed in the previous chapter). It also suggests that life in "conformation to Christ" includes participation in the divine activity of, or capacity for, discernment and recognition.

The implications of this move for the ethics of communication, specifically, will be considered in subsequent chapters. The negative aspect of the mystery of the resurrection – the intensification of the Christological *incognito* – implies, as suggested above, that we should be wary of establishing a priori stable analogies between divine and human acts of listening. It remains the case that the nature of "conformation to Christ" is understood in and through its enactment in particular lives and situations. With this in mind, I move in the next chapter to a consideration of how the "hearing of the Word of God" is thought and practiced. I shall argue that a developed account of how God hears God's own Word provides the theological basis for challenging the models of communication that collude with oppression and violence.

Chapter Four

HEARING THE WORD?

Introduction

In the last chapter I outlined the possibility, and the possible importance, of understanding the God of Jesus Christ as one who both speaks and listens. My task now is to examine how the reconciled *logos* of God might re-form the "halved" human *logos*; and what it might mean, in terms of practices of speech, silence, and listening, for the "reality" of the resurrection to be realized in the world. In this chapter I approach this issue by directing Morton's question, "Who hears? Who is heard?" at the hearing of the Word of God. Highlighted in the first chapter as particularly problematic for feminist theology, this remains a central theme for any theological consideration of silence and hearing. It is especially important if we want to take up the suggestion that Christology forms the basis for an ethics of communication.

In chapter 2, I described Fiumara's challenge to the "halving of the *logos*" in the contemporary communicative environment – the "*logos* that speaks and hardly listens." Fiumara argues that the necessary passivity of hearing, in a situation where the "power of speech" is all and the "strength of listening" is nothing, leads to the desire for benumbment – indifference to whatever presents itself to be heard. Benumbment defends the individual against the incursion of the powerful word, but does nothing to alter the communicative environment. If we are seeking a way beyond benumbment toward responsible hearing, what can a Christological rereading of the silence of God offer? The search for a theological articulation of what active hearing means will be conducted, in this chapter, in critical conversation with various theological appropriations of philosophies of language.

Here and in chapter 6, several of the "Bonhoeffer texts" to which I refer are received only from those who listened to him[1] – an observation that brings to the fore the issue of the activity of the hearer in any act of communication. Readings of these texts have tended to assume that any process of reconstruction by these listeners is either negligible in the first place or has been rendered so by the subsequent reconstruction, the editing of the notes for publication – so that these writings can be treated as the words Bonhoeffer "really spoke." The further implied assumption is that they would be of limited value were this not the case. It is worth recalling from the start, however, that the dependence of a speaker on specific listeners, and the possibility of new interpretation that that dependence implies, is inescapably at issue in the use of these texts, as, indeed, it is at issue in the interpretation of "Jesus texts" and "Socrates texts," or of the texts of any other teachers who wrote little or none of their teaching down.

Word and Silence in *Christology*

God "spoke, and it came to be" (Ps. 33:9). Reflection on the association between God's speech and God's action in and toward the world has been significant for the theology of all generations; and the identification of Christ as *logos* forces the question to the center of Christian concerns. Christology is always, implicitly or explicitly, a *logology*, thinking about words in and through its thinking of the Word. In the first of his lectures on Christology, Bonhoeffer pointed directly to this aspect of Christological thought. "Christology as the study of Christ is a peculiar discipline [*eine eigentümliche Wissenschaftsgebiet*] . . ."[2] and the "peculiarity" of Christology is centered on the identification of Christ as *logos*; "Christology is therefore *Logology*."

The lectures do not, however, begin with the reference to *logos*, but rather with silence: "Insofar as the Church proclaims the Word, it falls

---

[1] No manuscript (other than two undated sides of outline notes) for the *Christology* lectures exists; what we possess is two recostructions (published in *GS* 3, pp.166–242, and *Berlin: 1933, DBW* 12, pp. 279–348) based on notes taken by some of the 200-odd students who attended the course in the summer of 1933. See for a detailed account of the reconstruction processes *DBW* 12, p. 279, n.1 – and note here that some of the manuscripts available to the editors of *GS* were not available for *DBW*. The English translation *Christology* corresponds to the *GS* version. The lectures on *Spiritual Care*, considered in chapter 6, are reconstructed from the notes of Finkenwalde students – see chapter 6, note 2.

[2] *Christology*, p. 27; *GS* 3, p. 167; *DBW* 12, p. 280.

down silently . . . To speak of Christ means to keep silent; to keep silent about Christ means to speak . . . To pray is to be silent and at the same time to cry out."[3]

Silence, a carefully delimited and defined silence, is treated here as essential to the "beginning" of Christology per se. It is not referred to in the rest of the lectures – but its appearance here, at the beginning of an outline of the method and presuppositions of Christology, provokes reflection. In the discussion that follows, I shall draw out some of the possible meanings that could be ascribed to this silence – with the intention, eventually, of offering an interpretation that does justice to the account of the silence of God outlined in the previous chapter. Such an interpretation goes beyond the original intention of Bonhoeffer's lecture – though perhaps not beyond associations it would have brought for his hearers – and draws it into a wider and subsequent theological conversation.

A developing tradition, in the twentieth century, of thinking about language *in use*, words as they "do things" or as people "do things" with them, has given rise to a range of new theological articulations of what it means to say that God "spoke, and it came to be." I begin by examining the way in which two key aspects of contemporary philosophical accounts of language – broadly classifiable as concerned with linguistic *pragmatics*[4] or the theory of speech-acts[5] – have been appropriated theologically to explain or describe the unique effectiveness of God's "speech-acts" – and the implications of this for a theological ethics of communication.

The first aspect of this approach to language with which I am concerned here is the idea of the performative utterance, the effect of which is inseparable from its truthfulness. While the "effectiveness" of words has sometimes been treated as a result of their social location and the conventions that govern their use, it has in other analyses been thematized as

---

[3] *DBW* 12, p. 280; *GS* 3, p. 167; *Christology*, p. 27.

[4] Following Charles Morris' division of semiotics into syntactics, semantics, and pragmatics – without wishing to make assumptions here about the extent to which pragmatics can include or replace the other two aspects. See on this Stephen C. Levinson, *Pragmatics* (Cambridge: Cambridge University Press, 1983). A useful summary, in a theological context, of the philosophical background of emphasis on dialog is in Oliver Davies, "Revelation and the Politics of Culture," in Lawrence Hemming, ed., *Radical Orthodoxy? A Catholic Enquiry* ed. (Aldershot: Ashgate, 2000), pp. 117–18, n.14.

[5] Usually used to refer to developments of J. L. Austin's seminal lectures (J. L. Austin, *How to Do Things with Words* (Oxford: Oxford University Press, 1971)) and J. R. Searle's subsequent work.

the capacity of speech to bring about new possibilities of existence or relationship.[6]

The second idea to be considered is that words "mean" or "refer" only within relational contexts, only, we might say, in being addressed by someone to someone in some situation. The basic insight that meaning is a property not of words or sentences, but of utterances in interpretive contexts, leads, in the project of "universal pragmatics," to an account of the intersubjective character of rationality as such. Even where this general claim is not accepted, work in linguistic pragmatics that focuses on the intersubjective, social and institutional factors determining the meaningfulness of utterances presupposes the inseparability of "the word" from its speakers and interpreters in a particular time and place.

Why should theologians be attracted by these ways of thinking about language and its ways of meaning? The simplest answer would be: because each of the aspects outlined above enables some claim about the speech of God, found to be central to biblical accounts and to theological tradition, to be articulated. On the one hand, there is the claim that God's speech is effective; by speaking God creates, directs history, reshapes the world. On the other hand, there is the claim that God's speech is embodied, entering particular historical situations, addressing persons as themselves potential speakers and respondents, and having "meaning" only in this intersubjective framework.[7]

What becomes of a Christological account of the ethics of communication, if either or both of these aspects of divine speech is emphasized? The first of Bonhoeffer's *Christology* lectures helps us, on a first reading, to see some of the implications of shaping *logology* according to such a pattern. Bonhoeffer sets out Christological method and presuppositions according to a fundamental contrast – setting the "human *logos*" in opposition to the "divine *logos*." The contrast is defined, in the first instance, in terms of differing modes of enquiry. Bonhoeffer represents the human *logos* as shaped by the will to "classification." The "How?" question" is its paradigmatic form of enquiry – the question that leads to classification, to the location of its object within an existing system.

The encounter with Christ as *counter-logos* appears first, in this context, as the encounter with one who "denies the classification," and hence cannot be approached by means of the "How?" question. "The only real

---

[6] For a discussion of this contrast, see Stephen K. White, *Political Theory and Postmodernism* (Cambridge: Cambridge University Press, 1991), p. 25.

[7] For a full treatment of this latter point, see Oliver Davies, *A Theology of Compassion: Metaphysics of Difference and the Renewal of Tradition* (London: SCM, 2001), chapter 9.

question which now remains is "Who are you?"[8] This "Who?" question
is the Christological question, determining the content and method of
Christology. Christology becomes possible, Bonhoeffer claims, only on the
basis of the encounter with Christ, as the confrontation of the human
logos by the *counter-logos*. This confrontation is described in terms of an
inescapable and final decision: "There are only two ways possible of
encountering Jesus: man must die or he must put Jesus to death."[9]

A further implication of the *Christology* introduction, as presented, is
that Christology is only possible from the place where, in Bonhoeffer's
terms, the "Who?" question is put and answered. The effect of the whole
introduction is, then, to redefine the academic "discipline of Christology"
by grounding it outside the academy in the worshiping congregation –
and in silence.[10] The question thus becomes pressing: what is the communicative environment that Christology requires or creates? In what kind
of silence does Christology, which is in turn the "unknown and hidden
center of the *universitas litterarum*," begin?

The shape of the answer to this question is apparent from the
previous chapter; Christology begins in the silence of the incarnate,
crucified, and resurrected Christ. The first *Christology* lecture indicates
both the central, if implicit, importance of the resurrection for Bonhoeffer's grounding of Christology as an academic discipline, and the impossibility of understanding the resurrection apart from the incarnation and
Crucifixion. The silence in which Christology begins is the silence in
which the living Christ (to whom only the "Who?" question is appropriate) is encountered; it is also the silence of the Christ who is and
remains incognito.

Most importantly, in Bonhoeffer's introduction, Christology begins in
the encounter through which the human *logos* is judged and consigned to
silence. The introduction to the *Christology* lectures depicts, apparently, a
"war of Words" in which Christ as the divine *counter-logos* confronts the
human *Logos* in the latter's attempt to assert itself or assimilate what
opposes it. "Man must die or he must put Jesus to death;" one of the
logoi must emerge victorious by reducing the other to silence.[11] The silence
in which the human *logos* falls silent before the addressing Word, and

---

[8] *Christology*, p. 30, *DBW* 12, p. 282.
[9] *Christology*, p. 35, *DBW* 12, p. 288.
[10] See *DBW* 12, pp. 283–4 on the Church as the place where the "Who?" question can
be asked and answered.
[11] The imagery clearly belongs in the context of the developing German Church struggle, with the emergence of a specific and explicitly aggrandizing anti-Christian *Logos*.

becomes the object of address and encounter, is the basis for teaching and speaking. We can interpret the silence at the beginning of the *Christology* lectures, then, as that of the defeated human *logos* after the "war of Words." When the *counter-logos* appears, the human *logos* is destroyed; there is nothing more for human reason to say.

It is clear that, for the structure of argument Bonhoeffer is following here to work, both of the affirmations concerning language, discussed above, have to be maintained concerning the divine *logos*; the Word must be effective and must be located interpersonally. Later in the lectures, in his analysis of the presence of Christ as "Word,"[12] Bonhoeffer introduces an important pair of contrasting categories: the "word as address" and the "word as idea" – described as "the basic structures of the word," which "exclude each other." "Human thought only knows the one form of the word, as idea . . . Christ [is] Word in the sense of address."[13]

The word as idea, in Bonhoeffer's discussion, is the word considered apart from the identity of the one who speaks it or the one who hears it, the context of its utterance, or its effects on persons. It "rests in itself and is relative to itself." It is understood as "timeless truth," equally accessible in all times and places. The "word as address," by contrast, is the word "spoken in the concrete moment," in the context of personal encounter, from and to particular persons. "While the word as idea can remain alone, as address it is only possible between two." The word as address "is" only in its being spoken; its "truth happens only in community."[14] From the word as address come "response and responsibility" (*Antwort* and *Verantwortung*).

Bonhoeffer is claiming that, for at least one case or group of cases, truthfulness is a property not of a word or sentence but of an utterance; and hence by implication that there is at least some aspect of an utterance's meaning that is determined by the "concrete moment" in which it is spoken and heard. The reference to "response and responsibility," furthermore, points to aspects of the "truthfulness" and "meaning" of an utterance beyond what can be attributed to the "timeless truth" of the idea, aspects of truthfulness and meaning that are inseparable from the interpersonal context of the utterance. The "word as address" does not merely describe a state of affairs; it performs a relationship. More than

---

See Thomas Day, *Dietrich Bonhoeffer on Christian Community and Common Sense* (New York: Edwin Mellon, 1982), pp. 83–4.

[12] *DBW* 12, pp. 297–300.

[13] *DBW* 12, p. 298, my translation; compare *Christology*, p. 50, *GS* 3, p. 185.

[14] *Christology*, p. 51, *DBW* 12, p. 298.

this, again, it effects a change in relationship, since response and responsibility arise from it; it *does* something, and it is only understood properly if this is recognized. This aspect of the description might be restated in the terms of speech-act theory as the claim that the word as address is "not constative but performative."[15]

Bonhoeffer's claim that "human thought knows only the form of the word as idea," and the strong contrast he draws between the Christological "word" and all other forms of human reason, raises questions for the interpretation of this aspect of his thought.[16] Is the intention here to distance the divine *logos* from the human *logos*, or to make a claim about the truthfulness or otherwise of all speech? There are points in Bonhoeffer's account of the "word as address," here and elsewhere, where he appears to acknowledge that the possibility of truthfulness in *any* act of speaking depends on the "concrete moment," or that truth always "happens only in community."[17] At the same time, the silence in which teaching about Christ begins, in these lectures, marks a discontinuity, more fundamental than the assimilation of Bonhoeffer's "word as address" to a more general characteristic of speech would appear to allow.

This question of how Christ as *logos* interacts with the human *logos* is obviously important for my attempt to develop a Christologically focused

---

[15] Frits de Lange, *Waiting for the Word: Dietrich Bonhoeffer on Speaking about God*, trans. Martin N. Walton (Grand Rapids: Eerdmans, 2000), p. 21, using Austin's well-known distinction (Austin, *How to Do Things with Words*, pp. 6–7) Of course Lange's contrast is questionable; by the end of his lectures Austin is suggesting that "performativity" can be attributed even to those sentences previously classified as "constative" (Austin, *How to Do Things with Words,* p. 132).

[16] Walter Lowe, "Bonhoeffer and Deconstruction: Towards a Theology of the Crucified Logos," in Wayne Whitson Floyd Jr. and Charles Marsh, eds., *Theology and the Practice of Responsibility* (Valley Forge: Trinity Press, 1994), argues that the "war of Words" suggests a residual oppositionalism that sits ill with other aspects of Bonhoeffer's thought. "Reason" as a whole, and the human subject is taken to define, is set up as the opponent of Christ. "The result is that, as in any such contest, Bonhoeffer ends up mirroring his opponent . . . [and] yields too much to instrumental reason's complacent assumption that it itself is monolithic, internally consistent." Lowe suggests that Bonhoeffer's determination to set the Word of God in opposition to another reality runs against his determination, expressed elsewhere, to avoid any "thinking in terms of two spheres," any division of reality in order to "clear a space" for Christ or Christianity. The whole "classificatory" endeavor of human reason has been excluded from the space cleared in the world for Christ.

I would argue that this reading fails to take seriously Bonhoeffer's own insistence that Christology is a *Wissenschaftsgebiet*, albeit a distinctive one; or, to put it another way, this reading forgets that the Christology lectures continue beyond the introduction!

[17] "The concept of the word gains its full significance here" [i.e. in the recognition of the truth-character of "address"] – *Christology*, p. 50, *GS* 3, p. 185; compare *DBW* 12, p. 298.

ethics of communication. Following the basic Christological pattern set out in the previous chapter, I shall be suggesting here that existing communicative situations can be understood as affirmed, judged and transformed in the context of the divine *logos*.

The Word that Addresses

The presentation of the effectiveness of the divine word suggested in the Christology introduction – with the emphasis on the opposition between Christ as *logos* and the human *logos* – has potential to be both very significant for a Christological understanding of language and very problematic for feminist thought. In order to understand both the opportunities and the problems, we must consider more fully what it means to describe the word of God as effective within, and in bringing about, relations of communication.

The concept of the "performative utterance" was developed most famously in J. L. Austin's lectures on *How to Do Things with Words*, a thinking through of the everyday and unremarked experience that to say something is to do something. The subsequent interpretation and development of Austin's work enquires into the theoretical frameworks within which this can be said to be the case.

Here, I want to look most closely at the use of the idea of God's effective speech to convey the sense of a radical discontinuity between the word or act of God and any possible context of human words or actions – the interruption of an existing *logos* and the appearance of a "new thing," brought about by the encounter with Christ as Word. If we can find a structure within which to speak about a w/Word that brings about God's/its own effects, this creates a context within which the transcendent act of God, occurring without innerworldly preconditions, can be expounded.

The theologians of the "New Hermeneutic" in the late twentieth century sought to do exactly this. Beginning from the interpretation of human existence as fundamentally shaped by the condition of "being addressed" in language, they understood the divine word as that which reconstituted human existence through a new act of address. Drawing on their work and that of Austin, Jüngel's use of the category of "address" in *God as the Mystery of the World*, to ground the claim to theological knowledge and the possibility of naming God, is a good example of the theological use of this account of the addressing word as creative. In God's act of addressing the world, as Jüngel sets it out, the "perlocutionary-attractive" effect determines the hearer as one who is in free relationship to God. "Perlocutionary-attractive" is a term created by Jüngel to emphasize the power of the addressing word to affect the very being of the one addressed, and the fact that "[the] goal (*telos*) is not outside of the act but rather effected by it and included in the act."[18]

The key point about this appropriation of the idea of the performative is that the Word of God, unlike the speech-acts analyzed by Austin and his followers, constitutes for itself the communicative context in which its performative force becomes possible. Austin's key examples – the judge's verdict and the priest's performance of a marriage – both obviously depend on institutional conventions for their success as *performative*. His extended analysis of "infelicity" emphasizes this point. Subsequent speech-act theory has debated the relative significance of the speaker's intention and social or institutional "rules" in determining the illocutionary or perlocutionary force of a speech-act. The difficulty for theological appropriations is that where the speech of God is concerned it must be possible to say, not only (for example) that "God promises (successfully)," but that "God brings about the possibility of God's promising (successfully)."[19] God's speech must produce the communicative framework within which it can be effective, and not enter an existing framework that would determine its possibilities in advance.[20]

What would be the implications of this for our understanding of the hearing of this word? It is common enough to articulate the basic "passivity" of the individual and the community, with regard to faith, by reference to the act of hearing.[21] Hearing has been taken, particularly within the Reformation debates, as the designation of an "act" of knowing

---

[18] Eberhard Jüngel, *God as the Mystery of the World: On the the Foundation of the Theology of the Crucified One in the Dispute between Theism and Atheism*, trans. Darrell L. Guder (Grand Rapids: Eerdmans, 1983) , p. 11, n. 17.

[19] For a reading of Austin that rejects for this reason the interpretation, favorable or unfavorable, of his work in terms of the divine speech-act see Sandy Petrey, "Speech Acts in Society: Fish, Felman, Austin and God," *Texte* 3 (1984).

[20] For other uses of the "perlocutionary act" in relation to divine speech (here particularly for scriptural interpretation), see Francis Watson, *Text and Truth: Redefining Biblical Theology* (Edinburgh: T. & T. Clark, 1997), p. 103, Kevin J. Vanhoozer, *Is There a Meaning in This Text? The Bible, the Reader and the Morality of Literary Knowledge* (Leicester: Apollos, 1998), pp. 410–12.

[21] Compare Eberhard Jüngel, *Theological Essays,* trans. John Webster (Edinburgh: T. & T. Clark, 1989), p. 205: "the Church is primordially defined as the hearing Church. Only as the hearing church is it also a speaking church. As the *ecclesia audiens* it preserves the place of God as the primary acting subject . . . In its – very lively – passivity, the Church represents in a fundamental way the activity of God."

entirely determined by the specific self-presentation of the object of knowledge.[22] To name the community as *ecclesia audiens* is to refer to this primary condition of dependence on the creative Word.

Theological developments of the idea of the uniquely effective divine speech–act clearly have reason to appropriate this characterization of humanity's relation to God in terms of "obedient hearing." The implication of Jüngel's "perlocutionary-attractive act," for example, is that the being of the hearer is determined by the event of "being addressed" – which provides a way of articulating the basic passivity of humanity in relation to God.[23] Some of the implications of this use of the "word as address" can be seen from Bonhoeffer's characterization, most notably in *Act and Being*, of the attitude of humanity encountered by revelation as *actus directus*. The essence of the *actus directus* is self-forgetfulness – "clinging to Christ need not become self-conscious; rather, it is wholly taken up by completion of the act."[24] It arises from the encounter with that which comes from the "outside" and is completely unassimilable to classificatory thought. By contrast to the sinful condition of the *cor curvatum in se*, the *actus directus* is the heart turned completely outward, called into this condition by the "word as address." Hearing implies here forgetfulness of the self, or rather the redefinition of the self by its relation to the prevenient divine act of address.[25]

Some of Kierkegaard's discourses on silence can be used to amplify this reading of silence as *actus directus*. Bonhoeffer quotes Kierkegaard's call to silence in the second sentence of *Christology*; the latter's discourses on *The Lilies and the Birds* interprets silence before God in terms of the complete abandonment of self-reflection or self-awareness. Kierkegaard reads the lilies and birds – who "neither sow nor reap . . . neither toil nor spin" (Matthew 6:26ff.) as exemplars of silence. They live in the moment because of their orientation toward the future; they "wait" without asking

---

[22] On "hearing" in Luther, see especially Silvia Hell, *Die Dialektik des Wortes bei Martin Luther* (Innsbruck: Tyrolia-Verlag, 1992); Albrecht Beuchtel, *In dem Anfang war das Wort: Studien zu Luthers Sprachverständnis* (Tübingen: Mohr, 1991); and on the symbolism of the "ear," Margaret R. Miles, "The Rope Breaks When It Is Tightest: Luther on the Body, Consciousness and the Word," *Harvard Theological Review* 22, 3/4 (1984).

[23] For discussion and critique of this aspect of Jüngel see John Webster, "Justification, Analogy and Action: Passivity and Activity in Jüngel's Anthropology," in his *The Possibilities of Theology: Studies in the Theology of Eberhard Jüngel in His Sixtieth Year* (Edinburgh: T. & T. Clark, 1994).

[24] *Act and Being DBWE* 2, p. 158, *DBW* 2, p. 158.

[25] On the problems of combining a critical moment with the *actus directus*, see Wayne Whitson Floyd, *Theology and the Dialectics of Otherness: On Reading Bonhoeffer and Adorno* (Lanham: University Press of America, 1988), pp. 275–6.

or seeking to control "what will happen." The paradoxes Bonhoeffer uses in his introductory lecture – "To pray is to be silent and at the same time to cry out," "To speak of Christ is to be silent" – echo Kierkegaard's claims that the natural world is "silent," in this sense, before God even when sounds are heard.[26]

What this account of the hearing self apparently excludes is the "capacity for discernment and recognition" – the aspects of selfhood that enable the asking and answering of the question "Who hears?" Some of the problems this poses for the ethics of communication were mentioned in the first chapter, with the suggestion that the supposed priority of "obedient hearing" may be used to mask relations of power. To identify any speech as arising from a pure hearing of the prevenient Word is effectively to deny the possibility of power interests in any way shaping that speech. The challenge put by feminist theologies to the mainstream tradition has been: how can you claim to have listened to, and spoken out of, the Word of God when you have failed to hear the voices of those with whom the Word of God became identified? As I observed in the discussion of Heidegger and Fiumara, above, the rediscovery of the significance of "listening" for philosophy – even outside an explicitly theological context – and the critique of forms of "non-listening" rationality does not necessarily imply that forms of oppressive silencing are overcome.

Feminist theology has had particular cause for concern about the portrayal of humanity as silent or receptive hearer vis-à-vis the active Word of God. Repeatedly at all levels of theological discourse and ecclesial practice, hearers have been gendered as feminine, and the task of representing the obedient hearer of the word assigned to women. The association of hearing with the non-activity of humanity before God reinforces a pattern of authority where the power of the appointed speaker over those who hear is treated as unproblematic. Even – perhaps, especially – if the gender aspect of the assignation of roles in hearing and speaking is not made explicit, the model itself remains in need of critique. To ally hearing with "self-forgetfulness" is to invite the criticism made in many other contexts of traditional theological anthropology – that it reinforces the oppression of women by valorizing the self-denying behavior into which they have been socialized.

---

[26] Søren Kierkegaard, *Christian Discourses*, trans. Walter Lowrie (Oxford: Oxford University Press, 1939), pp. 324ff. For an extended comparison of Bonhoeffer and Kierkegaard on "obedience," see André Dumas, *Dietrich Bonhoeffer: Theologian of Reality* trans. R. M. Brown (London: SCM, 1971), chapter V.

That the determination of women as "hearers" can be supported with scriptural exegesis[27] makes the use of the active speaker/passive hearer model even more problematic; "learning in silence" will always recall "women." This in turn suggests that an effective feminist challenge to the construction of women as "silent hearers of the Word" requires a critique, not merely of the assignation of hearer and speaker roles according to gender, but of the model itself. Morton's critiques of existing understandings of the authority of a speaker were not, as we have seen, restricted to claiming for women and other excluded groups the right to exercise power by speaking. Rather, in common with other feminist and liberationist theologians, she at the same time challenged the assumption that hearers were non-agents.

Judith Butler's examination of the "hate speech" directed against racial minorities and those classed as sexually deviant[28] suggests that the notion of a "perlocutionary-attractive act," that carries with it the guarantee of its own success in determining the being of the one addressed, is particularly problematic for those whom mainstream discourse has silenced. Butler draws out some of the most problematic political and ideological uses of Austin's account of the "performative" in her consideration of what gives hate speech the effects it has. She claims that the "hate speech myth" – the supposition by both perpetrators and victims that hate speech effects what it signifies – is "theological" in origin, relying ultimately on the approximation of every speaker to the all-powerful divine speaker who "spoke and it was done." In both the perpetration and the recognition of "hate speech," the sovereign power of the speaker to determine the effectiveness of speech is assumed and reinscribed.

Butler's analysis is particularly disturbing to the theology of "divine speech" when we note that Jüngel's paradigmatic example of the "perlocutionary-attractive act" is the insult (albeit a fairly trivial insult, in his text):

> If one Swabian says to another, "*Halbdackel*" ["half a dachshund!"] . . . then he is impugning the being of that individual . . . If the word were only a sign, a denominating, then the person who was cursed could respond, "Wrong signification!" But normally the person . . . becomes worked up . . . because the word includes the person in its meaning and thus approaches him too closely.[29]

---

[27] 1 Cor 14:34–5.; 1 Tim 2:11–14.

[28] Judith Butler, *Excitable Speech: Towards a Politics of the Performative* (London: Routledge, 1997).

[29] Jüngel, *God as the Mystery of the World*, p. 10.

It might be claimed that the point about the appropriation of the capacity for the "perlocutionary-attractive act" to God is that it assures a benign "renaming," the antithesis of hate speech (as for example in Isaiah 62:4: "You shall no longer be termed Forsaken, and your land shall no more be termed Desolate; but you shall be called My Delight Is In Her, and your land Married"). This still leaves the problem of the fact that the structural possibility of "perlocutionary-attractive" action has been affirmed – with the consequent mystification of the power of hate speech.

Where does this leave the "war of Words" at the beginning of Bonhoeffer's lectures on Christology, or the "silence" in which teaching about Christ is supposed to begin? I want to argue that to say that "teaching about Christ begins in silence" cannot be fully explained as a reference to the redetermination of humanity as obedient or passive hearers. As it happens, Bonhoeffer specifically avoids identifying the silence in which Christology begins with the act of hearing, and especially with the hearing of proclamation.[30] Whatever the ambiguities, something more is going on here than the demand to "shut up and listen."

I have already stated that Bonhoeffer's concept of the word as address includes the claim that "truth happens only in community," implicitly referring to the true character of *all* words, in which Christ as Word shares. How might this affect our understanding of the significance of hearing in the communicative situation determined by Christ as *logos*?

The Weakness of the Word: Address as Dependence on Hearers

In the theological appropriations of pragmatics discussed so far, it is assumed that the Word of God needs hearers. This is why the Word must, for the thinkers I have been considering, have a "perlocutionary-attractive" effect, bring about the conditions of its own hearing, summon persons to be hearers and effect the communal context within which it can be spoken. What the reading of the silences of Christ, developed in the previous chapter in conversation with Bonhoeffer, suggests is that the need of the Word of God for hearers, the fact that the truth of this Word happens "only in community," can and should be read in a different way.

---

[30] "*Inasmuch as* [*Indem*] the Church proclaims the Word, she in truth falls silent . . . *To speak about Christ means to be silent*, to be silent about Christ means to speak . . . *To pray is to be silent and to cry out at the same time*, before God in the face of his Word" (my emphases).

If we begin from the silence of the incarnation – the Christ who lives incognito – we begin from one who is dependent on his hearers in such a way as to be vulnerable to all manner of *mis*hearing. He "takes on" the way in which words depend on the communicative contexts in which they exist, together with its potentially disastrous consequences. Jesus suffers the effects of people's wilful self-benumbment,[31] and of the exploitative listening that looks either to trap the speaker in error or to twist his words for one's own advantage.[32] Mishearings by those who are most committed to attend to his words are as common as mishearings by "those outside." Jesus does not, it seems, act or speak in such a way as to escape this vulnerability. Rather, in living and acting as Word incarnate he makes the vulnerability of his words to mishearing one with the vulnerability of his body to "misapprehension," to the violent laying on of hands.

This point deserves further reflection. We speak of misread and misappropriated words being "mangled" and "butchered," and elsewhere of the "violence" of interpretation – conveying the sense of the power of the hearer to alter the word and its capacity for material effects (its "body") through the manner of receiving it. There are plenty of examples, not least in the history of "Christian" heresy-hunting, of the mangling of someone's words being a prelude to and sanction for the mangling of his or her body. What appears in the account of the mishearing of Jesus, I would suggest, is the equation of word and embodied identity to the point where the reception and hearing of the one is united with the reception of the other. The dependence of the Word on hearers is closely linked to the idea of the dependence of this body on the bodies of others.[33]

---

[31] As described for example in Matt 13:13ff.: "the reason I speak to them in parables is that 'seeing they do not perceive, and hearing they do not listen, nor do they understand.' With them indeed is fulfilled the prophecy of Isaiah." The parallel passage in Mark (4:11ff.) suggests that the parables are intended to *prevent* hearing – "for those outside everything comes in parables, in order that 'they may indeed look, but not perceive, and may indeed listen, but not understand.' " If we imagine the communicative situation in which all hearing is either "benumbed" or in some way exploitative, the claim that truthful speech must be given in a form that cannot be "heard" makes sense – and does not directly contradict the Matthean emphasis on the diagnosis of mishearing as a basic problem.

[32] As for example in the encounter described in Mark 12:13ff.: "Then they sent to him some Pharisees and some Herodians to trap him in what he said."

[33] The Christological significance of the idea of "voice" – discussed most notably by Oliver Davies, *A Theology of Compassion*, chapters 9 and 12 – might be considered further in this connection; to think "voice" is to think both word and body, word not without its material and interpersonal context, body not without its signifying power.

At the moment of Jesus' death (convicted on the basis of false testimony about what he has been "heard to say"[34]) even his cry of despair is misheard. The Crucifixion, then, brings this history of mishearing to its culmination, in the failure of any of the available communal frameworks of communication to hear what is being said to and within them.

In the previous chapter, I discussed with reference to Bonhoeffer's work the contrasting motifs of the "weakness" and the "strength" of Christ as understood from the Christological incognito, and as associated with the incarnation and the Crucifixion respectively. I observed there that the incognito meant both that Christ "took on" the weakness of the world and that Christ was decisively set "over against" the world. The *Christology* introduction, with its "war of Words" opposing *logos* to *counter-logos*, would seem to emphasize the latter theme – which poses problems for its interpretation, as we have seen. However, we also find that the lectures as printed end with the contemplation of the "humiliated one."[35] The apparent strength of the *counter-logos* does not, it would seem, exclude Bonhoeffer's other motif of the weakness of Christ – Christ's "continuity" with the world.

It is particularly instructive, in this regard, to consider the *Christology* introduction in conjunction with what is said about Christ as Word in *Discipleship*. Here, the description of "human reason" as dominated by the "word as idea" is replaced by a more explicitly ethical contrast between the "weak Word" and the "conquering idea."[36] The two main passages in *Discipleship* in which weakness is associated with Christ both concern Christ as Word. In the first, the "witnesses of the Word" are described as "weaker than the propagandists of an idea." The disciples whom Christ sends out, unlike the "fanatics" who follow an idea, must recognize that there will be places where the Word is rejected and where it, and they as apostles, will be forced to "retreat or even flee . . . as long as their weakness is the weakness of the Word."[37] Later in the same work, the Word of God is described as "weak and lowly," having become so for the sake of lost humanity. Strikingly, this weakness can be perceived even before the coming of Christ, in the prophecies and laws of the Hebrew Bible.[38]

These two instances of the "weakness of the Word" point back to both our discussion of the silences of Christ in the previous chapter and the interpretation of the *Christology* introduction. The weakness of the

---

[34] See Mark 14:57.
[35] *DBW* 12, p. 348. The proposed concluding lectures on "The Exalted Christ" were never given.
[36] *DBWE* 4, p. 173, *DBW* 4, p. 181.
[37] Ibid. See also *DBWE* 4, p. 193, *DBW* 4, p. 205.
[38] *DBWE* 4, pp. 213–14, *DBW* 4, p. 227.

Word differentiates it from practices of communication that rely on the imposition of powerful speech; but its weakness also denotes acceptance of the "weakness" that in fact pertains to human speech as such. God's *counter-logos* is weak "in itself" inasmuch as it accommodates itself to the capacity of the world for hearing. In so doing, however, it runs "counter" to practices of communication that rely on the power of the monologue.

The implication of these passages on the "weakness of the Word" is that God makes God's word vulnerable to mishearing, and that communication that "conforms" to God's word is similarly vulnerable. The suggestion in an earlier reconstruction of the *Christology* lectures that human thought is dominated (*beherrscht*) by the "word as idea"[39] could perhaps be read, not simply as a claim about the radical discontinuity between the human word and Christ as Word, but as a reminder of the "dominating" tendencies of the human word that denies its own finitude. Christ as the "weak" Word is exposed, not only to the possibility of mishearing, but to the possibility of being silenced by the word that claims universal validity – and condemns that "whereof it cannot speak" to be passed over in silence. The stark alternatives put forward in the *Christology* introduction – "Either man must die or he kills Jesus" – draw attention to the violence of the human *logos* that reduces the person – here the person of Christ – to a mute object of enquiry.

I have emphasized the links between, on the one hand, the dependence of the Word on hearers and the body of Jesus on the bodies of others, and, on the other hand, the mishearing of the Word and the abuse of the body. This was done, in the first instance, to call into question the idea that the incarnate Word should be thought primarily as "effective" in the way that power-asserting speech is effective. There are, however, obvious risks in such a presentation. Could the condition of dependence come to be understood in purely negative terms – as an unfortunate encumbrance or barrier to effectiveness? Feminist theologians, in particular, are rightly sensitive to the equation of embodiment or materiality with vulnerability to abuse. In seeking an account of a communicative situation Christologically transformed, the dependence of speakers on hearers needs to be affirmed – as part of what communication means in the created world. We need to recall and reaffirm that "truth happens only in community;" and a description of the reconciled *logos* must include this affirmation of the interpersonal character of truth-speaking, the primacy of the "Who?" question, as well as the judgment pronounced against the exclusions performed by any existing communicative framework.

---

[39] *Christology*, p. 50, *GS* 3, p. 185.

In Bonhoeffer's lectures, Christ as Word is heard in a silence that marks the end of *wissenschaftlich* enquiry as previously conducted, and becomes the basis for a new mode of enquiry, characterized by "response and responsibility." The claim is that teaching about Christ *begins* in this silence, and does not end with it – and that, moreover, it is possible to pursue a *wissenschaftlich* investigation even after the appearance of the *counter-logos*. This raises in a more specific form the question posed in the previous chapter concerning the positive significance of the resurrection as mystery. The silence in which Christology begins – the silence of the resurrection – must become the basis for a transformed *logos*. To use the terms outlined in the previous chapter, the whole "penultimate" activity of worship and study, speaking and hearing, must be seen in its orientation toward, and dependence on, the "last word" that accompanies it. Teaching about Christ begins, not in a silence that marks a capacity for hearing that can equally be exercised within any other *logos*, but in the silence determined by the *logos* of God.

Bonhoeffer's *counter-logos* is not, then, on the basis of the lectures as a whole, a louder voice that shouts down the opposing voices of human reason. It is, rather, a new communicative situation – distinguished in this lecture series primarily over against the academic disciplines, but distinguished, as we shall see, specifically by the forms and practices of communication it brings about. Central to this new communicative situation, this transformed human *logos*, are practices of hearing conformed with God's act of hearing.

Christological Hearing

At this point I return to the claim in the previous chapter that in the resurrection God hears God's own Word; and my suggestion is that to begin from the claim that God hears God's Word permits more theological significance to be given to the human activity of hearing.

At first glance, this claim looks counter-intuitive. If the statement that God hears God's Word is not merely trivial, it sounds like an easy affirmation of the "triumph of grace." If the act of hearing is God's, what becomes of the "responsibility" to which that Word gives rise in humanity?[40] Does this not simply exacerbate the problem with the accounts of

---

[40] The first reference in Bonhoeffer's work to the idea that God hears – and the only clear reference to the idea that God hears God's Word – tends to reinforce this suspicion. In the discussion of Barth in *Act and Being*, Bonhoeffer paraphrases Barth as saying that

divine "perlocutionary-attractive" speech, discussed above – making humanity into passive recipients of a complete speech-act, in which both the Word and its effectiveness are determined in advance?

It is certainly the case in the tradition I have been discussing that the "hearing" that God creates for God's Word, insofar as it is ascribed to humanity, is not an activity and does not depend on a prior human capacity. The emphasis on "hearing" as the beginning and continuing ground of faith is intended precisely to indicate that the reception of faith is something "undergone."[41] To appropriate the hearing itself to God does not change this. That being so, what is the substantive difference between the claim that God ensures a hearing for God's Word and that God hears God's Word? I suggest that it lies, not in the understanding of divine and human freedom implied, but in the understanding of speech and hearing. The privileging of the speaker–hearer relationship as the key model for the relation of God to humanity is called into question. God's communicative activity is understood to consist, not simply in "acting upon," but in the activities characteristic of a hearer – in making room for new speech to occur, in acknowledging and welcoming, in the judgment of truth and falsehood. With this, also, and most importantly, the whole understanding of communication conformed to God's action must be rethought.

The Christ of whom the "Who?" question is asked and answered is the one whom, and in whom, God hears. I shall suggest at this point three implications of this for the ethics of communication, or for the Christological reshaping of the communicative situation, corresponding to the threefold identification of Christ explored in the previous chapter. Firstly, taking up the point about "incarnation," above, Christ as the Word becomes what human words in truth are – vulnerable to mishearing, dependent on their hearers for their effectiveness, bound to historical and

---

God "creates hearing and faith for Himself, indeed, himself hears and believes." (Karl Barth, *Die Lehre vom Wort Gottes (Die Christliche Dogmatik, 1)* (Munich: Kaiser, 1927), pp. 357–8, paraphrased in *DBW* 2, p. 77, *DBWE* 2, p. 83). Subsequent discussion makes it clear that, in Bonhoeffer's view, espousal of the idea that God "himself hears and believes" is part of Barth's failure to conceptualize the continuity of existence in the light of revelation. Saying that "God himself hears" is, for Barth as Bonhoeffer reads him, a way of safeguarding the "pure act" character of revelation; everything that might have allowed resurrection to be conceptualized as "being," as possessing continuity, is absorbed back into the divine act. (He himself also wishes to assert that "preaching is basically always heard" and that the Word does not fail; but at this point he locates the "continuity" of the Word in the church-community that hears it (pp. 110, 127)).

[41] See Bonhoeffer's use of *pati* in *Act and Being* – which should probably not be translated in terms of "passivity" as such. *DBW* 2, p. 113, *DBWE* 2, p. 116.

social contexts (and hence weaker than the "idea" that demands hege-
monic force). The "weak Word" does not silence the world by entering
the battle of powerful monologues; in Fiumara's terms discussed in my
first chapter, the incarnate Word is "mild, moderate, modest, available,
vulnerable, welcoming, patient . . . pitiful (with reference to *pietas*),
humble (with reference to *humus*)." God's "hearing" of the incarnate
Christ is the affirmation of this weakness of words as proper to creaturely
reality.

Secondly, the silence of the crucified Christ calls into question all the
frameworks that determine which words can be effective, what can be
performed through speech, what is hearable. The identification of this
silent Christ as the one whom God hears confirms the irreducible over-
againstness of the other in any act of hearing – what I have referred to
as the silence of unknowability, the silence that is recognized when the
victims of unjust silencing are recognised. Conformity to God's act of
hearing – responsible life – requires that the reality confronting us be
neither explained away nor passed over in silence.[42] This claim in turn
points to the need for practices of anti-idolatry – disciplines and actions
through which acts of silencing can be recognized and overcome, and
violent forms of communication subjected to critique.

Thirdly, the asking and answering of the "Who?" question itself points
to the re-creation of the capacity for hearing as an aspect of the worldly
"realization" of Christological reality. I suggested in the previous chapter
that the capacity for hearing could be thought as one of the gifts of the
Spirit that enables participation in God's act of self-acknowledgment.

The claim, on the one hand, that "truth happens only in community,"
and, on the other, that persons are constituted as hearers through being
addressed, are not in the first instance obviously Christological; they rely
on concepts of performativity developed outside a Christological framework. Having said that the "word as address" is inseparable from its
speaker, I have then, apparently, taken generalized concepts of "address"
and applied them to the Christologically determined communicative
situation.[43] Bonhoeffer's claim, however, is that "the question 'Who?'

---

[42] See Mary M. Solberg, *Compelling Knowledge: A Feminist Proposal for an Epistemology of
the Cross* (Albany: State University of New York Press, 1997), for a discussion of the
relationship between feminist epistemologies and Luther's thought, which begins with an
analysis of the relation of ethics to epistemology – "the ethical significance of not knowing"
(p. 4).

[43] Jüngel, in his exposition of the concept of "address," makes a distinction that illustrates
this point. "If the word is the location of the thinkability of God," he writes, "then we
should not only ask about what the word *as God's word* has to say to the person addressed

presupposes an answer that has already been given;"[44] in other words, that the possibility of "address" depends on the reality of the risen Christ and demands to be thought in terms appropriate to that reality. The silence with which the *Christology* lectures begin is silence that corresponds to the risen Christ, a silence which, Bonhoeffer wants to suggest, can be kept in particular communities.

What happens when we set this alongside the claim, outlined in the previous chapter, that the resurrection of Christ is the event in which God hears God's own Word? The claim in the *Christology* introduction would be, following this reading, that the "humble silence of the worshipping community" participates in God's act of hearing and is enabled thereby to discern, not only the person of Christ "over against" the world, but the world in relation to Christ as its center. The community that becomes conformed in its hearing to God's hearing is the community within which "truth happens."

But how could we locate or identify a community within which "truth happens?" I suggested in the previous chapter that the claim that "God hears" is itself understood only through practices that "conform" to it. God's act of listening remains inextricable from the *unknowability* of God – and hence from the impossibility of formulating comprehensively the principles that specify "conformity" to that act of listening.

Thinking about listening as a gift of the Spirit, however, we might want to claim that the reconciled *logos*, the communicative pattern that conforms to God's act of hearing, can be found in the worshiping community. Within Bonhoeffer's work, this claim would be reinforced by the independence of Word and community in his thought. Christ as "Word in the sense of address" is thought together, in the lectures as previously

---

in a material sense . . . but we must also clarify hermeneutically what function the word of God *as addressing word* has for the addressed ego." (Jüngel, *God as the Mystery*, p. 170). It is precisely that "hermeneutical" clarification, in its consequences for an ethic of communication, that we are seeking. The problem with Jüngel's distinction as it stands, however – and this is the crucial issue – is that by distinguishing "the word as God's word" from "the word as addressing word" it allows the concept of "address" in itself to avoid theological critique. As I suggested in the first chapter, an understanding of the structure of "communication as such" is here adopted for theology without itself being subjected to theological or other critique.

[44] Although it should be noted that certain statements in the *Christology* introduction might lead us toward treating the "Who?" question itself as an abstract principle, by formalizing it into a statement concerning whatever, in general terms, presents itself as coming "from outside" the boundaries of knowledge and classification. "That which addresses us can only be interrogated with the 'Who?' question;" "the phenomenon is opened up only by this."

in his doctoral dissertations, with "Christ existing as community."[45] It would seem that the concept of the church-community identifies the place where Christ exists as both the one "who hears" and the one "who is heard," the place where the world-constituting power of the Word is not in contradiction with the dependence of the Word on the hearers.

There are profound problems, however, with identifying the silence of "the Church" *tout court* as a silence that corresponds to God's act of hearing. We discover these problems in reflecting on the use of silence within ecclesial contexts as a tool of oppression; we also discover them, as Bonhoeffer did, in the culpable silences of the churches in situations of grave injustice. For Bonhoeffer, the failures of the German churches called into question early attempts to identify the church-community as the place where the Word of God becomes effective through being heard. The Church's irresponsible silence is at the center of Bonhoeffer's "confession of guilt," through which he analyzes and assumes solidarity before God with the condition of Germany under Nazism:

> [The Church] was silent when she should have cried out because the blood of the innocent was crying to heaven. She has failed to speak the right word in the right way and at the right time . . . she has not raised her voice on behalf of the victim . . . she has witnessed in silence the spoliation and exploitation of the poor and the enrichment and corruption of the strong.[46]

The historical experience of the weakness of the Word of God in an unjust world, recorded by Bonhoeffer in the *Ethics* and the *Letters and Papers*, involves the loss of a secure innerworldly "location" for the hearing of the Word. While the "word of address" in the *Christology* lectures can be asserted to create "response and responsibility" for itself *in the space of the Church*, the location of the effective hearing of the Word in Bonhoeffer's later writings is rather more ambiguous. This is not just a reaction to a particular situation of ecclesial "guilt" and secular "goodness" – and so, by extension, feminist theology's corresponding uneasiness about the location of the "hearing of the Word" is not just a reaction to particular instances of injustice. It is, rather, the consequence in communicative terms of recognizing the resurrection of Christ as the only possible "answer to δος μοι που στω."

If we do not want to assume that a church-community as such is the place where the transformed *logos* is realized, this does not mean that

---

[45]   *GS* 3, pp. 193–4, *DBW* 12, pp. 305–6. On the interrelation of community and word in Bonhoeffer, see Dumas, *Dietrich Bonhoeffer: Theologian of Reality*, p. 118.
[46]   *Ethics*, pp. 49–50.

nothing can be perceived of the transformed *logos* in the life and com-municative practices of church-communities and of individuals within them. In the next two chapters, I consider how this might be the case – beginning, not, for obvious reasons, with general claims about how the transformed *logos* would appear always and everywhere, but rather with specific analyses of historical situations and the different patterns of com-munication perceived within them.

Chapter Five

WISDOM AND FOLLY: SEEKING PLACES TO STAND

Introduction

What is the communicative situation within which we exist, and how might the reconciled *logos* be perceived within it – if not through victory in a war of words? Listening, as Morton recognizes in her account of hearing to speech, is political – and in this chapter I use two "character sketches" to explore the pervasive implications of a distorted communicative situation, one that requires and produces folly, and the subversive and liberating power of a listening *logos* that requires and produces the "hearing mind" of wisdom. I then consider, taking up again a conversation with feminist thinkers, how the affirmation of the resurrection as "place to stand" (as opposed – or as, I shall argue, precisely *not* opposed – to the adoption of an epistemological "standpoint') can make possible this genuinely liberating transformation of a communicative situation.

In one of his last essays, and in the fiction he wrote in Tegel, Bonhoeffer reflects on the communicative situation in which "Words no longer possess any weight. There is too much talk."[1] The baptismal address for his great-nephew indicates that this condition is shared by, but not confined to, the words in which Christians are accustomed to speak of God – "Our earlier words are therefore bound to lose their force and cease."[2] The problem of the inability to speak of God (in the "religious" sense) is, it seems in these later discussions, merely one aspect of the wider problem of the loss of the "word as address," of the truth that "happens only in community."[3] It is this wider loss of truthfulness that the *logos* of

[1] *Ethics*, p. 330, *Konspiration und Haft*, DBW 16, p. 624.
[2] *Letters and Papers*, p. 300, DBW 8, p. 435.
[3] See especially *Fragmente aus Tegel*, DBW 7, pp. 48–9, DBWE 7, pp. 50–1; DBW 16, pp. 619–29, *Ethics*, pp. 326–34.

God confronts. The profound incapacity of the world to hear the Word is revealed, in the later writings, to be intimately connected with the near-complete breakdown of the possibility of truthful speech that Bonhoeffer perceived in his context.[4]

Looking at contemporary times, Fiumara's analysis of the logocentric culture depicts, as discussed in my second chapter, the constant "production" of words that has become an end in itself – without concern for the capacity of those words to give rise to genuine understanding or to the "listening event." Both she and Bonhoeffer record the flattening (for Bonhoeffer, the Nazi *Gleichschaltung*) of the discursive space into a "monologue," and the proliferation of competing discourses. The portrayal of the "power of discourse" in Fiumara's work is clearly reminiscent of Bonhoeffer's discussion of the "victorious idea" – the practice of propaganda – in *Discipleship*. For both thinkers, the communicative situation dominated by the monologue is based on a false understanding of what communication is or should be. Equally, for both thinkers, the falsehood has come to dominate patterns of thinking and action to such an extent that any attempt to change it is likely to be drawn into the same set of fruitless conflicts.[5]

Clearly Bonhoeffer would not accept the implication in Fiumara's work that resistance to the "pull towards benumbment" is a matter of the development of a human capacity that pre-dates any or every cultural context and is therefore present to be "rediscovered." His conviction that the godlessness of the world – the situation in which the Word of God is excluded from the world – is overcome only in the resurrection must lead him, as we suggested at the end of the previous chapter, to extreme caution in identifying any *loci* in which the condition of "benumbment" is overcome and the Word of God becomes effective.

In the light of this extreme caution, commentators have sometimes emphasized the aspect of silent waiting in Bonhoeffer's response to this breakdown in communication; waiting for God to speak again, waiting for the "new language" that can have an effect in the world.[6] I noted in the previous chapter the appeals to patience, grounded in the patience of God, in Bonhoeffer's work. The problem with speaking about "patience"

---

[4] See Frits de Lange, *Waiting for the Word: Dietrich Bonhoeffer on Speaking About God*, trans. Martin N. Walton (Grand Rapids: Eerdmans, 2000), p. 121.

[5] Bonhoeffer's rejection of Christian "radicalism" reflects this; and see Gemma Corradi Fiumara, *The Other Side of Language: A Philosophy of Listening*, trans. Charles Lambert. (London: Routledge, 1990), pp. 52–4.

[6] For Bonhoeffer's prediction of a "new language," see *Widerstand und Ergebung*, *DBW* 8, pp. 435–6, *Letters and Papers*, p. 300. For discussion of this, see Lange, *Waiting for the Word*,

and "waiting" in this context, as the discussion of feminist thought in the previous chapter suggested, is the suspicion that they point to a kind of quietism – one that would refuse to engage with the given situation because of its imperfections, that would fail to resist specific instances of injustice and untruth. Fiumara's account of benumbment points to such a risk – the one who refuses to be affected by the present communicative situation also sacrifices any possibility of agency within it.

Specifying God as the object of "waiting" does not necessarily overcome this suspicion. We might recall Morton's comments on "theologians who claim that God is sometimes silent, hidden or withdrawn . . . and that we must wait patiently until 'He' deigns to speak again," and the implicit claim that such theologians were in some way avoiding responsibility by casting themselves as the passive recipients of divine speech.

Just as, in the last chapter, it was necessary to expand the account of God's patience with a discussion of what it meant for God to be the one who hears, so in examining Bonhoeffer's response to the "breakdown of communication" we must also attend to the question "Who hears?" This is where we need to return, with Fiumara and others, to the question of the listening self – what its characteristics are, how it becomes possible, and how an ethics of communication is to take it seriously.

Having suggested earlier that Fiumara can be read as a contemporary teacher of wisdom, I now examine, with her work in mind, the depictions in Bonhoeffer's work of "folly" and "wisdom" – both centered around contemporary problems of communication, and in particular the failure and success of listening. The portraits raise important questions about the adequacy or otherwise of Bonhoeffer's articulation of "communication conformed to Christ,"[7] which will be examined in the section that follows.

Portraying Folly

The fear of the LORD is the beginning of knowledge; fools despise wisdom and instruction. (Prov 1:7)

---

pp. 122ff. See also Gerhard Ebeling, *Introduction to a Theological Theory of Language*, trans. R. A. Wilson (London: Collins, 1973), pp. 67–8 – "even if forced to silence oneself, one could agree with Bonhoeffer [*sc.* on the need for a time of silence] only if the necessity for silence was tolerated unwillingly . . . keeping a close look-out for fundamental experiences which could . . . reveal the possibility of making a wholesome and saving use of words."

[7] Alistair McFadyen, *The Call to Personhood: A Christian Theory of the Individual in Social Relationships* (Cambridge: Cambridge University Press, 1990), see esp. pp. 58–61.

Bonhoeffer's "After Ten Years"[8] contains a series of memorable character sketches that together "map" the ethical failure of his society. The use of "character sketches" of ideal types or (less often) of particular individuals is a common feature of his ethical reflection.[9] Given the statement in the *Ethics* that this is the age in which "there are once more villains and saints,"[10] it is particularly shocking to find one of the character sketches in "After Ten Years" introduced with the claim that the problem it represents is "more dangerous to the good than evil." This is the description of "the fool" – a particularly clear rereading of the condemnation of folly in the book of Proverbs. Having elsewhere asked whether wisdom should be regarded as the "first" virtue,[11] Bonhoeffer now portrays folly as the first human evil.

The fool, as Bonhoeffer describes him, is one who has given up "trying to assess the new state of affairs for himself" and is deprived of "independent judgment." He has become a passive hearer and unthinking repeater of the Nazi "slogans, catchwords and the like, which have taken hold of him." It should be made clear that folly has nothing to do with intellectual capacity, but is, rather, as in Proverbs, a moral defect; the fool as described may well, like many prominent Nazis, be extremely "intelligent."

The most obvious characteristic of the fool is that communication with him is impossible. Like Adolf Eichmann, as Hannah Arendt observed him at his trial,[12] "One feels . . . when talking to him, that one is dealing, not with the man himself, but with slogans." The image is of one whom propaganda, the large-scale renaming of the world, and other forms of distorted communication, have fully depersonalized. There is, in the presence

---

[8]   In *DBW* 8, pp. 19–39; *Letters and Papers*, pp. 3–17.

[9]   See further on this Stephen Plant, "Uses of the Bible in the 'Ethics' of Dietrich Bonhoeffer." (PhD, University of Cambridge, 1993), chapter 3. See Clifford Green, "Two Bonhoeffers on Psychoanalysis," in *A Bonhoeffer Legacy: Essays in Understanding*, ed. A. J. Klassen (Grand Rapids: Eerdmans, 1981), p. 68, for the influence – mainly negative – on Bonhoeffer of Fritz Künkel's popular psychology. Künkel's characterological approach is mentioned with qualified approval in the *Ethics* (*DBW* 6, p. 169, n.19).

[10]   *Ethics*, p. 3; *DBW* 6, p. 62.

[11]   *DBW* 6 *Erganzungsband*, p. 26.

[12]   Hannah Arendt, *Eichmann in Jerusalem: A Report on the Banality of Evil*, 2nd edn. (London: Penguin, 1994). Arendt's final verdict on Eichmann, as is well known, is that his fundamental failure was, simply or horrifyingly, the "inability to think." This "inability" was discernible, for Arendt as an observer of the trial, in Eichmann's reliance on slogans and catchphrases to express what he believed to be his moral and political "judgments:" ". . . he was genuinely incapable of uttering a single sentence that was not a cliché . . . his inability to speak was closely connected with an inability to *think* . . . No communication was possible with him." (Arendt, *Eichmann*, pp. 48–9).The monotonous uttering of clichés was combined with the – for Arendt and other listeners, staggering – inability to appreciate the enormous distortions of moral judgment manifested in the accounts he gave of particular actions during the implementation of the "Final Solution." Eichmann, as Arendt

of the fool, no one "who is heard" – only the slogans, the representation of the disembodied idea.

There is also no one "who hears." Importantly, Bonhoeffer argues that folly cannot be overcome "by instruction," and neither "protests," "reasoning" nor "facts" can touch it. In other words, the fool has altogether ceased to listen, except in the impoverished sense of listening to rebut objections or to reinforce prejudices – "facts that contradict personal prejudices can simply be disbelieved – indeed, the fool can counter by criticising them, and if they are undeniable, they can just be pushed aside as trivial exceptions." A comparison with Fiumara's analysis of the problem of benumbment, discussed in my second chapter, serves to emphasize the political and social implications of this loss of the capacity to listen – and the fact that it can occur in a wide range of situations, not necessarily characterizable as "totalitarian." Fiumara perceives a situation in which "the interactive modes that are commonly envisaged . . . are . . . that of 'listening' and falling victim to a possessive and exclusivist discourse that binds the 'hearer', or alternatively 'listening' in order to be able to rebut by a more powerful offensive logic."[13] Or perhaps, as it appears in Proverbs 9:7–8: "Whoever corrects a scoffer wins abuse;/whoever rebukes the wicked gets hurt./A scoffer who is rebuked will only hate you;/the wise, when rebuked, will love you."

The claim that folly is a moral defect is linked, in Bonhoeffer's account, to the perception that folly is "acquired" or "learned" in particular communicative circumstances – "people *make* fools of others or allow others to make fools of them," "the power of some needs the folly of the others." Folly may occur in many times and places, and remains a constant danger, but it cannot be historically generalized: "[these thoughts] in no way justify us in the belief that most people are fools in all circumstances."

The discussion of the "fool" is an interesting indication of Bonhoeffer's growing awareness of a particular form of the "view from below" in

---

portrays him, cannot "hear himself speak," just as he could not at the time "see what he was doing." He is, for Arendt, variously a "clown" and a "fool," whose clownery and folly do not exempt him from, but rather subject him to, the most severe moral judgment.

For an interesting comparison of Bonhoeffer and Arendt on "evil," which, however, suffers from an excessive focus on *Creation and Fall* (and hence from a failure to recognize Bonhoeffer's political analysis of evil), see Charles Mathewes, "A Tale of Two Judgements: Bonhoeffer and Arendt on Evil, Understanding and Limits, and the Limits of Understanding Evil," *Journal of Religion* 80, 3 (2000). I am grateful to David Grumett for conversations on this subject.

[13]   Fiumara, *The Other Side of Language*, pp. 83–4.

ethics.[14] The "view from below" is famously described as the perspective of "the outcast, the suspects . . . the powerless, the oppressed . . . those who suffer;"[15] but even more significant is the recognition in the later works of the experience of those who are rendered irresponsible.[16] In the earlier works, especially, sin is the futile and inescapable desire to gain unlimited and self-founding control over self, others, and the world. While the self-affirming person of Bonhoeffer's earlier work can be "irresponsible" in the sense of refusing to accept responsibility *for others*, the "fool" refuses to accept responsibility *for himself*.[17] The problem is not self-aggrandisement, but self-protection through the refusal of responsibility for one's actions and decisions.

The identification of folly as a failure of responsibility also means that the cure for folly is not instruction, but an act of liberation, "inward liberation to live a responsible life before God," which "in the vast majority of cases must be preceded by outward liberation." Outward liberation cannot, however, consist in talking to the fool, instructing or commanding him. The fool, we may surmise, is not ready to receive proclamation; in fact, he will hear it only as "instruction." Bonhoeffer has already stated the impossibility of arguing with the fool, and we presume that proclamation will suffer the same fate as reasoned protest; the fool in his self-satisfaction will brush it aside. His liberation will consist, not in the replacement of the powerful word to which he is enslaved with another such word, but in the restoration of his responsibility – which implies, crucially for this description, his ability to listen and to know himself as one who is listened to.[18] The "halved *logos*" that makes his folly possible must be overcome by the *logos* that "begins in silence."

Bonhoeffer can give little indication of the concrete form of the "act of liberation." The obvious reference in this passage is to the overthrow of the Nazi regime, but it is clear that this will not in itself bring about the end of folly. The only "consolation in these thoughts on folly" is that they "in no way justify us in thinking that most people are fools in all

---

[14]   The title given by Bethge to the passage written in prison and printed at the end of "After Ten Years."

[15]   *Letters and Papers*, p. 17, *DBW* 8, p. 38.

[16]   Among the other relevant passages in his later work are the confrontation between Heinrich and Christoph – the proletarian and the bourgeois – in the drama fragment written in prison, and the extended discussion of the range of "responsible life" in the *Ethics* (*DBW* 6, pp. 256ff., *Ethics*, pp. 218ff.)

[17]   And in doing so, project that responsibility onto another – "My conscience is Adolf Hitler." (*DBW* 6, p. 278; *Ethics*, p. 212).

[18]   Again, Arendt sheds interesting light on this; Eichmann's folly is linked to his inability to "see himself from the standpoint of another." Arendt, *Eichmann*, p. 49.

circumstances." This is not primarily an appeal to a concealed but ineliminable human capacity, but more, as the following paragraph makes clear, a statement of practical intent. The conclusion drawn from the analysis of folly is not a judgment on humanity but a course of action – the practice of love that resists the temptation to enact "contempt for humanity."[19]

What forms might this practice of love take? I would suggest, on the basis of this discussion, that the act of liberation that enables the "beginning of wisdom" in the fool – that frees him to live a responsible life before God – will be an act that mediates the silence of God in the godless world. It will not attempt to claim the "power of discourse" (the fool will not listen to arguments) but will condemn the *logos* that produces folly and will summon the "fool" to respond to the God who awaits the world's response. Being "liberated" for responsibility in this way will, Bonhoeffer's argument suggests, involve the restoration of the ability to listen with discrimination.

It should be emphasized again that the statement of ethical intent here implied does not amount to a comprehensive plan of action; nor is the limited optimism it implies secure in abstraction from the practice toward which it points. "Inward liberation" remains the work of God. The overthrow of the Nazi regime, which is apparently Bonhoeffer's example of "liberative" action, was fraught with ethical ambiguity and practical uncertainty. As the previous chapter suggested, one consequence of an emphasis on the *silence* of God in the penultimate is that action in conformation to Christ cannot necessarily be predicted in its characteristics or outcomes.

We should also say, following the discussion in the previous chapter, that the "liberation" of the fool need not be the final goal of responsible action or the conclusion of an ethic of communication. Wisdom is not, prima facie, simply the absence of folly. The claim that "the fear of the Lord is the beginning of wisdom" raises questions about the shape and development of that of which liberation, the elimination of a particular oppressive "communication regime," is a beginning.

We can see something beyond the "beginning," a depiction of wisdom and of the responsible listener, in a contrasting and intriguing character sketch drawn from the novel fragment that Bonhoeffer wrote in Tegel.

---

[19] On "contempt for humanity," see also *DBW* 6, pp. 72–4, *Ethics*, pp. 11–13, an extended discussion of the contempt underlying Hitler's populism.

Portraying Wisdom

The ear that heeds wholesome admonition will lodge among the wise.
(Prov 15:31)

The fragments of fiction Bonhoeffer wrote in Tegel stand in contrast to
the rest of his writings, in their lack of explicit theological concern – but
in continuity with them in their interest in the depiction of character
types. At the beginning of the novel fragment, the reader is introduced
to Frau Karoline Brake, an upper-middle-class matriarch.[20] Frau Brake is
portrayed returning from church on a Sunday afternoon, after a sermon
on the subject of "liberty," based (falsely, in her strong opinion) on Mark
2:23–28. She recalls it with horror: "instead of saying that Christ may do
many things because he is Christ, but that does not give *us* the right to
do them by any means . . . he babbled on about the freedom of all human
beings, and that people may do whatever they think is right."[21] The
problem goes beyond this particular sermon, and Frau Brake interprets it
in the gravest terms: "It could no longer be denied that here in this suburb
. . . hot air had taken the place of God's Word."[22] She perceives the
loss of the word of God at once as God's judgment and as a call to
responsible action by those who would be hearers of the word: "Frau
Karoline Brake had asked herself tacitly whether it could be God's will to
bring judgement over this generation by withdrawing God's word from
them. But even if it were so . . . God would also want people to resist this
judgement, to take God at his word and not let him go until he blessed
them."[23]

Her thoughts are interrupted by an encounter with a neighbor, who,
after a few platitudinous speeches which establish her as the "foolish, garrulous" but "good-natured" person she is later said to be,[24] appeals for
Frau Brake's assent to her praise of the morning's sermon. It has eased her
worries concerning her grandchild, whose father has refused to let the
child be baptized. While she cannot give a clear account of the sermon,
she can repeat enough phrases to secure her continuing comfort.

---

[20] Supposedly modeled on Bonhoeffer's grandmother, Julie Tafel Bonhoeffer, and on Ruth
von Kleist-Retzow. See *DBW* 7, p. 75 n.12.
[21] *DBWE* 7, pp. 78–9, *DBW* 7, p. 81
[22] *DBWE* 7, p. 74, *DBW* 7, p. 77.
[23] Ibid.
[24] *DBWE* 7, p. 79, *DBW* 7, p. 82.

Frau Brake's initial sharp response: "Dear Frau Warmblut, didn't you notice that the minister only preached what the congregation wanted to hear, but not the word of God?" is followed by the onset of doubt: "Do I have the right to criticise the sermon she found so lovely? Am I called upon to jolt this complacent woman out of her peace of mind?" Her final remark to the neighbor is a sign of her loss of self-assurance: "and you know – perhaps your daughter is quite right."[25]

It has been clear from the beginning of the scene that Frau Brake's attitude to communication is very different from that of her neighbor or the minister. She is introduced as she enjoys the peaceful atmosphere of the park, planted at her request by her husband the mayor and placed at her request under one restriction: "there was to be no noise in the park on Sundays." Her reflections on the subject lead to a consideration of the deficiencies of modern life: "Why were human beings so afraid of silence?"[26] In the conversation that follows, the neighbor's loquaciousness is deliberately emphasized to contrast with Frau Brake's brief responses.[27]

The scene is one of the few pieces of evidence for Bonhoeffer's understanding of the role of the congregation – that is, the hearers – with regard to preaching. Frau Brake, while she does not necessarily seek to set herself "above" the minister, certainly assumes some capacity in herself to pass judgment on his abilities and sincerity, and to discriminate within what he says between the valuable and the worthless. She is capable of doing this, we are told, because "she had learned through the years how to ignore the talk and to focus on the few words which contained truth."[28] She has, in other words, learned to listen to preaching; and her exercise of the responsibility of listening is, we learn, about to require her to take action against the preacher. Very few others in the parish have developed the capacity to listen to the extent that they recognize the preacher's failings – although, significantly, her grandson, who very rarely attends church but has been brought up in a similar environment to hers, dismisses the sermons as "preacher wisdom."[29]

---

[25]   *DBWE* 7, p. 79, *DBW* 7, p. 82.

[26]   *DBWE* 7, p. 72, *DBW* 7, p. 75.

[27]   What is especially noticeable in the light of Bonhoeffer's other writings at the time is that the neighbor's frequent references to God – "hasn't God given us another wonderful day . . . what wonderful health God has given you . . ." are met with polite non-religious responses – this from the woman whose earlier "soliloquy" was distinctly theological. The response to the loss of the word of God is to keep *more silent* concerning God.

[28]   *DBWE* 7, p. 76, *DBW* 7, p. 78.

[29]   *DBWE* 7, p. 74, *DBW* 7, p. 76. The word for "wisdom" here is *Weisheit*, generally a negative term in Bonhoeffer – see for example *DBW* 6, p. 72: "a time in which . . . contempt for humanity or the idolisation of humanity is the summit of wisdom [*Weisheit*]."

It is possible that in the figure of Frau Brake we also have Bonhoeffer's attempt at portraying some of the qualities that will enable the Church to emerge from its "time of silence" at some point in the unpredictable future. She listens from a position of assurance, but she gains her assurance from her listening. She is capable of attending to the particulars with which she is confronted and of "reading" her situation Christologically. She recognizes that the last word is God's but will not on that account abandon the possibility of a true word or righteous action in the present. She respects "earthly goods" and happiness – the limited integrity of the penultimate – and does not act wilfully to disrupt them; but she also perceives the judgment of God on the folly and self-satisfaction of her times. Her uncertain responses to her neighbor – responses that eventually amount to silence – reflect her attempt to respond to this double perception in a way that corresponds to the word of God.

The portrayal of Frau Brake is not, however, particularly optimistic. We are given no reason to believe that she will succeed in halting the advance of "folly" in her neighborhood. More to the point, she represents a culture that is disappearing. The young people in the novel have less self-assurance, and noticeably less reticence.[30] In Bonhoeffer's funeral address for one of her real-life originals,[31] he identified the "world" she represented in terms chiefly of its speech-ethics: "the free word of the free man, the binding nature of a word once given, clarity and restraint of speech." This is a world that, Bonhoeffer declared, "went to the grave" with the woman who exemplified it;[32] from the novel fragment we gain some indication of the apparently insurmountable difficulties surrounding its representatives.

If for Bonhoeffer Frau Brake's world, with its "clarity and restraint of speech," was the object of mourning, for us it can scarcely even be the object of nostalgia; and Bonhoeffer can offer no program either for its restoration or for its replacement. What then is the theological importance of this character sketch? I suggest that it offers an example, which is deliberately ambiguous, of "conformation" to the silence of God in the penultimate; action that seeks to recall the world to responsibility before God by mediating God's presence-in-absence. The responsibility to which

---

[30]   The one notable exception is Frau Brake's granddaughter "Clara," who is protected from the upheavals encountered by the young men.

[31]   Julie Tafel Bonhoeffer; see *Illegale Theologenausbildung: Finkenwalde 1935–1937*, *DBW* 14, pp. 9–24.

[32]   *DBW* 14, p. 924; the equivalent in *GS* (4, p. 459) reads "did *not* go to the grave with her," but the *DBW* editors argue rightly (see their n.11) that this makes no sense in the context.

it seeks to recall the world is also, perhaps primarily, the responsibility of listening.

This still leaves open the question of the applicability of both Bonhoeffer's character sketches, in the light of their historical and cultural specificity, to a contemporary theological ethics of communication. If we cannot treat these texts as the sources of generalized ethical principles, without attending to the particular situation from which they are written and to which they refer, how are they to be used? This question is important in any attempt to understand how the reconciled *logos*, shaped by God's activity of listening, might be discerned in the lives of people and communities, because it draws attention again to the particular "presence, history and form" of silence – the ways in which listening, as well as speech, always arises within a historical and social location.

At around the time he wrote the character sketches, Bonhoeffer famously claimed that in opposition to Nazism he, and his fellow con-spirators, had come to see the world from the "perspective of those who suffer" – something he described as "an experience of incomparable value." This claim, of a specific and partial "standpoint" as the location of theological reflection, raises questions about the affirmation (discussed earlier) of the resurrection as the "answer to δος μοι που στω," the "place to stand." It might also be questioned in the light of Bonhoeffer's own social background and context – a background reflected in the prison fiction, with its focus on the lives and concerns of upper-middle-class families.

The idea of the "standpoint" from which knowledge arises has been central to debates in feminist epistemology, sometimes with an explicitly theological – or anti-theological – concern. In the next section, I link some of these feminist reflections on the social location of knowing and hearing with Bonhoeffer's claims about "standpoints" – both the claim to think "from the perspective of those who suffer" and the claim about the resurrection as "place to stand." How does the ethics of communication, and in particular the activity of listening, appear from the standpoint of those who suffer? And what does it mean to affirm, in any given situation, the resurrection as the "silent," non-thematizable place to stand?

Listening and Places to Stand

Standpoint epistemologies, as developed in feminist theory through engagement with Marxist thought, have traced out the possibility that "those who suffer" from oppression within a situation can come to have privileged knowledge of the reality of that situation. For the standpoint epistemologist, the interest of the oppressed is in unmasking, rather than maintaining, the falsehoods that sustain a system of oppression. Their position gives them the possibility of knowledge that – to quote one of the most influential articles on feminist standpoint epistemology – "exposes the real relations among human beings as inhuman, points beyond the present, and carries a historically liberatory role."[33]

To seek a feminist standpoint is, then, at its most basic, to accept the situated character and the partiality of knowledge – and to seek consciously to inhabit a particular position, the position of the subjugated, in order to understand the access to knowledge it can give.[34] It is to refuse, and to undertake the critique of, what Donna Haraway calls the "God trick" – the claim to know the world and to speak of it from a position of value-free objectivity.[35] To revert to the language of earlier chapters, to criticize the "God trick" is to draw attention to the acts of silencing on which a supposedly "obvious" or "neutral" position has been constructed; adopting a feminist standpoint is venturing the claim that the silence surrounding the obvious or neutral position is "not absence." It is easy to see how this critique of the "God trick" can lead to suspicion about the claim that the resurrection is "answer to δος μοι που στω" – particularly when this claim is made by a theologian working within a male-dominated tradition.

Crucially, however, for at least some advocates of a standpoint epistemology, one does not necessarily have to be part of the oppressed group whose standpoint one adopts.[36] One must start from critical reflection on

---

[33] Nancy Hartsock, "The Feminist Standpoint: Developing the Ground for a Specifically Feminist Historical Materialism," in *Discovering Reality: Feminist Perspectives on Epistemology, Metaphysics, Methodology and Philosophy of Science*, eds. Sandra Harding and Merrill B. Hintikka (Dordrecht: Reidel, 1983), pp. 283–310, here p. 284.

[34] See for further discussions and expositions of feminist standpoint epistemology, Sandra Harding, *Whose Science? Whose Knowledge? Thinking from Women's Lives* (Milton Keynes: Open University Press, 1991); Nancy Hartsock, "The Feminist Standpoint Revisited," in Hartsock, *The Feminist Standpoint Revisited and Other Essays* (Boulder: Westview, 1997), pp. 227–48; Alison M. Jaggar, *Feminist Politics and Human Nature* (Brighton: Harvester, 1983), chapter 11; Pamela Sue Anderson, *A Feminist Philosophy of Religion: The Rationality and Myths of Religious Belief* (Oxford: Blackwell, 1998).

[35] Donna Haraway, "Situated Knowledges: 'The Science Question in Feminism" and the privilege of partial perspective," *Feminist Studies*, 14, 3: 575–99.

[36] See on this Harding, *Whose Science?*, pp. 286–95. See also, for an important recent discussion of the "possibility of reversing standpoints" in relation to the hearing of the socially marginalized in religious discourse, Pamela Sue Anderson, "An Epistemological-Ethical Approach," in *Feminist Philosophy of Religion: Critical Readings*, eds. Pamela Sue Anderson and Beverley Clack (London: Routledge, 2004), pp. 94–6.

how the members of that group experience their situation; but, for example, a man adopting a feminist "standpoint" (if this is agreed to be possible) will not only attend to feminist women's analyses of patriarchy, but will also think through and from his own social location in relation to those analyses.

Looking at Bonhoeffer's claim to have entered into "the perspective of those who suffer" from the point of view of such claims about the "standpoint," we might say that he, through a combination of his own experience of suffering and the deliberate adoption of a position of solidarity with "those who suffer," had indeed acquired some "historically liberatory" knowledge of the operation of the Nazi regime. At the same time, there are critical questions to be asked, specifically from a feminist perspective, about what his adoption of this "standpoint" actually means – questions that emerge when we consider the gendered nature of the texts under discussion.

The "fool" Bonhoeffer describes is a man; but his condition, the condition of willfully persisting in a state of irresponsibility, clearly corresponds to what Valerie Saiving and others have identified as "feminine" sin, and what I discussed earlier as part of the analysis of the silencing of women.[37] The fool has been placed by others, and has come to place himself, in the position of the passive recipient of powerful speech. While his folly is in part caused by those in power, he himself, in his own speech and hearing, reinforces it. He is, in other words, complicit in the patterns of communication that deprive him both of his own voice and of his own ears. Considering the depth of the involvement of the silenced, and of those who are "made fools of," in their own silencing already exposes the difficulty of exercising communicative agency from such a standpoint. It is not surprising that the emergence of the fool from his folly is not portrayed. As feminist epistemologists are anxious to emphasize, there is nothing automatic about the emergence of "historically liberatory knowledge" from a position of powerlessness.[38]

Looking at Frau Brake, the "female" solution to the fool's "feminine" sin raises, in this context, as many questions as it answers. It is clearly not incidental – and not solely explicable in biographical terms – that the lost

---

[37]   Valerie Saiving, "The Human Situation: A Feminine View," *Journal of Religion* (1960); Judith Plaskow, *Sex, Sin and Grace* (Lanham: University Press of America, 1980). See for a discussion of "feminine" sin in relation to the Shoah, McFadyen, *Bound to Sin?*, chapter 7.
[38]   See Hartsock, *The Feminist Standpoint Revisited*, pp. 236–7. Anderson expresses the basic point clearly ("An Epistemological-Ethical Approach," p. 45): ". . . a feminist standpoint is the result of an epistemological struggle; it is not a spontaneous perspective which a woman possesses by virtue of being a woman."

"wisdom" of a passing age is represented in Bonhoeffer's work by a woman. At several points – most famously in the wedding sermon for Renate and Eberhard Bethge – he makes women, specifically as keepers of the home, representatives of the "silent" cultural and social background of thought and action. In the wedding sermon, a (selective[39]) quotation of Proverbs 31 is used to secure the home, and the woman as its guardian, as the *locus* of "not novelty, but permanence; not change, but constancy; not noisiness, but peace."

There is a tendency, then, to turn women and the sphere they represent into an unthematized "place to stand" – a space from which one can view a changing world from a critical distance.[40] The feminist reader suspects that women's own multiple perspectives are being ignored. Their assumed silence is, it would appear, used as the basis for maintaining Bonhoeffer's own – ideologically concealed – position as a socially and educationally privileged man, which will in turn allow him to avoid really entering "the perspective of those who suffer" and asking about their perceptions of the communicative situation.

Several of the problems with the structure of Bonhoeffer's ethics, noted so far, would seem to relate to this concealment of the privileges of his position. While, as I have indicated, the recognition of "folly" as an ethical problem is itself a significant move, it is relatively underdeveloped. We saw in the second chapter his portrayal of the "mandates" that govern life in the penultimate, and that seem to require "relations of superiority and inferiority;" and we should note, in connection with it, his continuing focus, in the portrayal of the fool, on the responsibility of "those in power."

Does this unacknowledged assumption of a male "place to stand," as if it were self-evident – and the ideological construction of women as the silent supporters and guarantors of that situation – render the character sketches worthless in understanding the innerworldly realization of the reconciled *logos*? My discussion of the portrayal of Frau Brake drew attention to two aspects that take it beyond these obvious limitations and render it more fruitful for our discussion: Frau Brake's location in an irrecoverable past, and her exercise of responsibility as a listener.

---

[39] Omitting, for example, the references to the woman's economic activities (vv. 16–18, 24: – "She considers a field, and buys it . . . she perceives that her merchandise is profitable . . . she makes linen garments and sells them") and her public visibility (v. 31 "let her works praise her in the city gate"), and emphasizing the passages that fit with the description of an idealized *Hausfrau*.

[40] When his friend Detlef Albers became engaged, Bonhoeffer wrote to him describing the home, for the married man, in terms of δός μοι ποὐ στῶ – *Barcelona, Berlin, Amerika, DBW* 10, p. 152.

The portrayal of the fool and of the "wise woman" can be compared to some of Fiumara's strategies, discussed in my second chapter, for showing the possibility of a philosophy of listening. Recollections of an idealized or schematized past are combined with diagnostic sketches of the present, which portray both its dangers and the persistence of opportunities for averting these dangers. In neither case will it, by definition, be possible to present the reconciled *logos* as a comprehensive alternative in the terms available within present discourse. The historical particularity of Frau Brake puts her in the past, and it is of the nature of her "wisdom" – the wisdom that allows her to recognize falsehood and educate others in listening – that, once lost, it cannot be restored as the unthematized "place to stand."

Bonhoeffer's use of character sketches is, however, significant. For him the only possibility for the reconstruction of a *logos* within which responsible listening is possible lies in the asking and answering of the question "Who?" The reconciled *logos* that in Fiumara might threaten to degenerate into a "How?" – how do we listen, how do we change our discursive patterns – is for Bonhoeffer only understood through and as the "Who?" question.

Frau Brake in herself, as part of an irrecoverable past, can provide no answers to the question posed above, of how the reconciled *logos* comes to be restored in the world Bonhoeffer and Fiumara both describe – a world in which words "no longer have any weight," and in which folly or benumbment has become so widespread that the problem can scarcely any longer be defined or recognized. This is not, in itself, a problem. If, following the discussion in the previous chapter, we want to argue that the only possible enduring answer to our "Who?" questions ("Who hears? Who is heard?') is "The God of Jesus Christ," and the only "standpoint" unquestionably given is the resurrection, we should not expect to be able to offer a definitive portrayal of the "listening self." The practices and forms of life that mediate that act of hearing – the "act of hearing" that enables responsible existence in the penultimate – are themselves of penultimate significance; limited, historically complex, and understandable only in the light of that toward which they point. Here and in my third chapter, the feminist critique of Bonhoeffer's assumptions helps to draw awareness to aspects of his partial "standpoint" that might otherwise be treated as possessing some ultimate importance. To say that, however, is only to make a negative claim – and I have been suggesting that these character sketches, however flawed, make a positive contribution to a theological and ethical understanding of the reconciled *logos*.

At the end of the passage on "the fool" in *After Ten Years* we read: "What will really matter is whether those in power expect more from people's folly than from their wisdom and independence of mind" (*Letters and Papers* 9). The insight that "the power of some needs the folly of the others" is identified as a "psychological and sociological law"(8) rather than, in the first instance, as a question requiring theological and ethical reflection. The focus is still, then, on the actions of those who would normally be defined as speakers. Elsewhere in the *Ethics* (in the section that also refers to the definite order of preacher "above" and congregation "below') we find that rebellion of those "below" is what disrupts the orders of life.[41] So far, those who are "made fools of" have been offered very little hope, and have been left reliant on the actions of "those in power." Little hope, that is – except in the unexplained activity of the woman who, from a position of no recognized power, refuses to allow herself (or, if she can help it, her neighbor) to be made into a fool.

By leaving the groups designated as "inferior" relatively undifferentiated and paying little attention to their particular exercises of responsibility,[42] Bonhoeffer avoided some of the challenges implied in Morton's question "Who hears?". But the tiny hint contained in the depiction of Frau Brake is that it would be foolish to expect the communicative situation to be changed simply "from above." Responsible listening from a position of supposed weakness – the refusal to allow one's folly to support the power of others – is action that overcomes the "halving of the *logos*." My first chapter already suggested that the attempt to claim for oneself a powerful voice, which in turn can silence others, is not an adequate solution to the problem of silencing. The practices of "hearing to speech"

---

[41] *Ethics*, pp. 256–7, *DBW* 6, pp. 395–6. Against this we must of course set the famous passage on the "view from below" (*DBW* 8, pp. 37–9, *Letters and Papers*, p. 17). The significance of this passage should not be underestimated, but it distances Bonhoeffer deliberately from those who *generally* view the world "from below" – those he terms "the eternally dissatisfied" (pointing back to the characterization of "rebellion").

[42] As stated above, Frau Brake's portrait is the only significant consideration of the responsibility of members of a congregation. The examples of substitutionary responsibility used in the *Ethics* are instructive in this regard; "a man is directly obliged to act in the place of other men . . . as a father, as a statesman or as a teacher" (*Ethics*, p. 194; *DBW* 6, pp. 256–7). An opposite set of examples would have been equally possible – a child (by whose actions the parent will be judged), a government official (who acts on behalf of the statesman), a pupil. In Bonhoeffer's examples the emphasis is on the curtailment of arbitrary action in the light of the needs of those in whose place one is empowered to act. In the second set of examples, the emphasis might be, rather, on the possibility of free action despite the context of dependence and obedience.

and the critical articulation of other possible communicative practices by the silenced suggests that liberation from silencing does not depend on the action of "those in power." The very identification of the problem of silencing implies that the silenced have recognized their own condition, and can begin to change it – can begin, for example, to "hear one another to speech."[43]

Here, in fact, a focus on the "Who?" question can help us to appreciate the contributions and limitations of an emphasis on the epistemological significance of the "standpoint," for an ethics of communication based on listening. It is, in the first place, true that a person can hear and be heard only as situated and embodied, and that the particular form of her capacity for hearing – the ear with which she is able to hear[44] – develops in a particular way according to that situation. In the second place, however, to ask "*Who* hears?" is to draw attention to the possibility of the communicative agent going beyond the given conditions of a situation, becoming more than the mouthpiece or the earpiece of some "standpoint," claiming responsibility for hearing things differently. Dauenhauer's double characterization of silence as signifying both finitude and freedom, or both the givenness and the openness of the world of signification, is helpful here – if we at the same time remember, with his critics, that the "openness" of any silence, simply *as* silence, is not to be taken for granted.

We cannot think of the listening self as disembodied, or as existing nowhere in particular; hearing, as both Morton and Fiumara make abundantly clear, is an embodied and historically located activity. We can, however, think of the listening self as one whose embodied location is "open" – open to being affected and changed in itself, and thus forming a place of openness to change within the world. In the same way, thinking about the resurrection does not mean thinking a "disembodied" Christ (the resurrected one is still the incarnate and the crucified) – but rather thinking the embodied Christ as the point of openness. To put it in other terms – the question "Who hears?" is not asked and answered without reference to some body, at some time, in some set of social and political relations; but nor can it be asked and answered exhaustively by a list of the various characteristics and innerworldly relationships of the person or group in question, the labels he or she might adopt.

---

[43] With no assumptions about how this becomes possible – see the discussion in chapter 1 of the complicity of the silenced in their own silencing.

[44] See Jacques Derrida and Claude Levesque, *The Ear of the Other: Autobiography, Transference, Retranslation – Texts and Discussions with Jacques Derrida* (New York: Random House, 1985), p. 5: "everything depends on the ear you are able to hear me with."

The claim with which this discussion began was not, however, simply that all knowledge is socially located; it was that knowledge developed from "the perspective of those who suffer" has a particular liberative or transformative force. What of this claim within a theological account of hearing? We might say that the resurrection as "place to stand" calls into question both the ideological concealment of one's own position, and the attempt to make a particular standpoint normative. With the vindication of Jesus in God's act of hearing, the voice of the victim, of the one previously suppressed or excluded from speech, is heard and affirmed, as a judgment on any action that would silence her in order to secure another's privileged position of speech. To call the resurrection the "answer to δος μοι που στω" is to call into question all accounts of knowledge that do *not* recognize the limitations of their historical standpoints, and that by this failure of acknowledgment suppress knowledge that is differently located. Thinking about divine hearing in fact deepens the critique of the so-called "God trick," because knowing and speaking from "nowhere" is precisely *not* a trick God plays.[45]

To refer to divine hearing is also, however, to question the attempt to make any social position, or any specified form of oppression, into a secure place to stand, because of the way this can itself limit the range of voices to which one is prepared to listen – producing its own kind of "folly." Here, in fact, a theological account of the resurrection as "place to stand" meets developments in feminist epistemology – critiques of attempts to define "women's" standpoint at the expense of attention to the multiple differences among women, the recognition that a commitment to any "standpoint" in search of genuinely liberatory knowledge will imply a commitment to engagement with all the "standpoints."[46]

If, then, we focus on a standpoint as a place from which we *hear*, rather than – in the first instance – a place from which we *speak*, it becomes clear that a standpoint is neither a fixed ideological position nor a foreclosed collection of experiences, to be defended over against the experi-

---

[45]   I discuss this point further, with reference to ideas of divine omniscience, in chapter 7. Note also that Anderson (*Feminist Philosophy of Religion*, p. 134) criticizes those who call the view from nowhere the "God trick" because this perpetuates the assumption that God is best thought as disembodied.

[46]   See on this Harding, *Whose Science?*, pp. 285–6. See also the discussion in my first chapter of the question of representation in feminist writing – the claim to "speak for" women, or even for particular sub-groups of women, becomes problematic once the unity of the subject of feminist discourse is called into question. For discussion of this in relation to theology, see in particular Mary McClintock Fulkerson, *Changing the Subject: Women's Discourses and Feminist Theology* (Minneapolis: Fortress, 1994).

ences or standpoints of others. To hear is necessarily to admit others into one's "standpoint," to be on common ground with them – and to accept the disruptions to one's own claims and self-understanding that this implies. In the Christological terms discussed in my previous chapter, it is to recognize and participate in a common space wherein affirmation, judgment and transformation occur. Beyond this, however, I want to suggest that to call the resurrection one's standpoint is to take on a call to participate in God's "historically liberatory" hearing of the silenced. It may also be, therefore, to be drawn beyond the concern for a particular act of historical "liberation" through relation to a wider divine dynamic of love.

In both this and the preceding chapter, we have seen the extent to which Bonhoeffer's understanding of the hearing and speaking of the Word retains assumptions about the respective superiority and inferiority of hearer and speaker, which in turn makes him less prepared to understand and depict the responsible "activity" of the listener. At the same time, Bonhoeffer's focus on the resurrection as the place from which the truthful speaking and responsible hearing becomes possible (defining the "ultimate" – and therefore not at present fully comprehensible – answer to the questions "Who hears? Who is heard?') enables us to take the gravity of the "loss of truth" seriously, while still giving an account of the hope in which practices of listening are grounded.

In the next chapter, I shall consider some different presentations of practices of communication that can be said to conform to the silence of God – and thus to reshape distorted communicative situations. I will suggest that those practices are both subversive and self-subverting; even when exercised by those "in positions of power" they call the relations of superiority and inferiority, which they appear to presuppose, into question. This subversion occurs, however, in the context of the formation of the "hearing mind," the realization in particular contexts of the reality given in the resurrection.

Chapter Six

HEARING WITH GOD'S EARS: INTERPRETING PRACTICES OF SILENCE

Christians have forgotten that the ministry of listening has been entrusted to them by the one who is indeed the great listener and in whose work they are to participate. We should listen with the ears of God, so that we can speak the Word of God. (Bonhoeffer, *Life Together*[1])

In the preceding chapters, I have put forward an understanding of the resurrection as the "place to stand" from which responsible action, grounded in God's hearing of the world, becomes possible. The silence of God, understood from the resurrection, is, I have suggested, not only the intensification of God's hiddenness, but also the action of God to transform the world. I have suggested, further, that the "form" toward which this transformation is oriented could not be understood apart from its realization in particular lives, and particular patterns of communication, "conformed to Christ." Having begun in the last chapter to consider what such lives and patterns of communication might look like, I now move to consider certain practices of silence that can be read in this way. Where and how do people keep God's silence, to "listen with the ears of God?" And what do we learn from such a keeping of silence, or such a listening, about existence "conformed to Christ?"

There are many silences that are said, by the people who keep them, to correspond to God; and in rather few cases can the way in which these silences correspond to God be reduced to agnosticism or to the discovery of the limits of speech (the possibilities admitted and discounted in my second chapter). The silences of worship are manifold and complex, as are the silences kept by those engaged in counselling and "spiritual

[1] *Life Together and Prayerbook of the Bible*, DBWE 5, p. 99; *Gemeinsames Leben & Gebetbuch der Bibe*, DBW 5, pp. 83–4.

care," and the silences that surround exercises of discernment. Thinking about listening as an activity of God, "realized" in the world, forces us to take these silences seriously – and to shape an understanding of divine and human communication that can recognize their importance. In the last chapter, I began to describe the listening self as a *locus* of transformation – transformation that is neither simply arbitrary nor specifiable in advance. I have also suggested that the formation of hearers is a process that extends beyond the initial move of disrupting misdirected listening. "Liberation" from folly or idolatry is coterminous with the process by which both the capacity of individuals for discernment and recognition, and the communicative situation within which they exist, are re-formed according to the reality of the resurrection.

In this chapter, I look more closely at some descriptions of what might be regarded as Christologically reconfigured practices of silence. First, I look at the use of silence in worship, and to the challenges this poses to a theological prioritization of speech. This discussion calls into question the tendency to interpret silence in worship in terms of the speech-acts for which it prepares, or of which it is the equivalent – or to treat it as individualizing or subjective. I consider silence in worship as an interruption to, or liberation from, expected patterns of communication and ways of experiencing time – and look beyond this to its positive significance as "keeping God's silence," participating in God's hearing of God's own Word in relation to the whole of creation.

I use this reading of silence in worship to develop a rereading of Bonhoeffer's lectures on *Seelsorge*, translated "spiritual care," together with descriptions of the "ministry of listening" in *Life Together*. In these texts, the silence of the spiritual carer is a major focus, and is taken to communicate the worldly ungraspability of God as constitutive of persons before God; it "uncovers sin" by revealing and destabilizing a person's attempts at self-creation. This in itself does not, however, do justice either to the fact that spiritual care is a practice of *listening* (and hence, among other things, a process wherein both participants are affected) or to the claim that spiritual care is a practice that *forms hearers*. Once again, an account of the hiddenness of God (the "silence of unknowability," to use the terms from my second chapter), and how a practice of silence reflects this, needs to be complemented by an account of the "silence of a listener."

The account of spiritual care found in Bonhoeffer's work, then, needs to be expanded – first, in terms of the "capacity for discernment and recognition" that spiritual care seems both to require and to develop, and, second, in terms of the relationship between the participants in spiritual care, moving beyond relations of "superiority and inferiority" to the practice of friendship. In each case I point out the importance of *love* as constitutive, both of who God is (God's hearing of God's own Word) and of the realization of this divine reality in human lives and societies (God's hearing of the world). An emphasis on divine love as a description of the "ultimate" helps us to develop the wider implications of Bonhoeffer's thought on wisdom, listening, and discernment, without losing his resistance to the formalization of ethics.

The practices of silence on which I have chosen to focus here are perhaps not those that come most immediately to mind in a consideration of silence in Christian spirituality. As I shall discuss in the next section, there is a common and understandable association of silence with solitude, with the individual, and with the "inwardness" of processes of transformation. In drawing attention, as I have from the beginning of this work, to the practice of silence as communal, interpersonal, and outward-looking, I attempt further to call into question what I take to be unhelpful ways of constructing the dichotomy of speech and silence – before returning to the question of the relationship between individual and communal "silences," in relation to issues in contemporary ethics, in the final chapter.

Interpreting Silence in Worship

I have suggested at several points in the foregoing discussion that the keeping of silence should be understood as communicative action that is not the equivalent of a speech-act. In chapter 4, having taken up the claim linked to speech-act theory that "truth happens only in community," I drew attention to the problems with an account of how truth "happens" that fails to recognize silence as itself a communicative activity. There are, we know, many situations in which the keeping of silence – in specific ways and with specific intentionality – is central to a communicative situation; consider, for example, Nelle Morton's group of silent listeners hearing someone into speech. There are, furthermore, many communities for whom the keeping of silence is a fundamental part, not only of practice but of self-understanding. Silence has been an organizing focus for theology and spirituality within Quakerism and many forms of monastic life, for example, not only as a shared practice but also as an organizing symbol for many other aspects of life and thought.[2]

---

[2] See for a detailed analysis of this in relation to early Quakerism, Richard Bauman, *Let Your Words Be Few: Symbolism of Speaking and Silence among Seventeenth-Century Quakers* (Cambridge: Cambridge University Press, 1983); and for a contemporary account written

In this section, I explore certain features of the use of silence in Christian worship. The underlying assumption – that the keeping of silence is a valid and important part of communal worship – may not be universally accepted. I start from the fact that silences *are* kept as part of Christian worship, and ask what sense this makes and what effects it has – while being concerned mainly with the broader question of a theological ethics of communication.

I noted in chapter 4 that Bonhoeffer's account of the "humble silence of the worshipping congregation," as the place in which the "Who?" question could be asked and answered and a different *logos* encountered, was rightly called into question in his later work. What is the point, then, of entering here into a discussion of the "silence of the worshipping congregation?" I want to consider silence in worship, here, in continuity with and illuminating a whole range of habits of communication and action – not, then, as a privileged or assured location for the realization of the transformed *logos*, but more as a way in which that *logos* is learned and signified. It is, in particular, a useful starting point if we want to see ways beyond those accounts of communication in which silence is thought solely as absence or passivity.

Treating silence as primary or focal in an account of communicative practices is, as I suggested in my introduction, both theologically and philosophically challenging. Part of the difficulty of talking about silence lies in the interplay between the function of (any given) silence as *sign* and the common-sense identification of silence with the absence of signification. Thus, having discussed at some length the "silence of God," we might wish to interpret some given practice of silence – say, perhaps, the silence at the beginning of a Quaker meeting for worship – as a sign of the silence of God as we had come to understand it from that discussion. The risk would then be that the practice of silence in question would itself be deprived of its character as silence – turned into a quasi- "speech-act," conveying a predetermined

---

as an introduction to Quaker practice, John Punshon, *Encounter with Silence: Reflections from the Quaker Tradition* (London: Quaker Home Service, 1987). On the monastic "rhetoric of silence," see Paul F. Gehl, "Competens Silentium: Varieties of Monastic Silence in the Medieval West" *Viator* (1987), 126; also Paul F. Gehl, "An Answering Silence: Medieval and Modern Claims for the Unity of Truth Beyond Language," *Philosophy Today* 30, 3 (1986). Gehl's claim, regarding monastic discourses on silence, is that the practice of silence becomes the symbolic focus for theology, worship, and ethics. It is associated with an emphasis on the "internalization" of texts ("Competens Silentium," pp. 142–3), on the transformation of the self ("An Answering Silence," pp. 229–30), and on an "ethics of collective action" ("An Answering Silence," p. 232).

message.[3] On the other hand, if we refuse to say that this silence "means" anything in particular, the conclusion is either that it means nothing or that it means whatever the individual wishes to impose on it. Neither of these approaches will, it seems, be adequate for talking about silence; both represent, in different ways, attempts to control it – and hence, in the terms suggested earlier, to reduce it to muteness. Discussions of the use of silence in communal worship make apparent the problems of speaking theologically about the keeping of silence as both significant and outside signification, both effective and resistant to instrumentalization.

Such discussions occur both within "mainstream" liturgical traditions and within the Quaker tradition, where the keeping of silence is the dominant feature of ordinary public worship.[4] In the former, it is, perhaps surprisingly, not uncommon for commentators to suggest that certain general characteristics of liturgical worship be appropriated in particular to the practice of silence. In the latter, there exists a comparable (if not commensurable) tradition of referring to silence in terms of "sacrament," "communion," "sacrifice of praise," and so forth – both as part of the apologetic (or polemical) advocacy of silence as the basis of worship, and in the well-developed genres of personal testimony.[5]

One of the aspects of the intentional keeping of silence that can most obviously be "transferred" to liturgy as a whole is, to refer back to Dauenhauer's phenomenology, its function as "interruption" or "cut." The interruption of the everyday and the delimitation of an alternative space – a characteristic of liturgy as a whole – may be said to be "performed," and not only represented, most fully in the keeping of silence. Silence in worship, thus understood, is an interruption of an otherwise inescapable succession both of the many claims to significance presented by and to the self, and of willed responses to them. It provides the opening for a radical simplification and refocusing of attention and desire. Subjectively, as is well attested, such a refocusing may be welcomed – people "need a break" – and simultaneously resisted in its full implications, because immersion in trivia is in fact what the mind and heart has learned to seek

---

[3] As, indeed, silences in specific conversational contexts sometimes do – see the discussion, in my introduction, of pragmatic and conversation-analytic approaches to silence.

[4] The significant differences between the practices of silence in question are discussed on p. 150.

[5] For some influential examples of the former, see the Epistle of London Yearly Meeting (1928), quoted in part in *Quaker Faith and Practice* 26, 15; *To Lima with Love: The Response from the Religious Society of Friends (Quakers) in Great Britain to the World Council of Churches Document "Baptism, Eucharist and Ministry"* (London: Quaker Home Service, 1987); of the latter, see Caroline E. Stephen, *Quaker Strongholds* (London, 1890), esp. pp. 12–13.

for itself. Quaker accounts of the need for silent worship have often described silence in terms of such a performed interruption – an interruption that relativizes the significance of whatever activity or speech it interrupts. Beyond this turning of oneself away from everyday concerns and burdens, the practice of silence in worship can be understood as entering a place and an attitude appropriate to the holiness of God, and the consequent liberation and transformation of one's concern.

In other discussions, the "holy uselessness" of the practice of silence is taken as emblematic of the "uselessness," that is, the non-instrumental nature, of worship.[6] Clearly it is possible to instrumentalize silence – to reduce listening to a technique for extracting information, or to use public silence solely as a means of producing a given effect. Particularly within a liturgical context, however – so, already within the context of an "interruption" – to keep silence is to refrain from pursuing any particular end, and, more than this, to act in a way that has a certain intrinsic resistance to being subordinated to a particular end. To spend time in silence and to refrain from the performance of any signifying action is, in everyday terms, to waste time. To perform liturgy is to waste time; it is to break into a series of causes and effects, the appropriation of present means toward a future end, and to reshape time in such a way as to call into question the assumptions about temporal sequence in relation to willed action on which the very notion of "wasting time" depends.

Silence in worship and liturgy, then, can be understood to have – and in some respects to share with liturgy *as such* – a critical and liberative function. Drawing on analyses of the liminal character of liturgical space, one commentator describes how the keeping of silence emphasizes the character of liturgy as risk.[7] Silence as an interruption to patterns of expec-

---

[6]   Nathan Mitchell, "Silent Music," *Worship* 68 (1993), p. 266; the idea of "holy uselessness" is from Max Picard, *The World of Silence*, trans. Stanley Godman (London: Harvill, 1948).

[7]   Joseph Dogherty, "Silence in the Liturgy," *Worship* 69 (1994), 147–8. For further discussions of the use of silence in liturgy, see Gustav Mensching, *Das Heilige Schweigens; eine Religionsgeschichtliche Untersuchung* (Giessen: Töpelmann, 1926); Charles Harris, "Liturgical Silence," in *Liturgy and Worship*, ed. W. K. Lowther Clarke (London: SPCK, 1932) (which includes a full history of the use of silence in eucharistic liturgy); Ignio Cecchetti, "Tibi Silentium Laus," in *Miscellanae Liturgica in Honorem L. K. Mohlberg*, vol. 2 (Rome: Edizione liturgiche, 1949), on the links between biblical and liturgical silences; Arnaldo Nesti, "Silence as Elsewhere", *Social Compass* 42, 4 (1995). Particularly interesting is the attempt in Marcia Sachs Littell, ed., *Liturgies on the Holocaust: An Interfaith Anthology* (Lewiston: Edwin Mellon, 1986), to explore the range of possible liturgical "silences" and to distinguish among them. See especially the introduction by Littell, and the liturgy devised by Fisher and Klenicki (pp. 27–40).

tation can bring people to a situation of "liminality" – being pushed to the limits of what can presently be known or brought within structures of thought and action.

Silence in worship presents one lived and reflected response to the question of how liturgy, or any other communicative action, can enact the opening up of space for the action of another. It is important, I would argue, not to think of this only as "falling silent so that God can speak;" if this were all, as the discussion in chapter 4 suggested, the concerns about the symbolism of silence in worship expressed by a recent feminist commentator would be well founded.[8] It is possible, rather, to understand silence kept in worship as a keeping of God's silence – a participation in God's "opening up of space" for the world. Silence in worship is not, in other words, only or mainly about the risk that people take in listening or attending to God; it is also about the risk God takes in listening or attending to people. To fall silent is, after all, to create a space in which *anything* can be heard, and to offer it a hearing that will not necessarily result in a verbalized resolution. It can, in this, be understood as an effective sign of God's hearing, of God's own Word and of the world.

To speak of "effective signs" in this context may seem doubly puzzling in the light of my earlier denials that silence is "like" a speech-act, and of the claim that silence makes space for the action of another. What can be signified and effected in silent worship, I have suggested here, is God's hearing for affirmation, judgment, and transformation. The act of keeping silence in itself (understood as a technique practiced by individuals or communities) gives no assurance that any such process will occur; and, indeed, in keeping silent people display their own *in*effectiveness.

To describe silence in worship only in terms of "risk" is to miss the central claim about God's overturning of expectations on which the keeping of silence relies; to enact resurrection faith is already to act from beyond the limits of what can presently be thought. As I discussed in chapter 4, the vulnerability of the Word of God in the world – to mishearing and the refusal of hearing, to being shouted down, to becoming a victim of the "war of Words" – is not denied by the resurrection; but the resurrection brings about patterns of communication in which the Word and the words consigned to terminal silence are heard again and opened up to new possibilities of signification. Reflection on silence in worship focuses attention on liturgy as a calling on God, in the expectation of a response that arises from God's boundless freedom and love,

[8] Monique Dumais, "Le Sacre et l'Autre Parole Selon un Voix Feministe," in *Silence, the Word and the Sacred*, ed. E. D. Blodgett (Wilfred Laurier University Press, 1980), pp. 149–60.

and is hence not encompassed by the particular expectations of the worshipers.

It is worth considering at this point the important contrast, not always appreciated by commentators, between various incorporations of silence into planned liturgy on the one hand, and Quaker "silent worship" on the other. The latter is only imprecisely described as "silent;" words may be spoken in all the various moods characteristic of liturgical worship (the indicatives of praise, affirmation of faith, the giving of testimony; the optatives of prayer; the imperatives of exhortation or command; and so forth). Such a practice of silence is reducible to neither a technique (for achieving some end external to itself) nor to a stably identifiable sign (of something that could perhaps equally well be verbalized).

By contrast, where silence is incorporated into a larger structure of liturgical worship – the taking of risks being "bracketed, for safety's sake, by the highly structured program" of ritual, and silence being treated, for example, more as a *symbol* of risk than as the actual taking of a risk[9] – there is frequent adversion to the need to control, delimit, or plan what the silence can mean or how it can be used.[10] Thus, for example, in Bonhoeffer's discussion of silent worship in *Life Together*, the concern is mainly to show that a proper keeping of silence is oriented to the word, rather than vice versa. "Mystical" silence – which Bonhoeffer understands as the "desire to get beyond the Word"[11] – is rejected; silence "in the end . . . means nothing other than waiting for God's word and coming from God's word with a blessing."[12] Silence is needed "mainly before and after hearing the Word."[13] Silence is accorded a preparatory and auxiliary function to the acts of collective worship to which the "ministry of the Word" is central.

I would argue that this "bracketing" of silence in interpretation and practice – with interpretations that define its function (symbolic, psychological, or otherwise) in relation to another desired end – will miss part of the significance of the practices of silence thus interpreted, significance that might be grasped by making "silence" the organizing focus in relation to which words are weighed or judged. Perhaps we can read the interplay of words and silence in worship – in any act of worship – as

---

[9] Dogherty, "Silence in the Liturgy," p. 148.
[10] See for example W. Jardine Grisbrook, "Silent Prayer," in *New Dictionary of Liturgy and Worship*, ed. J. G. Davies (London: SCM, 1986); J. D. Crichton, *Christian Celebration* (London: Chapman, 1971), pp. 103, 50.
[11] *DBWE* 5, p. 84, *DBW* 5, p. 67. Compare the comments on "mystical silence" at the beginning of the *Christology* lectures, *DBW* 12, p. 280.
[12] *DBWE* 5, p. 85, *DBW* 5, p. 68.
[13] *DBWE* 5, p. 84, *DBW* 5, p. 67.

one of reciprocal re-forming and structuring. One learns, through the interrelation of words, silences, and actions through time in relation to God, that "silence" is not undifferentiated (there are many *different* silences kept – even in a Quaker meeting!) and that "speaking" does not establish unchanging structures of meaning (there is time within which words are variously heard and reflected on).

Keeping silence in collective worship can, then, be understood as a way in which a different *logos* – in the broader sense I have developed, encompassing both speaking and hearing – is learned and enacted. What can we learn for a theological ethics of communication through attention to the silence in worship?

I have claimed in relation to Bonhoeffer's ethics that the form of the risen Christ is understood only through acts and lives "conformed" to Christ. Spiritualities centered on silence, together with the practice of "hearing to speech" and the silent ministry of spiritual care (to be discussed below), pose in a particularly acute way the question of the relationship between "orthopraxy" and orthodoxy,[14] between the loving service that may be carried out in silence and the ways in which the source and nature of love is named.

Beyond this, practices of silence in worship call further into question the idea that the "ultimate," God's "givenness," and its realization in the world, can be described best or only in terms of a *word* spoken – and raise the question of whether both the being-in-relation of God and the being-in-relation of human persons may exceed what can be spoken or signified. As in Bonhoeffer's lectures on Christology, the possibility is raised of a genuine asking and answering of the "Who?" question, in silence.

The insight that the keeping of silence is a "risk," in that its outcome cannot be predicted in advance, recalls the divine "silence of unknowability." This needs, I have suggested, to be counterbalanced by the recognition that our keeping of silence may be conformed to the creative self-faithfulness of God – so that its unpredictability need not render it empty or meaningless. The "risks" of the practices of silence and listening described here, are taken on the basis of the prior reality of God's action that provides the – silent – δος μοι που στω.

Reflecting further on the move beyond regarding silence as a "risk," a focus on silence allows particular attention to be paid to the transforming action of God as happening through time. The effects of the keeping

---

[14] See the discussion of this in Gehl, "Competens Silentium," pp. 157–60. He takes the term "orthopraxy" from Raimundo Panikkar, *The Unknown Christ of Hinduism: Toward an Ecumenical Christophany* (London: Darton, Longman & Todd, 1981).

of silence and the "work" of a listener are unthinkable apart from the time they take – even if, as I have noted, the time spent in silence is wasted, in that it is time during which no identifiable goal is pursued. I have already considered the importance of the divine attribute of patience for understanding God's relation to created time; a focus on practices of silence leads us to consider how patience is learned as part of the Christological reconfiguration of human communication.

In the context of considering how the practice of silence in worship can be understood as "keeping God's silence" and participating in God's act of patient listening, I have suggested that silence in worship calls into question any attempt definitively to separate the "hearing of the Word" from the discerning and creative "hearing" of others, or the hearing of a given situation. It is not a question of occasionally falling silent in order to receive or appropriate some particular instance or event of communication. The learning of a way of hearing appropriate to God's act of hearing – learning to "hear with God's ears" – becomes itself central to the transformation of selves and communities.

The question of the relationship between "the transformation of selves" and "the transformation of communities" in the keeping of silence is itself crucial. The unifying capacity of communal silence – the sense in which keeping silence together sets aside, for a defined period, a whole range of differentiations between persons that might otherwise impede the recognition of a community – is drawn on in a range of contexts. In some contexts the focus is on the suspension (however temporary) of hierarchical differentiations based on a presumed asymmetry of speaking and listening, direction and obedience.[15] The keeping of silence in the context of "ecumenical" worship, for another example, is sometimes justified in terms of the suspension of doctrinal divisions or denominational allegiances; silence forms one shared liturgical context in which these divisions are not made apparent.

In each case, to locate silence within worship is to locate the "suspension of differentiations" within a primary differentiation and relationship common to all – the relation of all and each to God that also grounds the possibility of community. Again, reflecting on the previous chapter's discussion of the "listening self," the claim is not that keeping silence necessarily means the denial of embodied particularity, but that it draws attention to the openness of that particularity to resignification.[16]

---

[15] See for example Dogherty, *Silence in the Liturgy*, p. 153.

[16] With regard to the historic Quaker practice and understanding of silence, an early and striking corollary of the "openness of embodied particularity to resignification" was seen

Claims about the capacity of silence to "bring people together" must be set alongside the assumption, if anything more common, that times of silence serve primarily to individualize what has otherwise been construed as collective action. Silence incorporated into liturgy is often "read" as a time for the offering of individual prayer, or for reflection by each participant on what has been read or heard. Bonhoeffer's *Life Together*[17] sets out such an association of silence with solitude, word with community.[18]

Associating silence solely with the individual, or the subjective, is bound to consign it to a secondary role, particularly in a theological age preoccupied with flight before the specter of the Cartesian subject.[19] I wish to maintain, over against the individualization of silence, the recognition that shared silence claims and enacts the reality of a given and non-verbalized common ground. To keep silence together is not merely for each to keep her own silence; it is to keep one another's silence, which in turn only makes sense if it is also a keeping of God's silence, a sign and enactment of the silence in which God hears the whole of creation. Without the latter, communal silence does indeed risk being nothing more than mutual tolerance on the basis of non-engagement, a mark of the *lack* of any common place to stand. Keeping communal silence in the context of God's hearing silence, by contrast, is recognizing and inhabiting a common place to stand that cannot be fully verbalized or articulated.

In all of this, however, the "subjective" aspect of silence is not lost – because the silence considered here is "hearing to speech," an opening up of space for each to become one who is heard. It is "objective" (the given, prevenient action of another) only for the sake of the "subjective" – and in silence that is shared, the distinction between the two is relativized ("Is this *my* silence, or somebody else's, or neither; and what sense does that question make?"). It is important to maintain that practices of silence need not be understood or described as *loci* of arbitrary freedom or the

---

in the preaching ministry and leadership of women. It is worth noting that written reflection on this, from the earliest period of Quakerism, includes some texts minimizing the importance of sexual difference (see for example Margaret Fell, *Women's Speaking Justified* (London, *c.* 1666)), but also (particularly in spiritual autobiography) draws attention to the specific bodily existence of the female preacher. I owe this insight to Shannon Craigo-Snell, who discussed it in "Writing the Female Body: Quaker Autobiography as Theological Disruption," unpublished paper presented to the AAR Feminist Theory and Religious Reflection Group, 2002.

[17] *DBWE* 5, pp. 81–92, *DBW* 5, pp. 65–76.
[18] *DBW* 5, p. 67, *DBWE* 5, p. 83.
[19] See Slavoj Žižek, *The Ticklish Subject: The Absent Centre of Political Ontology* (London: Verso, 1999), pp. 1–2.

complete subjectivization of the relationship to God. To claim this is to repeat the response to the contemporary "silence of God" that was found (in my first chapter) to be so problematic in feminist terms – the reassertion of an authoritative divine voice to control the plurality of human voices.

In drawing out the wider implications of silence in worship for the theological ethics of communication, I turn now to consideration of a practice of silence focused on the individual but with an intrinsic reference to a communal context. As I suggested above, the individual practice of silence played an important, if subsidiary and ambiguous, part in the life of the Finkenwalde community as Bonhoeffer established it. The texts I wish to consider here are concerned, not with silent individual reflection, but with the work of *Seelsorge*, "spiritual care." Bonhoeffer's discussions of *Seelsorge* are important for our theme because they set out particularly clearly a view of how silence that corresponds to the silence of God can work in communicative relationships. The themes already referred to in my discussion of silent worship – interruption and risk, the critical and liberative function of silence, participation in God's act of hearing, patience, and taking time, the centrality of love, and the interplay between "subjective" and "objective" silence, all arise in a close reading of these detailed reflections on pastoral conversation.

Seelsorge and the "Ministry of Listening"

Context

Bonhoeffer's lectures on *Seelsorge* were given at Finkenwalde between 1935 and 1937, and deal with all aspects of "pastoral care" from the perspective of the pastors-in-training.[20] I read them here alongside

---

[20] As noted in the previous chapter (n. 1), no copy of Bonhoeffer's own notes for the lectures exists, and commentators rely on reconstructions from student notes. The new *DBW* text (*Illegale Theologenausbildung: Finkenwalde 1935–1937, DBW* 14, pp. 555–91) uses a transcription from Friedrich Trentepohl's shorthand notes on the lectures as given in 1935/6, and inserts, in footnotes, expansions from later student notes where this is considered significant (see *DBW* 14, p. 555, n. 1). The editors of the GS did not have Trentepohl's manuscript, and produced a reconstruction mainly from 1936/7 notes. The comparison between the GS (V, pp. 364–414) and *DBW* versions is itself instructive for a consideration of the activity of listening. Is the reconstruction into continuous prose from plural sources (as attempted by the GS editors) an illegitimate attempt to reproduce "Bonhoeffer's own voice," or, perhaps, a more adequate representation of the reception of the lectures by an audience that was also a close-knit community?

relevant sections of the better-known and near-contemporaneous *Life Together*.[21]

Life Together introduces the "ministry of listening" as a central aspect of community life.[22] It is the first of the forms of ministry (*Dienst*), offered by community members to each other, to be analyzed – preceding, in that order, practical help,[23] the "bearing" of sins and faults,[24] and the ministry of the Word.[25] Like practical help and the "bearing" of faults, it is regarded as a precondition and determinant of the latter ministry; unlike any of these, it is explicitly described as *brüderliche Seelsorge*, fraternal "spiritual care."[26] Although *Seelsorge* as Bonhoeffer describes it encompasses more than the "ministry of listening," practices of silence and listening are central to it.

Both the *Seelsorge* lectures and the relevant sections of *Life Together* describe a particular form of service offered and received within a Christian community, between one individual and another. I shall be claiming that this form of service, as Bonhoeffer describes it, has the "mystery of the resurrection" – the irreducibly mysterious presence of Christ and the divine act of listening – as its basis, which both makes it possible and

I quote here mainly from the *DBW* version, but have on occasion chosen to "trust" the 1936/7 listeners and those who edited their notes. This is particularly important in considering the connection with *Life Together*, since the later revisions of the *Seelsorge* lectures seem to have brought them closer to the concepts and vocabulary of the latter text. (On this see *GS* V, p. 363).

[21] There has been very little discussion of the *Seelsorge* lectures in studies of Bonhoeffer's work. Even the main extended study of Bonhoeffer's concept of "spiritual care," Heinz Ruegger, *Kirche als seelsorgerliche Gemeinschaft: Dietrich Bonhoeffers Seelsorgeverständnis im Kontext seiner bruderschaftlichen Ekklesiologie* (Bern: Lang, 1992), treats them as an "unreliable" source (p. 210). The introduction to the English translation of the *GS* version (Jay C. Rochelle, ed., trans., and intro., *Spiritual Care* (Philadelphia: Fortress, 1985), pp. 7–29) gives a useful overview of the place of the lectures within Bonhoeffer's work, and within previous and subsequent work on the subject.

[22] *DBW* 5, pp. 82–4, *DBWE* 5, pp. 98–9. Clearly the formal definition of *Seelsorge* and the "ministry of listening" already raises a number of difficulties. The emphasis on the individual may appear to reinforce the portrayal of Christian faith as an individual's "private affair." Conversely, the placing of spiritual care within a Christian community – whether the parish or the Finkenwalde seminary – raises questions about the wider applicability of these texts. A resolution of either of these difficulties will require the texts to be read "beyond" themselves and in dialog with others.

[23] *DBW* 5, pp. 84–5, *DBWE* 5, pp. 99–100.

[24] *DBW* 5, pp. 85–7, *DBWE* 5, pp. 100–3.

[25] *DBW* 5, pp. 87–91, *DBWE* 5, pp. 103–7.

[26] *DBW* 5, p. 83. *DBWE* 5, p. 99 changes the sense somewhat by translating "*Brüderliche Seelsorge unterscheidet sich von der Predigt*" as "For Christians, pastoral care differs essentially from preaching.".

determines its course and consequences. I shall also be claiming that we can take the practice of silence in spiritual care seriously as integral to the participation of individuals and communities in the reconciled *logos* – and not as instrumental toward some other practice (such as "the proclamation of the Word').

The functions of spiritual care

In the first of the *Seelsorge* lectures, Bonhoeffer defines the functions of spiritual care, in a brief formulation that indicates its relevance to the themes I have been discussing. Spiritual care is to "uncover sin and educate into the hearing of the Word."[27]

It should be noted, first, that to "uncover sin and educate into the hearing of the Word" are of course recognizable as traditionally appropriated to the Holy Spirit.[28] Spiritual care thus described pertains directly to the key ethical question as identified by Bonhoeffer: "the relation between reality and realisation . . . between Jesus Christ and the Holy Spirit." I shall be exploring here the claim that spiritual care participates in the temporal realization of the "reality" of the resurrection.

Spiritual care – like the "ministry of listening" – is explicitly defined as concerned with the individual. "Uncovering sin" and "educating into hearing," which could both be understood as public or collective processes, are "individualized" in spiritual care. It is the specific sin of the individual that is named, and the individual who is "brought into hearing." In other words: in spiritual care, as practiced and discussed, the "Who?" questions outlined above come to the fore; in each given situation of spiritual care, it matters "who is heard" and "who hears."

The "individualization" of spiritual care need not separate it from social and political concerns. This is immediately apparent if we consider the reference to "uncovering sin" alongside Bonhoeffer's description of the "fool" in "After Ten Years." The "uncovering of sin" makes spiritual care

---

[27] *DBW* 14, p. 559, my trans. (*Erziehen zum Hören des Wortes*). The *GS* version has "*creates hearers* of the gospel" (*schafft aufs neue Hörer des Evangeliums*) (*GS* V, p. 366, see *Spiritual Care*, p. 32 – my emphasis). Is this Bonhoeffer's change of emphasis, or his listeners'? The *DBW* version fits better with the emphasis on spiritual care as *pedagogy* in this introductory lecture (*DBW* 14, p. 559; compare *GS* V, p. 366); the *GS* version stresses the possibility of complete transformation through spiritual care.

[28] Bonhoeffer's statement recalls the various uses, philosophical and theological, of the concept of *elenchus*; "conviction of sin" as in the Johannine account of the work of the Spirit (Jn 16:8), the exposure and elimination of error in preparation for the acceptance of truth as in the Socratic dialog.

a practice of inward and outward liberation. This gives spiritual care, like the "hearing to speech" discussed in my first chapter, a critical or negative aspect; it liberates from the idolatries that prevent genuine hearing.

As I shall indicate in what follows, the lectures as they stand (and *Life Together* to a lesser extent) leave open the possibility of understanding this anti-idolatry as the *only* function of spiritual care – so that "educating into hearing" is simply a matter of removing the obstacles to a "hearing" that is then treated as unproblematic. In a comparable way, it might be possible to understand silent worship only in terms of the "interruption" of ordinary life and patterns of communication. Since such an interpretation is unsatisfactory, either as an account of the practices described or in the context of a wider conversation on the theological ethics of communication, I shall attempt in subsequent sections to extend it.

The claim that spiritual care "educates into hearing" already suggests the possibility of such an extension. I suggested in the previous chapter that the formation of the "hearing mind" involves more than the act of outward liberation that removes the immediate causes of folly. "Hearers of the Word," as I wish to describe them, are those who attend to the world in its breadth and specificity and refer their "attending" to God, as both the one who hears the truth of what they hear and the one who is heard in whatever they hear. They are the *wise* whose wisdom is a gift of God and a correspondence to the wisdom of God shown forth in the world. My account of silent worship as "effective sign of God's hearing" began to indicate how such participation in God's act of hearing can be enacted and represented. By contrast, the fool, who absorbs and repeats the speech of others, is simply incapable of hearing – either the words of others or the Word of God. Clearly, if the hearing of the Word can be understood in this way, the function of spiritual care in bringing it about is extremely significant.

What is the theological basis of the practice that "uncovers sin and educates into the hearing of the word?" It can, I would claim, best be understood by beginning from silence. The first concrete guideline given in the *Seelsorge* lectures is an injunction to silence. "[It is a case of] hearing on the part of the pastor, and speech on the part of the community member. Spiritual care is, as *diakonia*, constituted by silent service and love [*stumme, helfende Liebe*]. Silence is required here."[29] Before they hear anything else about the context, purposes, theology, and practice of

---

[29] *DBW* 14, p. 557, my trans.

spiritual care, the pastors-in-training learn that its unconditional prerequisite is silence.[30]

What are the forms and purposes of this silence within spiritual care? In the first instance, I shall consider spiritual care as the process by which both parties are led away from the "attempt to make something of oneself," identified in Bonhoeffer's work as one of the key obstacles to right hearing.

Silence and self-creation

One must completely abandon any attempt to make something of oneself, whether it be a saint, or a converted sinner, or a churchman (a so-called priestly type!), a righteous man or an unrighteous one, a sick man or a healthy one. (Bonhoeffer, *Letters and Papers*[31])

The chapter on "service" in *Life Together*, within which the discussion of the "ministry of listening" falls, begins with a long enumeration of the respects in which the members of the community differ one from another – the differences between "strong people and weak ones . . . talented and untalented, simple and difficult, devout and less devout, sociable and loners."[32] Reading the quotation, above, from the prison letters alongside the section from *Life Together* emphasizes the fact that to "make oneself" a righteous person implies "making" another less righteous; to "make oneself" a sick person implies dependence on the healthy. I have already noted, with reference to the portrait of the "fool," that the tyranny of the ideologue and the irresponsibility of the fool are mutually required. "Making something of oneself," and "making" others according to one's needs, is a social process, and it is disrupted or reversed by changed social practices – including practices of silence.[33] The practice of silence that is the basis of spiritual care functions in several ways to disturb the process of "making something of oneself."

---

[30] Silence is described as *unbedingte Voraussetzung der Seelsorge* in GS V, p. 365 (*Spiritual Care*, p. 31).

[31] *Letters and Papers*, pp. 369–70, *Widerstand und Ergebung DBW* 8, p. 542.

[32] *DBWE* 5, p. 93, *DBW* 5, p. 77.

[33] The first of these "practices of silence" mentioned in *Life Together* is the famous "Finkenwalde rule" against gossip (*DBWE* 5, pp. 94–5, see especially p. 94 n. 3; *DBW* 5, pp. 78–9). This rule seems intended as much to free the seminarians from the temptation to compare themselves with others as to protect the "others" from being the objects of gossip – as much, then, against "making something of oneself" as against "making something" of others.

The spiritual carer's silence is in the first instance a tool against self-deception. Bonhoeffer claims that the pastor "hears through the uncovered need or problem a confession of sin which is not yet risked".[34] It is necessary "not to take the other's *questions* as seriously as he does, but to take the *questioner* more seriously than he takes himself."[35] The spiritual carer's silence refuses the easy word of comfort[36] that would allow an inadequate understanding of the self and its needs to be retained. It interrupts the succession of supposed wants, and actions to satisfy them, by which a self is produced.

The claim made early in the lectures that the spiritual carer is "better informed about others than they are about themselves"[37] sounds as if spiritual care might be intended to reinforce the "carer's" status as a person with superior wisdom or experience. It becomes clear within the lectures as a whole, however, that the reverse is the case.[38] Bonhoeffer's injunction to the "carer" throughout the lectures is to *avoid* providing answers,[39] to refrain both from "wise" advice and from calculating judgment,[40] to "come empty-handed."[41] The forms of self-deception or attempted self-making with which the lectures on spiritual care are particularly concerned are in fact the attempts to "make oneself" a sick or otherwise needy person; hence the spiritual carer's refusal to respond superficially to the other person's self-perceived need. The silence of the spiritual carer – the refusal to offer advice – subverts the other's adoption of a position of dependence. This is simultaneously, as noted above, the subversion of the other's attempt to "make something" of the pastor – the healthy, strong, or wise person, or the person whose responsible action can substitute for one's own.

Rowan Williams describes well the search for self-sufficiency (contradicted by its own structure, in that it still requires an imaginary other) that spiritual care, thus described, would seek to frustrate and redirect:

[34] *Spiritual Care*, p. 33, from *GS* V, p. 368; see *DBW* 14, p. 560.
[35] *DBW* 14, pp. 561–2.
[36] *DBW* 14, p. 581 – "no false comfort" is to be offered to the sick person; compare *GS* V, p. 395.
[37] *Spiritual Care*, p. 33, from *GS* V, p. 368; see *DBW* 14, p. 560.
[38] This is not to say, however, that the relationship portrayed is symmetric or "equal" – a question that will be discussed further below.
[39] "In general, the *Seelsorger* cannot give an answer to the question as it is posed" (*DBW* 14, pp. 561–2, my trans.; compare *GS* V, p. 368).
[40] "The *Seelsorger* will never confront the other in a calculating and investigative manner" (*DBW* 14, p. 563; identical in *GS* V, p. 370).
[41] *DBW* 14, p. 364; *GS* V, p. 371.

Even when I try to formulate my "real" self, what I am in effect doing is imagining an ideal other . . . a listener to whom I am making perfect sense . . . The danger . . . is that this imagined other, the perfect listener, blocks out the actual, less perfect, less sympathetic hearers, with whom I am actually and temporally doing business, so that my self-perception remains firmly under my own control.[42]

The ideal listener is projected by the person who desires to have her identity reconfirmed without the risk of miscognition or subjection to judgment. The silence of the spiritual carer frustrates this projection. In doing so, however, it returns the interlocutor to the "actual, less perfect, less sympathetic hearers" − of whom the spiritual carer is one − in negotiation with whom her identity is formed. The basic claim here is, then, that the silence of the spiritual carer is a disruption of self-making in two connected ways; it challenges the interlocutor's claim to know and adjudicate her own needs, and it prevents the spiritual carer from filling the role of the projected other who fulfills these needs.

Other specific practices of silence to which the *Seelsorge* lectures refer can be understood in this way. The confessional seal, and, closely connected with this, the confidentiality surrounding spiritual care, are defended vigorously. What is said in confession is to be guarded as "God's secret;" and the pastor can only be trusted as the one who keeps God's secret if he proves capable of keeping ordinary confidences.[43] Silence acquires a particular significance in conversations with the "indifferent" or "undecided."[44] In discussions with the "cultured despiser"[45] of

[42]   Rowan Williams, *On Christian Theology* (Oxford: Blackwell, 2000), p. 241.
[43]   See especially *DBW* 14, p. 565: "the question of trust in spiritual care, which often becomes decisive, is basically the question of the confessional seal" (my trans.). The implications of this theme for the theological understanding of privacy are discussed further in chapter 7. See further on private confession in the *Seelsorge* lectures and *Life Together*, Robin Joy Steinke, "Confessing and *Status Confessionis*: A Study in the Theology of Dietrich Bonhoeffer," PhD, University of Cambridge, 1998, p. 75.
[44]   *DBW* 14, pp. 575–7; see *GS* V, pp. 383–5.
[45]   The term does not appear in the lectures (which have simply *die Gebildeten*, *DBW* 14, p. 576.) Bonhoeffer's positive assessment of *Bildung*, most apparent in the *Ethics*, becomes clear here; *Bildung* is associated with "knowing one's limits" (p. 578), and is as such distinguished from *Aufklärung*. By the later lectures, the "cultured despiser" has become, more clearly, the one who is witnessing the collapse of "culture" and is drawn toward the Confessing Church. (*GS* V, pp. 384–5; see *DBW* 14, p. 578, n. 77). He more than any of the other characters in the *Seelsorge* lectures lives in the "world come of age" − he remarks wryly "But of course we are no longer children." (*Spiritual Care*, p. 52, from *GS* V, p. 385; compare *DBW* 14, p. 577). He is, perhaps, one of the future conspirators against Hitler; certainly one of the "good people" to whom Bonhoeffer later applies "Whoever is not against us is for us" (*DBW* 6, pp. 344–5).

Christianity and with the one who rejects the Church, the witness of the pastor is mainly silent; the "cultured despiser" is allowed to raise her own questions. Any words from the pastor risk being misunderstood or appropriated for "philosophical, semireligious conversation."[46] Likewise, in the case of the person who rejects the Church, the pastor's response is "the silent service of the deed."[47] There is even a deliberate avoidance of proclamation, at least in the first instance;[48] the aim is to awaken in the other the question "What's behind this?"[49]

What is the theological significance of this practice of silence? Reading the lectures in the context of Bonhoeffer's other work and of my wider discussion, the silence of the spiritual carer can be understood as a mediation of the silence of God discussed in previous chapters. The spiritual carer is the one in whose silence the divine "words" of affirmation and judgment are held together without being finally pronounced. She is fully present to the other, but her silence removes her from the attempt to integrate her into the other's project of self-creation. More than this, the spiritual carer refuses to leave the other in a condition of irresponsibility by speaking a word that compels a hearing; and, in conversation with the "cultured despiser," she refuses to enter the "war of words" on the terms established by the other. Her silence places the other in the world that must live "before God and with God without God."

The silence of the spiritual carer can be understood, further, as an act of "conformity to Christ," in that it institutes a form of communication appropriate to the communication of God in Christ. By keeping silent the spiritual carer practices communicative *kenosis*; she refuses to claim the power that might otherwise accrue to her, either as the bearer of an office (in *Spiritual Care*) or simply as the one who offers help (in *Life Together*). The one who holds power, who has the possibility of "playing God" through authoritative speech, gives up that power by falling silent. The act of giving up the power to speak in turn enables the other – previously "unheard" – to speak and be understood. Silence,

---

[46]   *Spiritual Care*, p. 50, *GS* V, p. 385, *DBW* 14, p. 577.

[47]   *DBW* 14, p. 579; see *GS* V, p. 386.

[48]   Compare the lectures on *Das Wesen der Kirche* (1932) on the nature of *confession* (*Ökumene, Universität, Pfarramt 1931–1932, DBW* 11, pp. 284–5) – "the first confession of the Christian community before the world is the deed . . . [the verbal confession] is not to be cried out before the world as propaganda." And see further on "enacted confession" Steinke, "Confessing and *Status Confessionis*," p. 107ff.

[49]   *DBW* 14, p. 577. There are interesting comparisons here with Kierkegaard's descriptions of the practice of "indirect communication." See in particular Søren Kierkegaard, *The Point of View for My Work as an Author*, trans. Howard V. Hong and Edna H. Hong (Princeton: Princeton University Press, 1998), p. 9.

again, makes explicit the relative nature of a given set of hierarchical distinctions.

It is important, however, when recognizing the extent to which the spiritual carer's silence functions to mediate the "silence of God" to the other, also to recognize how the *Seelsorge* lectures make a distinction between the work of the particular spiritual carer from the work of God in spiritual care. The practice of silence in spiritual care is intimately connected with the basic principle of interpersonal relationships within the Christian community, familiar from elsewhere in Bonhoeffer's work: "There is no immediate path to another person . . . That path is grounded in the mediatorial function of Christ. Christ the mediator stands between me and God, between me and my brother."[50] In the context of the *Seelsorge* lectures, the important effect of this is to render any essential dependence of the parishioner on the pastor in the matter of spiritual care impossible.

The silence of the spiritual carer also, then, marks a *difference* between her actions and the action of God, between her capacity for care or healing and the care or healing given by God. Spiritual care is not a technique that works apart from a relation to God; nor is it able to give the "carer" definitive significance in the life of the one cared for. The status of spiritual care as penultimate or preparatory is enacted by a constant redirection of the attention and dependence of the interlocutor away from the possibility of an authoritative human word and toward Christ. The aim is to place the other "before God."[51]

Like the process of "hearing to speech" considered earlier, spiritual care presupposes that the other can be understood only through the asking and answering of the " 'Who?" question. The classificatory enterprise ("*What* are you?") and the corresponding attempt to form the other according to a predetermined "image" are both relativized, if not excluded. The carer is not to attempt to form the other according to a "picture" (*Bild*) of her own – either epistemologically, by claiming a full understanding of him, or ethically, by trying to change him. Rather, she is to respect and await

---

[50] *Spiritual Care*, p. 35, *DBW* 14, p. 563 n. 25, *GS* V, p. 370.

[51] *GS* V, p. 371 – "*der andere soll nur vor Gott gestellt.*" *Spiritual Care* has "before God *alone*," which is unfortunately ambiguous – since the point is precisely that the other does *not* stand alone. This is one of the points at which Bonhoeffer would presumably wish to distinguish between the spiritual carer's "indirect communication" and that described in Kierkegaard's work. In *Sanctorum Communio*, the latter is criticized for according the relation to the other person only "relative" significance for the formation of Christian personhood, and hence (in Bonhoeffer's view) for an ultimate failure to escape idealism. (*Sanctorum Communio*, *DBWE* 1, p. 57, n. 12; *DBW* 1, p. 35).

the appearance of the unique "image" of Christ (*Ebenbild*) in him.[52] The *Seelsorge* lectures add a caution against attempting to gain knowledge of the other through manipulative listening or intrusive questioning.[53] For the "spiritual carer," the Christological mediation of the relation to the other renders "calculative judgement" impossible. The identity of the other – as one about whom the "Who?" question is asked – is secured by and in the identity of Christ.

Seeing the relation to the other in terms of the Christological mediation of communication enables a better understanding of the problematic claim, noted above, that the pastor knows the parishioner "better than he knows himself." This claim means that the course of spiritual care is not determined by a need perceived by the parishioner; but it might be taken to indicate, from the pastor's point of view, a claim to comprehensive understanding of the other.[54] What must now be emphasized, however, is that the pastor's "knowledge" of the other is knowledge of him as justified;[55] and this is the only form of superior "knowledge" the pastor is permitted to claim a priori. The fact of the other's acknowledgment and acceptance by God is the ground of, and presupposition for, spiritual care, but it is also the source of the limitation placed on the listener's activity. The possibility of approaching the other through the question "Who?" rests in the end on this divine recognition. Spiritual care takes this as a starting point – albeit as a starting point that is already the end point, as the "last word" concerning the person.[56]

What, in summary, does it mean to understand the spiritual carer's silence as a disruption of the process of "making something of oneself?" I have considered it here from two complementary perspectives, the one emphasizing the relationship between the spiritual carer's silence and the silence of God, the other emphasizing the difference between them. On the one hand, for the person who is "cared for," the spiritual carer's silence mediates the silence of the God "before" whom people are to live "without God." On the other hand, for the spiritual carer, the injunction to silence arises from the recognition of the other as standing in relation to God. The silence of God, understood as the withholding of the "ultimate" word of justification, is what makes the spiritual carer refrain, on

---

[52] *DBWE* 5, p. 95; *DBW* 5, p. 79.
[53] *DBW* 14, p. 563.
[54] This is how Ruegger, for example, interprets it – Ruegger, *Kirche als seelsorgerliche Gemeinschaft*, p. 252.
[55] *DBW* 14, p. 561.
[56] This focus on "God's knowledge of the person" as the starting point is discussed further in chapter 7.

the one hand from the analysis of the interlocutor, and on the other hand from the attempt to "make" the other according to a predetermined form. This leads the other, however, to recognize the falsehood of her own attempts to create a God according to the requirements of her project of self-creation.

"Hearing with God's ears" in spiritual care

This presentation of the critical and liberative function of spiritual care, however, risks ignoring an obvious aspect of the spiritual carer's silence. It was stated at the beginning of the lectures that the shape of spiritual care is "hearing on the part of the pastor, and speech on the part of the community member." Spiritual care is a ministry of hearing. In *Life Together*, Bonhoeffer states that "the beginning of love for [others] is learning to listen to them."[57] The emphasis on the significance of human listening is paralleled by the identification of God as one who listens. God "lends us God's ear"[58] as well as giving the Word; and the "ministry of listening" relates to that act of listening in the same way as the ministry of proclamation relates to God's speaking. There is thus a double obligation to the "ministry of listening;" one listens to the other both because he conveys the presence of God, and because one is entrusted with the "hearing" work of God toward him.[59]

What does this mean? I have already noted the importance, for the understanding of the process of spiritual care, of the mediation of communication in Christ. On the one hand, as shown above, this mediation means that there is "no immediate access to the other." Implicit in the very possibility of spiritual care, however, is the claim that Christ as mediator establishes the common ground on which communication takes place. The critique of attempts to secure "solidarity" with the other (through, for example, claiming personal knowledge of his situation) is based on the recognition of a solidarity "in Christ." The "answer to δος μοι που στω"

---

[57]   *DBWE* 5, p. 98, *DBW* 5, p. 82.
[58]   *DBWE* 5, p. 98, *DBW* 5, p. 82.
[59]   The repeated use of the image of the "ear" of God in *Life Together* emphasizes the Christological character of all such statements; God's work becomes fully "incarnate" in the community in which Christ is present. *Listening* as described in the texts I am discussing here is essentially an embodied activity, requiring physical presence (the *ear*) and affected by the physical environment and the presence of others (see the discussions of "home visiting" and "visiting the sick" in the *Seelsorge* lectures, *DBW* 14, pp. 571–5, 580–2).

– the resurrected Christ – becomes the place for *us* to stand, the place that makes renewed communication possible.

Having made this claim we must then ask, as in the earlier discussion of the resurrection as "place to stand," about the "relation between reality and realization." The common ground that makes communication possible is taken as a given and indisputable "reality" in spiritual care as Bonhoeffer describes it. There is considerable emphasis, as we have seen, on the "ultimate" word of justification as the basis for the spiritual carer's silence. At the same time, the description of spiritual care as a practice of communication related to God's act of hearing invites us to consider the change that occurs in and through it – the relation between the "reality" it presupposes and the "realization" it brings about. What really *happens* in spiritual care?

Asking this question raises issues, firstly about how we interpret the spiritual carer's silence, put forward above, and secondly and more broadly about how this practice of silence forms hearers. I have described the silence of the spiritual carer, on the one hand as a sign of the silence of God, and on the other hand as a means by which certain effects are produced in the other. These ways of interpreting the spiritual carer's silence, however, appear to assimilate it to a speech-act – as act of reference and/or as "performative." They make spiritual care a direct equivalent of proclamation.[60] I have suggested, however, that the assimilation of silence to a speech-act fails to do justice to the particular importance of the act of listening.

The spiritual carer's silence, as a listening silence that seeks to "hear with God's ears," both represents and effects the openness of the practice of spiritual care to transformations not anticipated in advance. It is important to note in this connection that, in the *Seelsorge* lectures, the silence of the spiritual carer affects *him* even as it affects the interlocutor.[61] The

---

[60] This is one area in which there is perceptible tension between the claims of *Life Together* and of the *Seelsorge* lectures – and, I would argue, within the lectures themselves. The lectures state that spiritual care is "proclamation [*Verkundigung*] to the individual" (*DBW* 14, p. 555); *Life Together*, as I have noted, places it with preaching under the general heading, not of "proclamation" but of "ministry." See on this Ruegger, *Kirche als seelsorgerliche Gemeinschaft*, p. 251.

[61] The significance of this becomes apparent in the section relating to *Seelsorge an Seelsorgern*. (*Spiritual Care*, pp. 65–9; *GS* V, pp. 403–5, *DBW* 14, pp. 586–8). The pastor is in particular danger because of his preaching; he is required to proclaim something that is not necessarily known as real in his own "experience" (*DBW* 14, pp. 587–8). He is tempted, for this reason, to close the door against the very possibility of the subjective appropriation of grace; to make himself a martyr in the service of the strange Word (*DBW* 14, p. 588 – "he . . . wants to justify himself as the martyr, the self-denying, the one who serves others

act of keeping silence, described above as communicative *kenosis*, is a real surrender of communicative power in that it allows the spiritual carer to be affected by the other.[62] This prevents us from understanding spiritual care, either as a direct equivalent of proclamation, or as a "technique" that remains within the control of the practitioner.

Recognizing that spiritual care affects the "carer," however, also draws attention to the fact that we have not yet seen what it means, positively, for spiritual care to "bring [somebody] into the hearing of the Word." The description of spiritual care as a practice of anti-idolatry does not supply an answer to the question "Who hears?," with which my last chapter ended – the question of how to understand the development of the "hearing mind."

In fact, the positive understanding of listening as the primary act of love, and with it the reciprocal aspect of spiritual care are at best implicit in earlier versions of the *Seelsorge* lectures.[63] The emphasis is, rather, on the significance of the pastoral *office*, and the extent to which this secures and structures the practice of spiritual care. The *Seelsorge* lectures have been criticized for their explicit reinforcement of a clear separation of the roles (here) of pastor and parishioner;[64] the "relation of superiority and inferiority," implied, according to Bonhoeffer, by proclamation, is also made to structure the practice of spiritual care. The preservation of this "relation of superiority and inferiority," as might have been expected on the basis of the previous chapter, is associated with a relative lack of attention to the activity of listening, its effects, and its theological implications. We are back to Morton's recognition that "hearing to speech is political" – that to consider listening seriously and to practice it is to challenge an established set of "relations of superiority and inferiority" and to open up the possibility of a social and political re-ordering.[65]

---

at the expense of his own experience'). Ruegger regards this section, with some justification, as one of the points at which the thought of the *Seelsorge* lectures comes closest to that of *Life Together*. Ruegger, *Kirche als seelsorgerliche Gemeinschaft*, p. 254.

[62] In the *GS* reconstruction, in fact, it is initially surprising to note that the first "need" that is met in silence is not a need of the parishioner but of the pastor. The latter is silent "in order to become free of all *Pfaffentum* and conceited clericalism." *Spiritual Care*, p. 31; *GS* V, p. 365.

[63] In *DBW* 14. Here it is striking, for example, that the *parishioner* is referred to as *Hörer* or *Hörende* (*DBW* 14, pp. 555, 558).

[64] Ruegger, *Kirche als seelsorgerliche Gemeinschaft*, p. 252; Rochelle, *Spiritual Care*, p. 18.

[65] On this whole section, see the discussion of Bonhoeffer's understanding of "interiority" in relation to hearing in Rowan Williams, "The Suspicion of Suspicion: Wittgenstein and Bonhoeffer," *The Grammar of the Heart*, ed. Richard H. Bell (London: Harper & Row, 1988), esp. p. 50.

In the rest of this chapter, I shall ask how a recognition of the unthematized common "place to stand" – the resurrection of Christ – can be used to develop the implications of the *Seelsorge* lectures and of the practice of silent worship further. To focus – as Bonhoeffer tends to – on what I have termed the "silence of unknowability" obscures important indications of a real transformation of individuals and situations, both occurring through and affecting particular practices of silence. I shall trace this, first, through a consideration of the capacity for discernment as an important aspect of the "hearing mind" (and one that is central to spiritual care), and, second, through a closer look at what it can mean to disrupt existing "relations of superiority and inferiority."

Becoming Hearers: Conscience, Discernment, and Love

I have already discussed the idea that spiritual care or the ministry of listening aims as much to heal "irresponsibility" or "folly" as to overcome pride; and the implication of my discussion of silence in worship was that its function cannot be merely that of anti-idolatry. The destruction of whatever idols the fool happens to worship, and the refusal to set up new ones, is itself insufficient to change the situation that makes folly possible. The outward liberation of the fool is succeeded only by enslavement if she does not acquire the wisdom associated with the capacity to listen and discern.

In this section, I look more closely at the idea of the capacity to listen and discern, and its relationship to hearing and being heard. The question of the interplay between the supposed "individualism" of silence or spiritual care, and participation in the life of a community, has been raised several times in this discussion, and to turn to conscience at this point may seem to take the reading of silence further in an individualizing direction. I want to claim, however, that the "otherness in the self" irreducible to the "otherness of other people" – as Ricoeur, again supplying useful starting points for theological discussion, describes the conscience[66] – is

---

[66] Paul Ricoeur, *Oneself as Another*, trans. Kathleen Blamey (Chicago: University of Chicago Press, 1992), p. 341. Like the "Who?" questions discussed previously, this definition has the merit of retaining the significant questions raised by modern philosophical anthropology without importing solipsistic presuppositions. The "irreducibility" of conscience to the "otherness of other people" means neither the separation of the one from the other, nor the prioritization of one at the expense of the other. Descriptions of conscience in terms of inner dialogs – conscience as the voice that calls or the hearer that

vital to an account of how people participate in the reconciled divine *logos*. Being in relation to the silence of God involves, I want to argue, both liberation from the tyranny of the (wrongly individualized) conscience, and the renewal of the conscience as the capacity to "hear with God's ears."

In theological and ethical writing following Kant (Bonhoeffer's work being no exception), conscience appears frequently as a *call*, of indictment, protest, or warning; the call of the self to itself to regain or safeguard an imperilled unity-with-self. Conscience, in this portrayal, arises in the moment in which action and the course of life cease to be self-evident; it reacts to, and thereby testifies to, an experience of division, and it demands that the self become unified as an autonomous self-legislator.

In spiritual care as I have described it, the call of conscience to the unity of the self, and its judgment on the self's disunity, is put in question by being placed in relation to the silence of God. The suggestion found in Bonhoeffer's work, to which this account of spiritual care also points, is that it is possible to act *against* the conscience, to become in these terms a "breaker of the law," for the sake of God – which is to say, also, for the particular demands of responsible action in the world. The call of conscience – which Heidegger characterized as silent (locating silence at the center of the struggle for individual authenticity) – is interrupted, but it is interrupted by a deeper silence that in fact transcends the project of "self-creation."

The social and political significance of this disruption of (a particular construction of) conscience can be seen in a contrast, drawn by Bonhoeffer, between the Christian who claims "Jesus Christ has become my conscience" and the national socialist who says "My conscience is Adolf Hitler." The former claim, in the light of my discussion of the silence of Christ, means in fact that the will or assertions of any given other cannot acquire mastery over the conscience – hence cannot take away my responsibility for my actions. By contrast, the "fool" says "My conscience is Adolf Hitler" and thereby sacrifices his capacity for decision-making and responsible action.[67] Thus Arendt, famously, observed that Eichmann not only had a "functioning" conscience, but attended to its dictates; he was, according to his own statement, governed in moral matters by his – relatively accurate – interpretation of the Kantian

---

pronounces judgment – already suggest a complex relationship between the "otherness of conscience" and the otherness of other people.
[67]   *DBW* 6, p. 278, *Ethics*, p. 212.

categorical imperative. What happened as he became more closely involved with the Final Solution amounted to the replacement, in his mind, of "the universal moral law" by "the will of the Führer."[68]

The disruption of the conscience's call to self-achieved unity, to which Bonhoeffer points with the claim "Jesus Christ has become [the] conscience," also prevents the absorption of the "otherness" of conscience into the "otherness of other people." Similarly, the silence of the spiritual carer, as I described it, functions to preserve the distinction and the interconnection between the "otherness in the self" and the "otherness of other people." The presence of the spiritual carer brings about an encounter with the particular other that disrupts a process of self-construction based on "the person's own ego and its law." The silence of the spiritual carer, we might suggest, allows the emergence of conscience as the capacity to "think from the standpoint of another" without becoming bound to the standpoint of this particular other. Unlike the ideologue the spiritual carer refuses to "become" the other's conscience, but seeks rather to bring about the recognition that "Jesus Christ has become the conscience."[69]

But what is the positive significance of this recognition? So far, all that it appears to denote is the possibility of ignoring the demands of conscience – perhaps, accepting the incurrence of guilt – for the sake of responsible action conformed to Christ. Once again, we need to move beyond the "critical" or "liberative" move to ask about how this responsible action is shaped and determined. Saying that "Jesus Christ has become [the] conscience" names a reality, and we must ask about its realization; or, to use more familiar terms, we must ask about the

---

[68] Arendt, *Eichmann*, pp. 135–7. John Milbank argues (John Milbank, *Being Reconciled: Ontology and Pardon* (London: Routledge, 2003), pp. 22–3) *contra* Arendt that Eichmann's position not a distortion of the Kantian account of conscience but is rather its logical consequence. In wagering on the theological significance of the – admittedly in important respects specifically modern – affirmation of the "otherness in the self," I obviously allow, with Bonhoeffer, far more to Kant (perhaps even to the "Cartesian" specter) than would Milbank. See further discussion of the issues around "individualism" in chapter 7.

[69] The recognition of the *other's conscience* that spiritual care implies is the recognition in Ricoeur's terms of the "other as a oneself." See also Paul L. Lehmann, *Ethics in a Christian Context* (London: SCM, 1963), pp. 357–60, for a discussion of the ethical significance of the neighbor's conscience, with reference to 1 Cor 8 and 10. Lehmann (a friend of Bonhoeffer's who develops various aspects of the latter's thought – see *DBW* 8 290) claims that "the neighbour's conscience is the concrete bearer of *whatever* ethical significance and function may be claimed for conscience" (Lehmann, *Ethics in a Christian Context*, pp. 129–30, my emphasis). I would argue that this overstates the case and risks the "evacuation of interiority" that Ricoeur identifies in Levinas; knowing "the other as a oneself" must be correlated, in Ricoeur's terms, with knowing "oneself as an other."

sanctification, or the participation in God's life and action, that corresponds to the justification that liberates conscience.

An indication of this possibility appears in the important section on "proving" the will of God in the *Ethics*.[70] The proving of the will of God begins from the recognition that the world in its complexity – "as it is in God" – calls for response and responsibility. The response cannot be determined, as we have seen, according to general ethical principles; and, in any given situation, reality does not always present itself *as* incontrovertible demand. "It is not said at all that the will of God forces its way into the human heart without further ado ... The will of God may lie very deeply concealed beneath a great number of available possibilities."[71] To replace the call of conscience with the "voice of God," characterized as equally incontrovertible and unequivocal, is to fall victim to a "psychologising misrepresentation of the new life."[72] In other words, once again, the discernment of the will of God in a given situation is not necessarily a question of excluding all other voices in order to hear a single authoritative word.

Hearing and recognizing the will of God – the "concrete commandment" that calls forth responsible action – in the particular instance must be acknowledged as a task, the precondition for which is "conformation with the form of the new man, Christ."[73] Discernment takes place, as Bonhoeffer puts it, solely on the basis of ... a complete inward transmutation of one's previous form."[74] Using the terms of my discussion, we could say that discernment of the will of God in a given situation – and hence action "conformed to Christ" – involves being formed as a hearer, as one who can hear a given situation "with God's ears."

In fact, Bonhoeffer's description of the exercise of "proving" includes "careful attention to the given facts," the exercise of intelligence and reason with the willingness to make judgments, the recognition of the temporal character of acquired knowledge through reference to past experience, and the maintenance throughout of a spirit of humility.[75] Echoes are heard here of the threefold Christological account, discussed earlier, of God's relation to the world – the compassionate "taking on" of

---

[70] *DBW* 6, pp. 323–9, *Ethics*, pp. 161–6. Conscience, curiously, does not as such appear here – although self-examination and self-proving, unusually in Bonhoeffer's work, are accorded a significant place within the life of the Christian.

[71] *Ethics*, p. 161, *DBW* 6, p. 323.

[72] Ibid.

[73] *Ethics*, p. 162, *DBW* 6, p. 324.

[74] Ibid.

[75] *Ethics*, pp. 163–4, *DBW* 6, p. 326.

the complexities of reality, the exercise of judgment, the practice of patience.

This passage, taken by itself, could be an account of decision-making "technique" applicable to any situation regardless of the end in view – whereas I have been asking what, if anything, is distinctive about that "proving" that stands in relation to the reality of the resurrection. Bonhoeffer rightly describes all the faculties used in discernment as "human powers" that could be identified apart from any particular relation to the proving of the will of God.

Here I would suggest that it is particularly important to place the discussion of discernment in the wider context of divine love, the love of God in Christ given as the love with which God and the neighbor are loved. "Doing the will of God" is acting in love; correspondingly, by implication, the exercise of "proving" is done rightly if it is done in and through love. The claim discussed earlier that "our love for the other consists first of all in listening" can be reread in this context as the claim that the divine love as gift shapes the exercise of hearing and discernment. The wisdom that makes responsible hearing possible can be rightly perceived only in relation to this love.

Bonhoeffer's emphasis, in the *Ethics*, on the indefinability of love – because the only "definition" of love is the love of God revealed in the living Christ – is used here (in a pattern now familiar) primarily negatively, to resist the reduction of the divine love to a set of ethical principles.[76] At the same time, however, to speak of God's love as the basis of transformed existence is inescapably to say something positively about how the very life of God – "God *is* love" – "realizes" itself in the world. Understanding the resurrection, as discussed in my second chapter, as a reality *for God* becomes significant here. From the resurrection we can understand something of what it means to love God and the other with God's own love – in the terms I have been using here, what it means to "hear with God's ears" – without thereby reducing the love of God to a set of principles for ethical action. The love that God is in Godself – the love in which God hears God's own Word – is inherently creative without being arbitrary or "formless" – and the same can be said of the practices of listening and discernment that conform to it.

This emphasis on the divine love as the ground of listening brings us back, however, to the question of the relationship between individual and

---

[76] " 'God is love' . . . For the sake of clarity this sentence is to be read with the emphasis on the word 'God' . . . *God* is love; that is to say not a human attitude, a conviction or a deed, but God himself is love" (*Ethics*, p. 173, *DBW* 6, p. 337).

community in the keeping of silence. Discernment as described here, even if it is spoken of chiefly as a process beginning with the individual, is never merely individual – nor, insofar as it requires "hearing with God's ears," is it merely "between me and God." Like the silence kept in worship, it is an expansion of the attention to draw in everything that is heard by God along with one's own concerns.[77]

It is here that the idea of spiritual care as "bringing into hearing" becomes important. Spiritual care as a process of discernment can be understood as a practice through which the participants come to "hear with God's ears." This can, of course, include the "hearing of the Word" to which Bonhoeffer's lectures most proximately refer – the hearing of preaching. What my formulation makes clear, however, is that spiritual care, and similar practices of silence associated with discernment, are not a silencing of the conscience in preparation for the "voice of God" spoken from outside.

What can be said on this basis about the relationship between the participants in spiritual care, and the extent to which "relations of superiority and inferiority" can be definitive of that relationship? If "the beginning of love for [others] is learning to listen to them," and that love for the other is a real reflection of the love that is God's own life, what does this mean for the relationships that structure practices of listening?

Hearing One Another: The Possibility of Friendship

As noted above, the *Seelsorge* lectures begin with an inversion of the expected roles of "speaker" and "hearer," but this inversion is not permitted to abrogate the distance between them, regarded as essential for the practice of spiritual care. This raises the question, as we have seen, of the real effect of spiritual care, and particularly of the ground of its claim to "bring into hearing."

One reconstruction of the *Seelsorge* lectures makes them refer to the possibility of reaching "the point where we do not know which is pastor and which is parishioner. But we should not make a method of this *ultimate possibility and grace*."[78] I have already suggested, in my third chapter,

---

[77] It is notable that Bonhoeffer's whole discussion of discernment makes no reference to any interpersonal or communal context for the process – perhaps reflecting the sense of isolation surrounding Bonhoeffer's own key decisions around this time, to return to Germany and to join the conspiracy against Hitler.

[78] *GS* V, p. 372, my trans. and emphasis. Compare *DBW* 14, p. 564, n. 33. This is one of the points at which I have chosen to use the work of Bonhoeffer's listeners to extend

that to understand the "ultimate" solely in terms of the word of justification – and, in connection with this, the resurrection solely as event *pro
nobis* – is to miss the full significance of the resurrection as "answer to
δος μοι που στω," the sense that the resurrection is the basis for a transformative sharing in the divine life. I now wish to explore this further
through the idea that the "ultimate possibility" of spiritual care is not the
word of proclamation but friendship.

This claim is best supported not from the lectures but from Bonhoeffer's
own life, and particularly from his relationship with Eberhard Bethge. Here,
a relationship structured by numerous socially ordered "distances" – teacher
and student, community director and assistant, older and younger (and
linked to different generations of a family) – became one concerning which
Bonhoeffer could write "having spent almost every day and having
experienced almost every event and discussed every thought together . . .
one needs only a second to know about each other."[79] The practices of
communication between these two friends, as both described and "enacted"
in the prison correspondence, both resemble and transcend the practices of
communication described as *Seelsorge* and the "ministry of listening." Each
relies on the other as listener – as confessor, as "bearer" of sufferings, and as
partner in a common theological task. The capacity to "know about each
other" in "only a second" means neither the conclusion of the conversation
nor the denial of the "unknowability" – in the sense explored in my chapter
2 – of each.

What does *this* "ultimate possibility" of spiritual care mean?[80]
Bonhoeffer's attempts to understand friendship, as something different
from relationships to which a definite socially determined "order" belongs,
occur fittingly enough in the prison correspondence with Bethge, and

---

his thought beyond its explicit scope – since the *wording* here cannot be claimed as "his
own."

[79] *Letters and Papers*, p. 145, *Widerstand und Ergebung*, DBW 8, p. 210. Much has already
been written about this friendship; the best testimonies to it are perhaps Bethge's own.
Particularly important is Eberhard Bethge, "My Friend Dietrich Bonhoeffer's Theology of
Friendship," in *The Changing Face of Friendship*, ed. Leroy S. Rouner (Notre Dame: Notre
Dame, 1994), which considers the prison correspondence in relation to Bonhoeffer's friend-
ships, especially that with Bethge.

[80] It should be noted that Bethge (Bethge, "My Friend," p. 146) is careful to differenti-
ate the account of friendship in Bonhoeffer's prison writings from "Finkenwalde" or "*Life
Together*." From context, what Bethge is rejecting here with "Finkenwalde" seems to be an
account of friendship based on the brotherhood of Christians, which would pull friendship back toward the sphere of necessity or duty. The lectures on spiritual care may, for all
the reasons that have previously given rise to scholarly suspicion, be more useful than *Life
Together* here.

begin from practical difficulties pertaining to that correspondence.[81] Bethge writes that friendship "has no *necessitas*," and this is the starting point for Bonhoeffer's consideration of the "classification," in terms of the scheme of divine mandates used in the *Ethics*, not only of friendship but of culture, education, art, and "play."[82]

Bonhoeffer begins by suggesting that friendship is a "subheading of culture and education," but is then faced with the problem of where to place the latter – "I don't think they can just be classified under work [one of the 'mandates' together with family, state and church], however tempting that might be." The eventual conclusion is that "they [sc. culture, education, and friendship] belong, not to the sphere of obedience, but to the broad area of freedom."[83] Friendship, Bonhoeffer concludes, "must be confidently defended . . . without claiming for it the *necessitas* of a divine decree, but only the *necessitas* of freedom . . . within the sphere of this freedom friendship is by far the rarest and most priceless treasure . . . It cannot be compared with the treasures of the mandates, for in relation to them it is *sui generis*."[84]

The curious idea of the "*necessitas* of freedom" most obviously refers to the importance of friendship and other "free" activities in the complete human life; freedom is itself a human *necessitas*.[85] The reader of Bonhoeffer's thoughts on friendship may feel, however, that they fail to do justice even to the friendship that gave rise to them – let alone to the variety of forms that friendship can take. How can friendship be characterized as free *over against* the family, work, and government, the sphere of "necessity," without an account of its role in those contexts? Is this not

---

[81] Bethge's problems obtaining permission to visit Bonhoeffer, and access to his letters. *DBW* 8, p. 267, *Letters and Papers*, p. 181.

[82] *DBW* 8, pp. 290–2; *Letters and Papers*, pp. 192–3.

[83] *Letters and Papers*, pp. 192–3, *DBW* 8, pp. 290–2. Bonhoeffer suggests that the Church in Germany "has been so dominated by the four mandates that the sphere of freedom has retreated into the background" and asks tentatively whether the Church can and should now reclaim that sphere as part of the Christian life. This is the counterpart of the move described in the *Ethics* (*DBW* 6, pp. 342–3., *Ethics*, pp. 177–8); culture and its associated values are "reclaimed" by the Church just as they themselves "return" to the Church in search of a home.

[84] *Letters and Papers*, pp. 192–3, *DBW* 8, pp. 290–2.

[85] Sabine Bobert-Stützel, "Liebt ein Freund mehr als ein Bruder? Zur Problematik der Verhältnisbestimmung von Bruderschaft und Freundschaft bei Dietrich Bonhoeffer unter pastoraltheologischen Aspekt," in *Theologie und Freundschaft*, eds. Christian Gremmels and Wolfgang Huber (Munich: Kaiser, 1994), pp. 99–100, makes the helpful distinction between the *necessitas ad salutem* and the "practical" *necessitas*, noting that in Bonhoeffer's work both friendship and – significantly for this discussion – private confession are explicitly excluded from the former and included in the latter.

an unacceptable restriction of the possibilities of friendship?[86] The whole attempt to find friendship a "sphere," separated from the sphere of obedience to the mandates, appears problematic.

At this point the contribution of Maria von Wedemeyer to the discussion conducted from Tegel, noted by Bethge in his own subsequent reflections, becomes significant. Confronted with Bonhoeffer's claim that parents and children – placed in a specific relationship of "superiority and inferiority" within the mandate of the family – cannot and should not be friends, von Wedemeyer "contradicts him very quickly and severely." She writes "I have only ever had one friend, and that was Father."[87] Von Wedemeyer's comment effectively displaces "friendship" – together with the "*necessitas* of freedom" it represents – from a protected sphere, and reveals its "ultimate possibility" as a dynamic operating within the various structured relationships of the mandates.[88] The "non-necessity" of friendship does not mean that it is absent as a transformative possibility from those relations that *have* been defined as "necessary."[89] If it cannot be spoken in the same language as can the various social institutions within which it operates, still it can neither be treated as an insignificant "absence" nor passed over in order to dismiss it.

[86] Recent lesbian/feminist theology has been particularly instrumental in revealing the extent to which (especially) women's experiences of friendship, and the challenges they pose to patriarchal social orders, have been marginalized in theology. See Mary E. Hunt, *Fierce Tenderness: A Feminist Theology of Friendship* (New York: Crossroad, 1991).

[87] Bethge, "My Friend", p. 150, quoting *Brautbriefe Zelle 92:Dietrich Bonhoeffer, Maria von Wedemeyer, 1943–1945*, eds. Ruth-Alice von Bismarck and Ulrich Kabitz (Munich: Beck, 1993), p. 128. Bethge then (pp. 150–1) reports a correspondence between himself and Andreas Pangritz, wherein Pangritz wrote of von Wedemeyer "In the final analysis she crossed out the entire doctrine of the mandates. And it seemed to me to be no coincidence that Dietrich probably ran out of arguments." Bethge comments (one suspects, from his own knowledge of his friend!) that Bonhoeffer would not in the end have "run out of arguments" and would not have been prepared altogether to eliminate the "mandated" aspect of the parent–child (or the husband–wife?) relationship. See also on von Wedemeyer in relation to Bonhoeffer's views on friendship, Regine Schindler, "Verhaftet und Verlobt: Zum Briefwechsel zwischen Dietrich Bonhoeffer und Maria von Wedemeyer, 1943–5," in Gremmels and Huber, eds., *Theologie und Freundschaft*.

[88] Jamie S. Scott, " "From the Spirit's Choice and Free Desire': Friendship as Atheology in Dietrich Bonhoeffer's *Letters and Papers from Prison*," *Studies in Religion* 22, 1 (1993), 61, claims that the *Letters and Papers* "offers us a vision of Christianity as the activity of friendship in all areas of life, under all the divine mandates," where friendship is characterized by "flexibility and play" and "greater openness." The problem with such a reading is that, without a corresponding discussion of friendship as grace, it tends to turn friendship into a new kind of "Christian program."

[89] The non-necessity of friendship is linked in certain recent reflections (see Gilbert Meilaender, *Friendship: A Study in Theological Ethics* (Notre Dame: Notre Dame, 1981),

What do these reflections on friendship mean in terms of the grounding of the complete human life in God; specifically, in terms of the resurrection as the "place to stand?" I suggest that what is here left implicit is the recognition of friendship as "ultimate possibility and grace" grounded in God's own "*necessitas* of freedom," that is, God's determination and confirmation of God's freedom as love. Friendship is a "practice" recognizable from a theological perspective as exemplifying the realization of that reality of divine love.

It is important to note that friendship, as described in Bonhoeffer's prison writings and elsewhere, becomes, itself, an innerworldly "place to stand," a "ground under our feet" that in some respects replaces the lost cultural "ground" without becoming its equivalent.[90] The discussion between Bonhoeffer and Bethge, referred to above, begins with the former's claim that their friendship is "one of the stable things in life;" it is this claim that Bethge counters with the reminder that friendship has no social *necessitas*. What emerges in the subsequent discussion is that the particular "stability" of friendship – that which maintains it *as* friendship – is precisely its lack of a form of social recognition that would render it interpretable or speakable as part of a social structure. This is what leads Bonhoeffer to emphasize the centrality of "freedom" in his understanding of friendship; friendship remains genuine friendship insofar as it is in this sense mysterious, unknowable, not definitively located within an existing set of social functions or relations.

Von Wedemeyer's comments, however, raise the question of whether "freedom" is a sufficient starting point for a definition of friendship – and Bonhoeffer's struggles with the "*necessitas* of freedom" themselves indicate the limitations of the concept. What it risks missing is the very "stability" of *this* friendship, with which Bethge began and to which the letters themselves testify; it is only from the stability of given friendships that Bonhoeffer is able to analyze the "mysterious" character of friendship as such. I would argue that the category of grace – the free gift that brings about a kind of freedom *not* contrasted with necessity – is required to

---

pp. 104–5) with its supposed "spiritual" character, as opposed to the "embodied" character of familial and political relationships. Such a view (which owes much to C. S. Lewis, *The Four Loves* (London: Collins, 1977)) is an attempt decisively to perform the "spatial" separation of friendship and the mandates.

[90]   See the reflections on this in "After Ten Years" (*DBW* 8, pp. 31–3, *Letters and Papers*, pp. 11–13). Ernst Feil, "Freundschaft – ein Thema der Theologie?," in Gremmels and Huber, eds., *Theologie und Freundschaft*, pp. 125–6, treats friendship as both the consequence and the "paradigm" of the relation to Christ in which a new "ground under our feet" is given.

"place" friendship theologically, and that Bonhoeffer's own friendships testify to this. It is also, I would suggest in the light of earlier discussion, necessary – obvious as this may seem – to recognize friendship as *love*, and hence to set it at least in possible relation to the realization of the divine love given in the reality of the resurrection.

Once again, it would seem, an emphasis on the unknowability of the "place to stand" needs to be complemented and extended – here in considering a penultimate "place to stand" as it relates to and reflects the ultimate. Friendship can, I would suggest, be understood as exemplifying the positive significance of existence in the penultimate.[91] What are sometimes regarded as its limitations as a form of love – its need for reciprocity, its preferential character, the impossibility of being "everyone's friend,"[92] its social and cultural specificity – place it within the realm of "innerworldly" human possibilities.[93] While not self-enclosed or self-sufficient, it persists for its own sake, and loses its significance if it is instrumentalized. It arises from and acknowledges a given reality ("one of the stable things in life") but "realizes" that reality in ever new ways. This creative possibility of friendship, which does not confine itself to a particular sphere but enters all aspects of human existence, is manifested (though not discussed) in the creative process of the prison correspondence itself.[94] The friendship between Bonhoeffer and Bethge enables the re-evaluation and development of inherited wisdom, through the careful analysis of a given situation in constant reference to their common "place to stand." Friendships,

[91] Bobert-Stützel, "Liebt ein Freund mehr?," pp. 102–3 suggests that friendship in Bonhoeffer's later work has the character of eschatological prolepsis – "Christian friendship partially anticipates fulfilled history. It allows redeemed social relations to be, to some extent, *experienced*" (my trans., original emphasis). While agreeing with the basic point made here – that friendship is a point at which the "realization" of redeemed reality can be perceived – I would argue that it is better understood in terms of the penultimate, to allow proper significance to be given to its finitude and temporality.

[92] Even if, following von Wedemeyer's correction, one can be "anyone's friend." On this, see Janet Martin Soskice, "Friendship", paper presented at the *Consultation on the Future of the Study of Theology and the Religions* (Cambridge: 2000). With reference to Bethge's reluctance to treat "Finkenwalde" as a model for friendship, it should be noted that he refers in the same article to the problem of jealousy among the ex-students of Finkenwalde. A close preferential friendship here appears to have come into conflict with the prescriptions of more general "brotherly love." See on this Bobert-Stützel, "Liebt ein Freund mehr?," pp. 95–6.

[93] See Soskice, "Friendship." This is opposed to the "spiritualization" of friendship following Lewis.

[94] Hunt discusses generativity as one of the characteristics of friendship (Hunt, *Fierce Tenderness*, pp. 99, 151–2). Her use of the language of "gratuity" and of indefinability is particularly striking here.

to put it simply, change things. The possibility of human creativity in the penultimate, which I discussed earlier in connection with the naming of God as a listener, emerges in friendship as something both gratuitous and entirely "worldly."

What are the implications of taking this "ultimate possibility and grace" seriously as a real possibility? This discussion suggests that the *Seelsorge* lectures can be reread as an invitation to friendship, the basis of which is the invitation to friendship in John 15:14ff. Christ is the one who names the disciples "friends" – *his* friends, but the invitation is to love *one another*. The promise of friendship with Christ, realized in love for one another, is bound up with the disciples" "hearing" and "being heard" – which in turn has its basis in the mutual "hearing" of Father and Son.[95]

The advocacy of an "ethic of friendship," or of friendship as an ecclesial model,[96] is distinctly ambiguous; what Bonhoeffer's cautious discussion indicates is that friendship is devalued to the extent that it is legislated for in advance of its occurrence. Attempts to construct an ethical system around "friendship" in general will inevitably establish a norm of friendship that omits or marginalizes some particular, lived friendships,[97] and which tends to ignore the difficulties of friendship – the time it takes to establish, its continuing vulnerability, its implication in power struggles. However, it is important, as von Wedemeyer's response to the discussion shows, to counterbalance this caution with an acknowledgment of friendship as a God-given possibility for the re-ordering of persons and societies.[98]

I have discussed friendship here as an analog and extension of the practices of silence considered earlier – as a relationship that relies on a given and unthematized common ground, that is embodied and self-transcending, that has an "openness" not arbitrary but grounded in God's self-determination as love, and that has the capacity to be critical and transformative of existing social structures. To associate friendship only with "silence," though, would seem strange; friends hear one another to speech, and speak expressions of their friendship. But then, spiritual care is not *only* silent; nor are many forms of "silent" worship. What is sought

---

[95] Jn 15:15, 16.

[96] As in Jürgen Moltmann, "Open Friendship: Aristotelian and Christian Views of Friendship," in Rouner, ed., *The Changing Face of Friendship*.

[97] Lewis, *The Four Loves* has become notorious for this, but models proposed by Hunt and other feminist writers on friendship can become equally limiting – as Hunt herself acknowledges (Hunt, *Fierce Tenderness*, p. 113).

[98] As, paradigmatically: "Behold a glutton and a drunkard, a friend of tax collectors and sinners."

here, as previous chapters suggested, is not a "counter-*logos*" asserting the place of silence over against the dominance of speech, but rather a "reconciled *logos*" to correspond to the act in which God hears God's own Word; a reconciled *logos* that may not be available as a set of general principles, but that may nonetheless be discerned, learned, and practiced.

Summary and Conclusions

At the end of a discussion of iconoclasm and its dangers, Donald Mackinnon proposed the task for theology of determining "what sort of silence, what sort of repudiation of every sort of image best conveys the ultimacy not of judgment but of love."[99] I have explored responses to that question in terms of practices of silence – asking how they convey the "ultimacy not of judgment but of love" given in the resurrection.

I considered, firstly, how silence in worship can become the focus for perceiving and understanding the innerworldly realization of the given reality of the resurrection – and how this might challenge the subordination of silence to the word. Central to the challenge was the importance of learning to "hear with God's ears," as central to the transformation of selves and communities.

The silence of the spiritual carer, as described in Bonhoeffer's lectures, is described as that which "uncovers sin and brings into the hearing of the Word." The "uncovering of sin" can be seen in the anti-idolatrous function of the spiritual carer's silence; it defeats the attempt to "make something of oneself" or to make the other's voice into the voice of God. The basis of this practice of silence is the understanding of communication as mediated in Christ, which establishes a "distance" between the participants in conversation. To say that communication is mediated in Christ, however, is also to say that the resurrection establishes a common "place to stand." From here, the transformation both of the communicative relationship itself and of the individuals within it – a transformation which I associate, on the basis of discussion in previous chapters, with "bringing into hearing" – becomes possible.

Reading "beyond" the *Seelsorge* lectures, in more senses than one, I then attempted to reach a fuller understanding of that possibility – of what really *happens* in spiritual care. This extension of Bonhoeffer's reflections on spiritual care called for fuller accounts, firstly of the capacity for discernment – which spiritual care apparently seeks to develop – and

[99]   Donald Mackinnon, *Explorations in Theology*, 5 (London: SCM, 1979).

secondly of the relationship between the participants in spiritual care. On both of these points, the "silence of unknowability," which the spiritual carer's silence preserves, remains significant. However, in order to do justice even to the realities to which the *Seelsorge* lectures point – to say nothing of other practices of silence to which it is analogous – it is necessary to recognize in spiritual care the "silence of the listener" as it both conveys and is formed by God's act of listening.

All of the practices of silence I have discussed could be described as ways of acknowledging and coming to know, entering and coming to inhabit, a common place to stand before God. The "commonness" that makes silent worship possible or makes spiritual care possible is not fully specifiable, but neither is it simply unknown. Believing in the "ultimacy not of judgment but of love" entails an engagement in processes through which people learn in and through love – learn, indeed, the making and enacting of judgments – but not in a way that presumes the conclusion of this process in the capacity to cut off relation to another and deny the common place to stand.

The contrasting understandings of silence discussed here and in previous chapters may be focused through consideration of two different silences in the biblical narratives of the resurrection. The Gospel of Mark ends in the silence of those who are confronted with an empty tomb and the "open road to Galilee"[100] – a given reality so mysterious as to confound all attempts to objectify it, and an invitation to its "realization" that sends those who accept it out into an apparently godless world. The Markan resurrection intensifies the silences of the incarnate and crucified Christ; the silence of the immediate response to it "expresses" its mystery. The Gospel proclaimed and written is clearly a performative contradiction if this silence in response to mystery is *all* there is; but the Gospel proclaimed and written, even with the addition of the "shorter ending" or the "longer ending," nonetheless has to maintain this silence.[101]

In John 21 the disciples are brought into silence in the presence of the risen Christ – "Nobody dared ask 'Who are you?'; they knew it was the Lord." This restoration of friendship, experienced as unpredictable grace, does not bring about a withdrawal from ethical responsibility,[102] a "solu-

---

[100] The expression is from Elisabeth Schüssler Fiorenza, *Jesus: Miriam's Child, Sophia's Prophet* (New York: 1994), p. 187.

[101] I am grateful to Janet Scott for discussions of this passage.

[102] Jn 21:15ff: "Jesus said to Simon Peter, 'Simon son of John, do you love me more than these?' He said to him, 'Yes, Lord; you know that I love you.' Jesus said to him, 'Feed my lambs.' "

tion" to the problem of suffering,[103] or even the immediate reconfiguration of this community into a society of equal friends.[104] The mediation
of communication in Christ, which restores friendship, at the same time
preserves the unknowability of the other.[105]

The question of the relationship between the individual and the communal keeping of silence – seen here as the relationship between "restor-
ing friendship" and "the unknowability of the other" – has arisen several
times in this discussion. I have suggested, in fact, that contemporary sus-
picions of silence have much to do with the flight from the "Cartesian"
specter, and the emphasis here on the possibility of interpersonal and
communal silence – rooted in the interpersonal silence of God – has been
directed against that suspicion. Nonetheless, the "silence of unknowability," and the question "Who keeps silent?," have been retained here as
central categories. My final chapter will consider how a particular *locus* of
contemporary debate about the unknowability of the other – the question of privacy – appears from the perspective of the resurrection silence
and the practice of communication to which it gives rise.

---

[103] Jn 21:18ff. " '. . . when you grow old, you will stretch out your hands and someone
else will fasten a belt around you and take you where you do not wish to go.' "
[104] Jn 21:21ff. Peter's question about the fate of the beloved disciple (v. 21) receives an
equivocal answer (v. 22): " '. . . what is that to you? Follow me!;' "So the rumour spread
in the community that this disciple would not die" (v. 23).
[105] As with the refusal of a direct answer to the question concerning the beloved
disciple (Jn 21:22, 23).

Chapter Seven

PRIVACY, OMNISCIENCE, AND THE SILENCE OF GOD

"Does God Violate Your Right to Privacy?"

Does the call to "keep God's silence" have anything to do with privacy? Personal privacy is an increasingly important and contested concept within contemporary ethics and public policy – and one on which Christian theology has, apparently, had relatively little to say.[1] It is easy, at least on a superficial level, to find reasons for this reticence. On at least two counts it can be argued that, for Christian faith, privacy as a concept can have no anthropological significance; that God and the right to privacy are incompatible. First, the belief that God sees and knows everything, even the secrets of the heart, appears to subvert any attempt to delimit a sphere of individual privacy, concealed from all except the one to whom it "belongs." If God is omniscient, whatever I "keep to myself" is in fact known to God.[2] Second, it might be claimed that privacy as a concept is fundamentally opposed to the account of redeemed existence as participation in the community "without reserve" that is the life of the Trinity.

In this chapter, taking forward all that has been said so far into this key contemporary question for the ethics of communication, I argue for a theological engagement with the fundamental concerns of the privacy debate.

---

[1] Recent articles include Charles Taliafero, "Does God Violate Your Right to Privacy?," *Theology* 92 (1989); Margaret Falls-Corbitt and F. Michael McLain, "God and Privacy," *Faith and Philosophy* 9 (1992). David Lyon, *The Electronic Eye: The Rise of Surveillance Society* (Cambridge: Polity, 1994), explicitly draws on the Christian theological tradition but describes his work as sociological. See also Church of England Board of Social Responsibility, *Cybernauts Awake! Ethical and Spiritual Implications of Computers, IT and the Internet* (London: Church of England Board of Social Responsibility, 1999), pp. 71–4.

[2] See H. Tristram Engelhardt, "Privacy and Limited Democracy: The Moral Centrality of Persons," *Social Philosophy and Policy* 17, 2 (2000), 126.

I suggest, first, that certain understandings of *knowledge* commonly assumed in that debate must be challenged, and, second, that the demand for privacy nonetheless reflects insights and needs to which theologians should attend – beginning with the need to recognize persons as irreducible to "objects of knowledge."

The naming of God as listener, here developed further in relation to biblical texts in which God's knowledge is associated with hearing or listening, provides the basis for my theological rethinking of privacy. I argue that knowledge thought in terms of divine hearing is fundamentally different from the knowledge understood as possessed information, on which privacy debates tend to rely. "Hearing knowledge" can be understood only within the relationship of knower and known, to which love, the acceptance of responsibility to and for the other, and the exercise of patience are integral. To speak of knowledge and knowing in terms of property and its accumulation – as many discussions both of divine omniscience and of privacy do – cannot do justice to such a non-acquisitive way of knowing. If there is a divine "knowledge economy," we might say, it cannot be based on competition for scarce knowledge commodities.[3]

Thinking about God's knowledge in this way, I argue, opens the way not only for a response to contemporary debates about privacy, but for further development of our theological understanding of human existence in the "penultimate" – that is, in complex temporal reality determined by its relation to the resurrection as "ultimate." Privacy matters, in other words, in our thinking about eschatology. "Hearing knowledge" implies, as my previous discussion has suggested, giving time to the other – and we are those to whom God gives time in this way, living among others to whom God also gives time. Recognizing privacy is recognizing this gift of time, and its implications. At the end of the chapter, I suggest that, in the final analysis, the theological importance of privacy arises from the mystery that God is in Godself, without which the "mystery" of a person is not fully understood.

The Privacy Debate

The debate over privacy, its nature, limits, and significance,[4] is conducted at all levels – from high-profile controversies over investigations of the

---

[3] I am grateful to Lewis Ayres for his comments on this.

[4] For the purposes of this discussion I am using "privacy" to refer to what the Anglo-American legal and philosophical literature generally calls *informational* privacy, that is, the

"private lives" of public figures, to attempts to specify the "right to privacy" in US constitutional law[5] and human rights law,[6] to analyses of the concept of privacy that call its usefulness and coherence into question.[7] Developments in information and surveillance technology make the question, apparently, ever more pressing and complex.[8]

The reference to the "right to privacy," above, already hints at the extent to which discussions of privacy – those most closely related to the development of policy, in any case – are dominated by the understanding of personhood associated with the autonomy of the self-legislating individual. The language of the privacy debate has indeed tended to begin from the language of rights, privacy being thought in the first instance as the "right to be left alone."[9] Privacy has been associated, then, with a particular kind of "negative" freedom – the freedom *from* interference or unwanted communication.

Clearly there is a close connection in this regard between the concept of privacy and that of the ownership of property. To describe something as "private property" is to invoke discourses, not only of negative freedom but of sovereign control, that also dominate discussions of privacy in the narrow sense. The language of privacy is used to denote the sphere within which the rights of individual ownership can be exercised. Defenses of

---

restriction of the access of others to "information" concerning a given person. I am not using it, except where indicated, to cover the more general questions of *autonomy* often linked to "privacy" in the US context (especially). I shall, however, be calling into question the assumptions behind the idea of "informational privacy."

[5] For a summary of which see Scott D. Gerber, "Privacy and Constitutional Theory," *Social Philosophy and Policy* 17, 2 (2000).

[6] A survey of the current place of privacy in human rights law, and the problems of defining the "right to privacy," is given in David Banisar, *Privacy and Human Rights 2000: An International Survey of Privacy Laws and Developments* (Washington DC: EPIC and Privacy International, 2000). The "right to privacy," or to protection against interference with privacy, is referred to in article 12 of the Universal Declaration of Human Rights (1948) and article 8 of the European Convention on Human Rights and Fundamental Freedoms (1950).

[7] A key example being Judith Jarvis Thomson, "The Right to Privacy," in *Philosophical Dimensions of Privacy: An Anthology*, ed. Ferdinand D. Schoeman (Cambridge: Cambridge University Press, 1984); see the discussion of this in James Rachels, "Why Privacy Is Important," in Schoeman, ed., *Philosophical Dimensions of Privacy*.

[8] As in, most recently, the debate in the UK over the Regulation of Investigatory Powers (RIP) Bill. See on the wider issue David Friedman, "Privacy and Technology," *Social Philosophy and Policy* 17, 2 (2000); Judith Wagner DeCew, *In Pursuit of Privacy: Law, Ethics and the Rise of Technology* (Ithaca: Cornell University Press, 1997), pp. 145–64.

[9] Samuel D. Warren and Louis D. Brandeis, "The Right to Privacy (the Implicit Made Explicit)," reprinted in Schoeman, ed., *Philosophical Dimensions of Privacy*.

privacy frequently use the language of ownership, theft, contract, and exchange.

What is it, though, to which this language of "property" is being applied, when it is used – for example – in debates about employers intercepting their staff's electronic mail, or about the activities of investigative journalists? The commonplace answer would be *personal information*, "owned" by one person, perhaps "stolen" by another, "sold" to somebody else. We are accustomed enough to the idea that "information" – by which is meant, roughly, knowledge considered in abstraction from its knower[10] – can be treated as a commodity in this way.[11] It is striking, however, that in privacy debates, in particular, the language of property in relation to "personal information" begins to break down. Commentators remark, sometimes with a perceptible air of frustration, that information does not function like "ordinary" property.[12] Even if the problem is "solved" by setting up a model of privacy precisely in order to make information behave, as far as possible, as "other property" does,[13] the sus-

---

[10]   The word has an interesting history. The SOED lists an obsolete Late Middle English sense, "formation or moulding of the mind or character," and two still-current senses from the same period, both containing intrinsic reference to communication – "communication of the knowledge of some thing or event" and the knowledge thus communicated. ("For your information . . ."). From the early sixteenth century "information" was used to mean "an item of news." In the early twentieth century a new sense appeared – "*Without necessary relation to a recipient*: that which inheres in or is represented by a particular arrangement, sequence, or set, that may be stored in, transferred by, and responded to *by inanimate things*" (my emphasis; the example given in SOED refers to "genetic information"). It would seem that the shift in the understanding of "information" represented by the loss of intrinsic reference to communication (and hence to the relationship between a "giver" and a "recipient" of communication) was what allowed it to be used of "inanimate things" – and is also what allows the attitude to "information as property," discussed in this chapter, to emerge. I am grateful to Melissa Demian for discussions of this topic.

[11]   Many of the issues around the idea of "personal information as property" apply more widely to various forms of "intellectual property" – which will also tend to stretch the limits of a paradigm of "property" that applies most readily to medium-sized dry goods.

[12]   For example, giving a unit of information to one party does not entail taking it from another (Alexander Rosenberg, "Privacy as a Matter of Taste and Right," *Social Philosophy and Policy* 17, 2 (2000), 80–1; any unit of information can be reproduced endlessly at no expense (Friedman, "Privacy and Technology," pp. 193–5.); the rights of ownership (if possession is not to constitute the whole of the law) are hard to establish (DeCew, *In Pursuit of Privacy*, p. 54; R. G. Frey, "Privacy, Control and Talk of Rights," *Social Philosophy and Policy* 17, 2 (2000), 64–5).

[13]   As Rosenberg, "Privacy as a Matter of Taste," appears to: "the regulations that govern information reflect the nature of information as an unusual commodity" (p. 83). It would seem, also, that the proclamation of a "knowledge-based economy" necessitates the transformation of knowledge of all sorts – not merely personal information – into a properly manipulable commodity.

picion remains that the paradigm has been stretched somewhat beyond its limits. As I shall show in later discussion, this problem proves on closer analysis to have major implications for the theological response to privacy debates.

The inclusion of privacy in declarations of universal human rights invites reflection on the sense, if any, in which privacy is indeed a human "universal." Attempts to define privacy as a *natural* right run into difficulties when the most rudimentary examination of the history of the concept reveals the extent of its social and cultural specificity. Sociological and social-historical analyzes of privacy are concerned, not most fundamentally with individual "rights to privacy," but with the social construction and definition of spheres of life opposed to or contrasted with "the public."[14] This in turn suggests that the processes by which the spheres of public and private are constituted are themselves possible objects of analysis and critique.

It is here that feminist critiques of the institution of privacy become important, as part of the broader analysis of the social processes by which women are silenced. The connection between "the feminine" and "the private," for example through the construction of the sphere of the domestic in opposition to the public realm, has been, it is claimed, a significant factor in the silencing of women.[15] The "private" is defined as that which is in most circumstances not to be spoken of – which has meant that acts of violence and injustice *within* the "private" have been rendered publicly unnameable, and that the concerns of women and others assigned to the "private" have been systematically excluded from expression or recognition. The well-known slogan "the personal is the political" denotes the feminist attempt to challenge the "silencing" effect of the institution of

---

[14]   See the introduction to Stanley I. Benn and Gerald Gaus, *Public and Private in Social Life* (London: Croom Helm, 1983), pp. 3–27, for a clear example of the descriptive approach to privacy as a social phenomenon, and an overview of the most significant work in the field. See also for a summary of various accounts of the emergence of modern "privacy," John Brewer, "This, That and the Other," in *Shifting the Boundaries: Transformation of the Language of Public and Private in the Eighteenth Century*, eds. Dario Cataglione and Lesley Sharpe (Exeter: University of Exeter Press, 1995), pp. 1–21.

[15]   See for example Jean Bethke Elshtain, *Public Man, Private Woman: Women in Social and Political Thought* (Princeton: Princeton University Press, 1981); Carol Pateman, "Feminist Critiques of the Public/Private Dichotomy," in Benn and Gaus, eds., *Public and Private in Social Life*; Catherine Mackinnon, *Towards a Feminist Theory of the State* (Cambridge: Harvard University Press, 1989), p.187; and the analysis and critique of these in DeCew, *In Pursuit of Privacy*, pp. 81–94. See also Lyon, *Electronic Eye*, p. 184 on feminist opposition to the association of privacy with personal autonomy.

privacy. It does not, however, necessarily imply a challenge to the idea of a "right to privacy" as such – indeed, the demand may be for *more* privacy for women, highlighting the fact that those who have constituted the "private sphere" for others have themselves often been given no privacy within it.

The ambivalent relationship of feminist theory to notions of privacy can be linked to the wider question of feminist attitudes to the "modern" ideas of autonomy, the individual as possessor of rights, and so forth. The privacy debate, as I initially described it, is itself ambivalent in this regard; it arose from a modern liberal paradigm, and has become a *locus* where that paradigm is called into question. However the discussion of privacy strains the language of rights, the irreducibility of the individual person as in some sense a bearer of value is clearly an important aspect of what a defense of privacy is intended to defend. The question then arises as to how this significance of the person as bearer of value can be defended, while recognizing the social constitution, and openness to critique, of all particular institutions of privacy.

Is this a point at which theologians can or should enter the debate? In the light of divine omniscience, it might be said on the one hand, the claim that we have private lives is a self-aggrandizing illusion. In the light of the redemption of humanity into perfect community, it might be said, on the other hand, privacy is numbered with the forms of human exis- tence that are specifically condemned or brought to an end with the inau- guration of the new humanity in Christ. The attempt to establish private lives for ourselves is, on either account, a modern manifestation of the basic sin of pride – the desire to establish the human individual as capable of self-determining existence outside community with God or the neigh- bor. Privacy, or so it might well be claimed on the basis of my summary of recent debates, is inextricably bound up with an individualistic anthro- pology, with social relations as extrinsic and self-possession as an ideal. The specter of the Cartesian subject looms large.

However, the debate over privacy calls into question some of the assumptions of an individualistic paradigm – such as the understanding of "property," and the separation of "private" and "public" spheres – pre- cisely as it attempts to defend them. This suggests prima facie that privacy is a topic with which theologians who are concerned about the limita- tions of "individualism" might well be concerned. In beginning such a reconsideration of privacy, I turn first to an essay by Bonhoeffer wherein a positive evaluation of privacy is based on a very different understanding of knowledge and truth from that discussed so far.

"What is Meant by 'Telling the Truth?'"

The essay "What is Meant by 'Telling the Truth?'"[16] was one of Bonhoeffer's last extant pieces of academic work, written in Tegel prison while under interrogation. Its publication with the *Ethics* in earlier editions reflects the fact that it is often read as an example of the application of Bonhoeffer's basic principles of theological ethics to a particular problem.[17] In using it here I, by contrast, treat the specific subject matter – truth-telling, falsehood, and privacy – as itself of wider significance for theological ethics.

The most striking feature of the essay at first glance is the assertion that "telling the truth" in particular circumstances may include concealment, secrecy, possibly by implication statements contrary to fact.[18]

> If my utterance is to be truthful it must in each case be different according to whom I am addressing, who is questioning me, and what I am speaking about . . . It is only the cynic who claims to "speak the truth" at all times and in all places to all men in the same way.[19]

Knowing that the essay was written under interrogation tends to sharpen our awareness of its applicability to what might be termed "limit situations" – such as that in Kant's famous example ("do we tell the murderer where to find his victim?").[20] Bonhoeffer does quote Kant's example, but what is in fact most striking about the essay is the "banality" of his examples of evil and the lie:[21] "a teacher asks a child in front of the class whether it is true that his father often comes home drunk. It is true, but the child denies it."[22] The banality of the examples points, paradoxically, to the seriousness with which Bonhoeffer takes the issues under consideration. The possibility of truthfulness and the threat

---

[16] Printed with the *Ethics* in old editions of Bonhoeffer's work – *Ethics*, pp. 326–34. In the new edition it appears in *Konspiration und Haft*, DBW 16, pp. 619–29.

[17] See for example James T. Laney, "An Examination of Bonhoeffer's Ethical Contextualism," in A. J. Klassen, ed., *A Bonhoeffer Legacy: Essays in understanding* (Grand Rapids: Eerdmans, 1981), pp. 294–313.

[18] Bonhoeffer placed careful theological restrictions on the use of the word "lie." See DBW 16, p. 626, *Ethics*, p. 331.

[19] *Ethics*, p. 328.

[20] For a discussion of the essay that treats Kant as Bonhoeffer's primary "dialog partner," see James Burtness, *Shaping the Future: The Ethics of Bonhoeffer* (Philadelphia: Fortress, 1985), pp. 126–63.

[21] This again recalls the comparison with Arendt – see chapter 5.

[22] DBW 16, pp. 625–6.

of the lie are conditions that affect, and are affected by, the totality of our social existence.

We might conventionally think of a debate about the scope of privacy as a debate about the relative claims of truth-telling and some other value or principle – social harmony, or respect for personal freedom. In this essay, by contrast, questions of privacy are subsumed under the question, "How does my word come to be true?" Bonhoeffer is claiming, not simply that it is sometimes *right* to conceal information or withhold speech,[23] but that it is sometimes *more truthful* to conceal information or withhold speech.

The question of truth-telling is, then, a particularly significant context in which the "relationship between reality and realisation" can be explored. "Our word has the assigned purpose [*die Bestimmung*] of expressing, in unity with God's Word, the real as it exists in God." The expression of "the real as it exists in God" is a possibility belonging not to the propositional content of what is said, but to the act of speaking as perceived within the social structures and relationships that shape it. Truthfulness depends, according to the section "How does my word come to be true?," on the recognition of "who gives me cause to speak" and of "the place at which I stand." Within the essay, this is immediately linked to the specific limitations on speech that the social order requires. Speech, Bonhoeffer claims, bears an essential relation, not only to the subject matter concerning which assertions are made, but to the person to whom it is spoken. Truthful speech is possible only where both these relations are accurately perceived and enacted. As suggested in chapter 4, Bonhoeffer's understanding of truthfulness makes speech dependent on its hearers and hence vulnerable to mishearing.

With reference to the discussion of philosophical debates on privacy, above, it should be noted at this point that Bonhoeffer's essay clearly differentiates *truthfulness* from the possession or communication of correct *information*. "The truth" is not separable, as infinitely reproducible items of information, from the people who know and speak it or the relationships in which it is formed and used. If it is this kind of "truth" that is at stake in discussions of privacy, it is already apparent that it will be necessary to call into question the terms in which those discussions are often conducted. The similarities between the "information" possessed, stolen, and protected in privacy debates, and the "word as idea" identified in the Christology lectures (discussed in chapter 4) become apparent; information "rests in itself and is relative to itself,"

---

[23]   *Pace* Laney, "An Examination of Bonhoeffer's Ethical Contextualism."

is "timeless truth," and can be considered apart from the one who speaks it or the one who hears it.

The different ideas of "truth" at stake become even clearer when we consider the possibility – unthinkable within the privacy debates outlined above – of the "truthful silence." Words are, as I have said, given in this essay the assigned purpose of "expressing the real as it exists in God;" but this claim is immediately followed, in the essay, by the further assertion that "our silence should be the sign of the boundary which is imposed on the word by the real as it exists in God."[24] Silence or the withholding of speech is, it is claimed here, in certain circumstances more truthful than speech.

Without further qualification, this might sound like the claim that the inevitable failure of words to express the reality of God – or the inevitable impurity of words in a sinful world[25] – means that silence is the ultimate truthful communication. Such a claim would clearly be very far from Bonhoeffer's understanding of the truthful silence. His truthful silences are precisely that – truthful silences, which, no less than acts of speaking, depend for their truthfulness on their fitness to a particular time and place in worldly "reality as it exists in God." Privacy becomes significant, within this understanding of "truthfulness," as the respect for and preservation of the proper limitations of speech. Respect for privacy is contrasted with the cynical truth-telling – a "truth of Satan" – that "wounds shame, desecrates mystery, breaks confidence, betrays the community," and enacts in doing so the "death of the real."[26]

What, however, has actually been said about this "reality as it exists in God," and what is its connection with privacy? Bonhoeffer's move to describe "who gives me cause to speak," and "the place at which I stand," in terms of the social rights and responsibilities involved in a particular instance of possible speech[27] raises questions in the light of my earlier discussion. "Who gives me cause to speak" and "the place at which I stand" have been asked and answered, in my discussion, in relation to the

---

[24]   The Horton Smith translation suggests a parallelism of "assigned purpose of words" and "assigned purpose of silence" here, which is not found in the original. See *DBW* 16, p. 627; compare *Ethics*, p. 332.

[25]   Which is a slightly different problem – the former pertains to creatureliness, the latter to fallenness.

[26]   *Ethics*, p. 328, *DBW* 16, pp. 623–4.

[27]   A definition of privacy in terms of the maintenance of a plurality of social relationships is put forward by Rachels, "Why Privacy Is Important." Particularly interesting for my purposes is Rachels' denial (pp. 293–4) that "the fact that we observe different standards of conduct [referring, from context, chiefly to the different things we are prepared to *say or reveal*] with different people is merely a sign of dishonesty."

resurrection. The world as it is in God, I suggested in chapter 3, is in the terms of Bonhoeffer's *Ethics* a world preserved in its fallen and disunited state, judged for its disunity and reconciled within itself and to God in Christ.

The essay on "telling the truth," as I have described it so far, is mainly concerned with the problems of what I earlier analyzed as the aspect of ethical thought relating to the incarnation – that is, the affirmation of the world in its given complexity. A key claim implied in the understanding of privacy described here is that the "real as it exists in God" is not simply a unified whole; its disunity is as integral to its reality as is its condition of being redeemed and healed, and the expression of this disunited reality is part of the "assigned purpose" of words. It is particularly significant that the "truth of Satan" – which mistakes itself for divine truth – is condemned for its attempt to judge the world without also enacting God's "taking on" of the world in the incarnation.[28]

The extent to which privacy is linked, for Bonhoeffer, to social order and the divine "mandates" of family, work, state, and Church is clearly conveyed in the essay. In his developed example – the child improperly questioned about his family in front of the class – the problem with the breach of privacy is that it imperils the order that preserves the home as a separate sphere with its own privileges and concerns. Society becomes untruthful when words become "rootless and homeless" – when the "word that is born in the warmth of personal relationships" enters the "cold air of the public realm," when "the being and limitations of the different words are no longer clearly perceived."[29] Privacy both marks and maintains the boundaries that the "order of preservation" requires. It could not itself be described as a mandate; rather, it is the means by which the spoken word is rendered obedient to the mandates and to this extent "truthful."

The desire for privacy, Bonhoeffer implies here and elsewhere, occurs as a consequence and reminder of the imperfection of human community. Institutions of privacy are part of the divinely appointed "orders of preservation" that enable the world to persist in its fallen existence without succumbing to chaos. Elsewhere, Bonhoeffer repeatedly alludes to the origins of shame and privacy in the expulsion of Adam and Eve from Eden – "God Himself made clothes for humanity . . . since the fall there

[28]   "[The false truth] gives itself the appearance of executing the judgment of God upon the sinfulness of the real. But God's truth judges creation out of love . . . [it] became flesh in the world" (*DBW* 16, pp. 623–4).
[29]   *Ethics*, p. 330, *DBW* 16, p. 624.

must be reticence and secrecy."[30] The fact that *God* made the clothes is understood as a sign – perhaps *the* sign – of God's will to preserve the fallen world.

How does the understanding of privacy suggested by an analysis of Bonhoeffer's essay relate to the issues in philosophical treatments of privacy, discussed earlier? First, it should be noted that if privacy has to do with the preservation of the world in and despite its disunity, and its proper scope and limits are determined by God, the right to privacy is meaningless save in the context of a broader responsibility for privacy. Bonhoeffer's concern for the value of personal reserve – the capacity to remain silent where appropriate about one's own "private" affairs – is as deep-seated as his concern for the responsibility of each for the privacy of her neighbor, if not more so. The moral failure of the cynic who "breaks confidence" is perhaps not qualitatively different from that of the "shameless" people who talk openly about aspects of their *own* lives that "ought to be concealed."[31] At the same time, the preservation of privacy relies on the recognition of the particular other – "who causes me to speak" – and by implication her justifiable claim on my silence. This again reflects the fact that privacy and reserve are not being considered here primarily in terms of the possession or control of information.

Thus far, however, the analysis of privacy seems to lead us no further than a divinely sanctioned social conservatism. To assign privacy to the "orders of preservation" rather than to the humanly derived consequences of human sin (to draw attention to the fact that "God Himself made clothes for humanity") is admittedly to allow it greater potential significance. However, if privacy is still simply a sign, positive and negative, of the disunity of the world that is overcome in Christ, it is hard to see whence we can derive the theological resources for the analysis or criticism of any given institutions of privacy.

The problem is that efforts to reassert the importance of existing institutions of privacy – in the face of their erosion by the increasing scope of the powerful "public word" – risk becoming an uncritical reaffirmation of the power relations inherent in those institutions. Feminist analyzes of the role of traditional constructions of privacy in the silencing of women would suggest that such a reaffirmation is just as dangerous as, perhaps more dangerous than, a complete abandonment of the concept of

---

[30] *Letters and Papers*, p. 158, *DBW* 8, p. 228. See also the important section on "shame" in *DBW* 6, pp. 304–8.

[31] *Letters and Papers*, p. 146, *DBW* 8, p. 211. See also *Letters and Papers*, pp. 212–3, *DBW* 8, pp. 324–5.

privacy. The issue is brought out particularly clearly if we look again at the example of the child and the teacher. What if the teacher had asked whether the child's father abused the child sexually or beat the child's mother – and what then if the child had replied in the negative, and continued to do so, when the opposite was true? It would not then be possible to affirm with the same confidence that the child was simply reflecting an awareness of the particular requirements of the sphere of the family, which has to be protected against the encroachments of the "public sphere".

The reflection on "telling the truth," begun in this reading of Bonhoeffer's essay, seems to require, for its completion, reflection on the significance of the crucifixion and the resurrection – the divine judgment and transformation of the world – for practices and institutions relating to privacy. How are the limits of speech redetermined by that judgment and transformation? Can we go beyond both the blanket condemnation of privacy, and the maintenance of existing conventions of privacy in the interests of preserving a social order together with its injustices? To see how this might be possible, I return to the connection made earlier between the doctrine of divine omniscience and theological debates about privacy. In order to develop an understanding of the theological signifi-cance of privacy, we need to think through what is meant by claims about God's "knowledge."

How Does God Know?

Hearing and omniscience

The divine attribute of omniscience, as a subject of theological reflection, has tended to be linked closely to the attribute of omnipotence, and to be considered mainly in the context of debates over freedom and neces-sity in human action.[32] The question of whether God's foreknowledge excludes creaturely freedom, bearing as it does on such areas of funda-mental dispute as the doctrine of predestination, has received considerable attention. More recently, divine omniscience has also been introduced into discussions of the intelligibility of theopaschite positions.[33] To the extent

---

[32] For recent discussions of omniscience in this context, see John Martin Fischer, ed., *God, Foreknowledge and Freedom* (Stanford: Stanford University Press, 1989); William Hasker, *God, Time and Knowledge* (Ithaca: Cornell University Press, 1989).

[33] For example, in Marcel Sarot, *God, Passibility and Corporeality* (Kampen: Kok Pharos, 1992), pp. 57–9.

that all such debates occur within the tradition of analytic "philosophy of religion," the account of knowledge, and hence of omniscience, that they assume remains unchallenged. Knowledge, and hence God's knowledge, is, here again, the possession of information about an object of knowledge. The acquisition of this information is itself indifferent to any further relationship between the knower and the known. God's omniscience with regard to me is God's possession of comprehensive information about my thoughts, feelings, actions, and so forth.

I have already indicated the parallels between this understanding of knowledge, and hence of divine omniscience, and the patterns of communication that, as Bonhoeffer describes them, produce the cynical "truth of Satan." This knowledge is timeless, has no intrinsic dependence on the relation of knower and known, and can hence be spoken "truthfully" as soon as it enters the possession of the one who thinks it. "Possession" is clearly a significant term here; the knowledge economy that is envisaged is one in which relatively scarce information is acquired and controlled as a means of self-aggrandizement or of meeting a perceived lack – a "need to know" – and God's omniscience is read as an aspect of God's supreme success in this task. The claim that God hears offers a different possible starting point for the thinking of divine omniscience, one that understands God's knowledge within the context of God's relation to what – and whom – God knows.

> The Israelites groaned under their slavery, and cried out. Out of the slavery their cry for help rose up to God. God heard their groaning, and God remembered his covenant with Abraham, Isaac and Jacob. God looked upon the Israelites, and God took notice of them.[34] (Ex 2:23–5)

In the narrative of the exodus as it stands, this is a significant turning point. It is the first reference to the intention of God to save the people of Israel from slavery, and it immediately precedes the account of Moses' vision on Mount Horeb. This is, then, the preface to the narrative of the saving action that became central to Israel's understanding of God, and of herself as a people of God – a narrative that is inaugurated by the act of divine hearing.

The significance for Israel's understanding of God of the statement that "God heard" the people of Israel in slavery can be seen in subsequent

---

[34] See also the discussion of this text in Peter Ochs, *Peirce, Pragmatism and the Logic of Scripture* (Cambridge: Cambridge University Press, 1998), pp. 304–7, where it is used to indicate the scriptural and traditional antecedents for the reading practice he advocates.

passages dealing with the exodus. In Moses' vision on Horeb, God prefaces the announcement of Israel's deliverance and the sending of Moses: "I have observed the misery of my people . . . I have heard their cry on account of their taskmasters. Indeed, I know their suffering" (Ex 3:7). Subsequently, the messengers sent by Moses to the king of Edom give a brief account of the exodus: "the Egyptians oppressed us . . . and when we cried to the Lord, he heard us . . . and brought us out of Egypt" (Num 20:16). Of particular interest is the formula for the harvest offering, given in Deut 26:7: "When the Egyptians treated us harshly . . . we cried to the LORD, the God of our ancestors; the LORD heard our voice and saw our affliction." In this extended account of Israel's formation, the first mention of God is as the one who hears the cries of the oppressed in Egypt.

An examination of the passage from Exodus reveals the complex interrelation between knowledge, judgment, commitment, and action involved in the claim that God hears. There is no implied moment of non-evaluative divine knowledge; God's hearing is already God's judgment, and hence also already God's self-determination toward justice and compassion.[35] One consequence of this understanding of divine hearing is that, for those who are the victims of injustice, the promise that God knows and observes their suffering is itself significant. The assurance that the truth is known, in itself, provides the assurance that the efforts of the unjust to impose control, both on events and on their interpretations and histories, ultimately fail.

In the book of Genesis, the association of the motif of divine hearing with victims of injustice and with those in some sense excluded from the central narrative is particularly striking. God is first said to hear the blood of Abel "crying out to me from the ground" (Gen 4:10).[36] The next significant narrative of divine hearing is the story of Hagar, whose son is named Ishmael, "God hears" (Gen 16:11); Ishmael himself is subsequently

---

[35]   Other passages link God's hearing directly with an evaluative judgment and the consequent action. "When the LORD heard your words, he was wrathful and swore 'Not one of these . . . shall see the good land' " (Dt 1:34ff.); ". . . the LORD said to me: 'I have heard the words of this people, which they have spoken to you; they are right in all they have spoken' " (Dt 5:28ff). Particularly important for this relationship between knowledge and judgment is the Song of Hannah, 1 Sam 2:1–10, especially v3: "Talk not more so very proudly/let no arrogance come from your mouth/for the LORD is a God of knowledge/and by him actions are weighed."

[36]   David Daube, *The Exodus Pattern in the Bible* (London: Faber & Faber, 1963), p. 27, argues that the verb translated "cry out" in Gen 4:10 and the Exodus narratives has primarily legal associations, and should be understood as denoting an appeal to God as the righteous judge.

heard by God (Gen 21:17). The other name in Genesis that refers to God's hearing is that of Simeon, the son of Leah who declares "the LORD has heard that I am hated" (Gen 29:33).

The same link between God's hearing and God's justice – particularly toward those who have no power to make themselves visible or to ensure that their voices are heard – becomes the basis of an ethical imperative to act justly toward those who have the least power. Having been the "aliens in the land of Egypt," whom God heard, the Israelites must "not abuse any widow or orphan. If you do abuse them, when they cry out to me, I shall surely heed their cry" (Ex 22:21ff.).[37]

At the same time, the motif of hearing establishes a link between God's knowledge and God's action, in the context of the establishment of the covenants with Israel and thus of the relationship of mutual faithfulness and responsibility between God and God's people.[38] In our passage from Exodus, God hears and "remembers the covenant;" God's knowledge is placed within a narrative of God's promise and the move toward its fulfillment.[39] Being "remembered" has both a retrospective and a prospective reference; to associate God's knowledge with remembrance is to assert that being known by God carries with it the promise of future liberation or transformation.

This brings us to the close connection between hearing and *answering*, here and elsewhere. The "hearing" of the Israelites functions in the story and its renarrations as a sign of God's determination to act to save them. The psalmists know they have been heard when God acts.[40] In the case of human "hearing," the commitment to respond is regarded as integral to the act of hearing; "Hear, O Israel" calls Israel to make the response that hearing demands. The God who hears Israel, then, is the God who acts on Israel's behalf. The promise to hear Israel is an acceptance of "responsibility" – an undertaking to respond to the prayers and cries of this people.

---

[37] See Ochs, *Peirce,* pp. 304–5, on the links between Ex 2:23–5 and 22:21–3, 23:9.

[38] William Propp, *Exodus,* Anchor Bible Commentaries (New York: Doubleday, 1999), p. 179 notes that it is unclear from the passage "whether the Hebrews in fact cry out to God or just cry out." Calvin's "two ways in which God looks down upon men, for the purpose of helping them; either when they, as suppliants, implore his aid, or when he, even unasked, succours them in their affliction" (*Commentary on Genesis* v. 16:11, p. 433) describes Propp's alternatives clearly. In this instance the question is probably undecidable; universal "hearing" and hearing related to the covenant must both be considered.

[39] See also for the use of *yāda,* "know" to imply election, Gen 18:19; Ex 33:12, 17; Jer 1:5; Amos 3:2.

[40] Ps 86:1; 102:1–2.

A consideration of the motif of divine hearing, then, suggests that the concept of God's omniscience is impoverished if it is considered apart from God's covenant faithfulness, liberating action, hearing of prayer – apart, in other words, from God's acts of relating Godself to the world.[41] This forms the basis for a consideration of the implications of the claim that the resurrection is the event in which God hears Godself as the basis for God's hearing of all creatures.

Christological accounts of God's knowledge have been used in the debate over divine possibility and impassibility, where the incarnation becomes a means by which God comes to "know" pain, limitation, and suffering.[42] Even this use of Christology suggests the inclusion within God's knowledge of something more like "knowing by acquaintance," knowledge that implies participation, than "knowing about;" Christ is "acquainted with grief" by participating in it. One of the most important consequences of understanding the doctrine of God's omniscience Christologically is further to focus the suggestion, developed above, that God's knowledge of the world cannot be considered apart from God's entering into a relation with the world characterized by intimacy and risk – as, in the passages discussed above, God's compassionate "knowing" is determined by the covenantal relationship. God's act of knowing is inseparable from what I discussed earlier as the act of *Annahme* – "taking on" the limitations of created existence and "accepting" them.

Following the Christological pattern set out in my second chapter, this is the aspect of divine omniscience associated with the incarnation. It is, however, as we have already seen, inseparable from the act of judgment in which all is brought to light. The claim that God "hears" the cries of the victims of injustice, who by definition cannot be heard in the world that has silenced them, is focused in the claim that God hears the cry of Jesus from the cross and judges those who have condemned him to silence.

---

[41] Ochs, *Peirce*, p. 293 gives a summary of the relationship between knowing and healing put forward in Ochs' discussion of the Exodus texts: "A sign of real problems is a call for help, which is, first, a call for someone to *hear* that someone is suffering. It is, second, a call for someone to *examine* the content of the call and figure out what is really the matter. It is, third, a call for someone to *do* something to resolve the matter and alleviate the suffering." In other words, in practices of reading and listening shaped within communities that hear and are heard by God, the knowledge of suffering imposes a corresponding responsibility toward the one who is thus known.

[42] As in Sarot, *God, Possibility and Corporeality*. The basic idea that certain forms of what is ordinarily regarded as "knowledge" require a *finite* knower is, of course, also debated without reference to Christology. An interesting example – for its title if nothing else – is Henry Simoni, "Omniscience and the Problem of Radical Particularity: Does God Know How to Ride a Bike?," *International Journal for the Philosophy of Religion* 42, 1 (1997).

These two "moments" of God's knowledge-by-hearing are together, I have suggested, both intensified and transformed in the resurrection, as the event in which God acknowledges Jesus' work as the completion of God's own work. I have already suggested that one of the most important implications of this aspect of divine "knowledge" is that its completion (the fulfillment of God's "self-recognition") does not result in *stasis* but is itself creative. This becomes the ground for a divine "knowing" of the world that makes innerworldly responsibility and creativity possible.

One particularly important aspect of divine "hearing knowledge" that emerges here is its connection with divine patience. Omniscience conceptualized in terms of the possession of information, I noted earlier, is fundamentally atemporal – and hence apparently opposed to the "knowing" of persons as temporal beings, or to aspects of human "knowledge" that inherently take time. This separation of God's knowledge from time is mirrored in the separation of issues of "informational" privacy from those aspects of personal "knowledge" that are inseparable from the formation of persons over time. By contrast, omniscience thought in terms of divine hearing, as described here, makes the temporality of created existence not irrelevant but central to God's knowledge of creation – and grounds this in God's own acceptance and transformation of temporality.

Escaping the Panopticon: God and the control of knowledge

The preoccupation of privacy debates with the language of rights and of property, noted above, points to an associated set of assumptions about what it is to know or be known. "Personal information" is, as I have noted, treated as controllable and defensible property. More than this, the acquisition of information about another person is understood as the acquisition of control over her. Underlying the whole debate is the dystopic image of the Panopticon,[43] the environment in which every life is subject to the all-seeing gaze that remains itself unseen. The development of remote surveillance and data-gathering technologies reinforces the separation of informational "knowledge" from interpersonal relationships of any sort. The questions "*Who* hears? *Who* is heard?" become both

---

[43] Foucault's use of Bentham's design as an image of contemporary social control is well known (see Michel Foucault, *Discipline and Punish: The Birth of the Prison*, trans. Alan Sheridan (Harmondsworth: Penguin, 1979), pp. 195–228). On the importance of the Panopticon in modern privacy debates, see Lyon, *Electronic Eye*, pp. 201–11 and *passim*.

increasingly meaningless – within the framework that understands knowledge as information – and increasingly urgent, as the concern for privacy
in fact reveals.

Consider, for example, the growing importance of the "data image" –
the sum total of information about a given person held on files, an
"image" that both describes and prescribes in various ways that person's
social and economic position. The contemporary concern for privacy
reflects, it would seem, the need to recognize oneself and be recognized
as "more than" the data image, more than the kind of object that panoptic knowledge of this sort constructs.[44] Following this line of reflection,
we might put the question "Who is heard?," in the context of the privacy
debate, by asking whether the data image as such – whether jealously
guarded by the individual, bought and sold for marketing purposes, or
maintained by the organs of state power – is "who" its referent is.

To describe the problem thus, however, is to reveal the inadequacies of
the language of property and control – perhaps also of the language of
information – for resolving the deeper concerns raised by privacy debates.
Designating information about myself, or the "contents of my consciousness"[45] as my *property* reinforces the understanding of knowledge as
sovereign control. The privacy debate is reduced to a battle for territory between a monadic individual and an impersonal "society," the
boundaries of *my* space secured by an uneasy truce or by ever more
sophisticated fortifications. Defending informational privacy against the
contemporary technologies of the Panopticon reflects, on the one hand,
a genuine and justified resistance to the attempt to reduce persons to mute
objects. On the other hand, however, it may end up reinforcing the same
problematic logic of communication and knowledge that created the
panoptic gaze in the first place.[46]

As has often been observed, the Panopticon is a secular appropriation
of a particular model of divine omniscience – the God who sees all and
judges all while remaining unseen. Conversely, debates about the implications of divine omniscience for debates about privacy have reappropri-
ated the model of omniscience thus parodied in critiques of the

---

[44] On responses to the "data image," see Lyon, *Electronic Eye*, pp. 215–16; Church of
England Board of Social Responsibility, *Cybernauts Awake!*, pp. 73–4.

[45] Falls-Corbitt and McLain, "God and Privacy," p. 380.

[46] The feminist critiques of institutions of privacy, mentioned on p. 186, are important
here in indicating the "silencing" effects of certain *defenses* of privacy – such as the
concealment of domestic violence within the "private property" of the home – while at
the same time recognizing the *lack* of privacy experienced by some women as itself part of
their "silencing."

surveillance society.[47] A fuller theological response to the debates in question would require a reconsideration of possible ways of knowing and being known.

It might appear initially, from Bonhoeffer's essay on "telling the truth" that the main solution Christian theology can offer, on the lines he provides, is a divine sanction for the preservation of a particular set of "boundaries" that protect certain areas of life from being exposed to public vision. However, the concern shown in that essay for the concrete situa-tions and interpersonal relationships in which truth is spoken and heard – "Speech must be justified and occasioned by the other person" – and the close connection of this with the Christological understanding of truth and knowledge, suggests otherwise. To start from the premise that we are first known by God, and then and only as such given to each other to be known, is to shift the focus of discussion and to raise the possibility of asserting that the truth is best known and served by preserving privacy.

As I have already argued, however, the mere assertion of the impor-tance of privacy as such, without a critique of the role of particular insti-tutions and practices of privacy in unjust silencing, is insufficient. The "incarnational" account of privacy provided in the essay on "telling the truth," as it stands, requires supplementation by an account of how rela-tions of privacy are judged and transformed.

My discussion of God's omniscience as "hearing knowledge," above, suggested that knowledge must also be understood in terms of judgment. How might this be developed in the context of the question of privacy? If we begin our consideration of privacy from the figure on the cross, stripped naked and exposed to all eyes, we seem to see the loss of all privacy. Certainly all defensive privacy is destroyed; the crucifixion is the breaking down of all defensive boundaries and the consequent exposure of the violence that erects them. The truth is revealed, and judgment is passed, concerning whatever guilty secrets and false securities have been maintained with practices of concealment. The disunion of the world from God and the desperate attempt to overcome it are made public. The cru-cified Christ becomes an object seen but not heard, controllable and divis-ible, without past or future. In this respect he represents the world before God seen for what it is, without concealment, before the panoptic gaze. This is, it would seem, the point from which the theological critique of

---

[47]   See also Anne-Marie Hunter, "Numbering the Hairs of Our Heads: Male Social Control and the All-Seeing God," *Journal of Feminist Studies in Religion* 8, 2 (1992), for an analysis of the role of the "panoptic" God in women's religious psychology.

oppressive secrecy can begin – not merely of the systematic secrecy of totalitarianism, but of the unchallenged concealment of personal and social evils behind the veil of "private life."

How is the recognition of God's complete and truthful knowledge of the world to be negotiated with the need to preserve privacy in a dis-united world – or, in terms familiar from previous discussion, what does it mean for relations of privacy that the realities of the incarnation and crucifixion are both intensified and transformed in the resurrection? I shall develop the answer to this question through a return to several themes, indicated in previous chapters as central to an understanding of the ethical implications of the "hearing silence" of God.

Knowledge and responsibility

In contemporary privacy debates it is generally accepted as the "common-sense" view that privacy is violated in many circumstances in which infor-mation about a person is acquired without her consent, even if there is no intention of using the information for any further purpose, and even if the person in question suffers no inconvenience as a result.[48] One possible deduction from this is that we do, "naturally," regard information about ourselves as property, and unauthorized efforts to discover such information as the equivalent of theft. A theological discussion of privacy might, however, start at a slightly different point – with the understand-ing of truthfulness and knowledge implied or rejected by the act of "invad-ing privacy."

On this view, the "invasion" of privacy is wrong most fundamentally, not because it steals knowledge-property that belongs to somebody else, but because it treats the person as one who can be known about without the acceptance of a corresponding responsibility. It is the equivalent of the cynical desire, identified in the essay discussed above, to "speak the truth" without regard for the person to whom one speaks. It implies the sepa-ration of questions of truth and truthfulness, and of knowability, from questions of responsibility and of right relationship.

Bonhoeffer's articulation of the relationship between knowing, acting, and judging is useful in helping to draw out some of the implications of

---

[48] Such examples are often used in attempts to demonstrate that the question of privacy is irreducible to more general questions of social freedom. See Schoeman, *Privacy and Social Freedom*, p. 13.

the essay on telling the truth. An important section in the *Ethics* puts forward the contrast between the "Pharisee" and Christ,[49] as the contrast between disunited and united human reality – and, as intrinsic to this, as the contrast between the one who judges and the one for whom knowledge passes into action without the intervention of judgment. The Pharisee's knowledge – of others and of herself – is always oriented toward the "knowledge of good and evil," the passing of judgment on others and herself. "Judgement passed on another man always presupposes disunion with him; it is an obstacle to action."[50] To "presuppose disunion" is to refuse responsibility – because to be responsible in relation to another is to affirm that one can be required to stand or act in her place. Christ, by contrast, does not pass judgment save in the paradoxical "judgement by not judging, a judgement which is the act of reconciliation;"[51] and he accepts complete responsibility by acting and suffering "for" humanity. His knowledge of the human heart and the human condition is inseparable from his acceptance of responsibility (in the most radical sense – standing and acting entirely in the other's place) for that condition.

In terms of the relationship between action and judgment described here, we can see that the invasion of privacy and the act of cynical speech both arise from the desire to establish oneself as a knower of good and evil, and in doing so to refuse the possibility of responsible relationship. To seek knowledge irresponsibly, or to speak "the truth" without reference to the situation and to the person to whom one speaks, is wilfully to assert or re-assert one's capacity to know (primarily, to know good and evil) apart from the mediation of such knowledge in Christ. As discussed above with reference to spiritual care, the Christological mediation of communicative relationships – and the call to "hear with God's ears" – in the first instance places limitations on the possibility of "direct" knowledge of the other.

A rethinking of questions of privacy in terms of the questions "*Who* is heard?" and "*Who* hears?" would, then, recognize the limits of "information," its possession, transfer, and exchange, as the basis for an account either of the knowledge of persons or of how people know. The one "who is heard" is not known as the sum of information about her; and the one "who hears" does not simply acquire information. The model of "hearing knowledge" places us within a different knowledge economy. It asserts the inseparability of knowledge from responsibility and love, and

---

[49]   *DBW* 6, pp. 311–22, *Ethics*, pp. 151–61.
[50]   *Ethics*, pp. 154–5, *DBW* 6, p. 316.
[51]   *Ethics*, p. 157, *DBW* 6, p. 319.

from the formation of persons in the temporal processes of "being known" and "coming to know." A concern for the protection of privacy may, in this context, point toward communicative practices conformed to the reality of God's act of hearing, in the refusal to reduce others or to be oneself reduced to a fully comprehensible mute object.[52]

How would this approach to privacy debates relate to the theological dismissals of "privacy" discussed earlier? There are many situations in which it might be claimed that the fulfillment of a responsibility or the completeness of love demands that one person can and should expect to be able to "know all about" another. With regard to the former, we might consider the relationship of a carer or doctor to a person with a mental illness; with regard to the latter, the suggestion that friends or spouses should have no secrets from each other.[53]

To what extent can or should such claims, to the justifiable elimination of the boundaries of privacy within certain relationships, be sustained within a theological understanding of privacy? Two interconnected answers to this question have already been indicated in earlier chapters, and will be developed in what follows; they reflect, once again, the centrality of the questions "Who is heard?" and "Who hears?" for an understanding of personhood in the light of the resurrection. The first is that the mediation of all knowledge of the other through Christ precludes the adoption of a position of total responsibility (and the corresponding claim to total knowledge) as much as it precludes a position of definitive judg-

---

[52] One example of a consequence of this approach to questions of privacy might be seen in reflection on the concept of "the public sphere" and the characterization of persons as "public figures." Knowledge "in the public sphere," words spoken "in public," are understood as open to the appropriation and judgment of everyone in general and no one in particular. The speaker and hearer, in their functions as "public" speaker and hearer, have no relationship to each other besides that defined by these two functions. What we receive through "publicity" is presented primarily for our judgment; often, for our condemnation. The one who speaks or acts "in public" is, by implication, made fully and irretrievably responsible for all the subsequent understandings and misunderstandings of her words. It is not clear that the only adequate theological response is the condemnation of the indifferent "public sphere," its growth and influence, but it does seem clear that the theologian must resist the suggestion that any life can or should be lived entirely in the public gaze. See on this Oliver O'Donovan, "The Concept of Publicity," *Studies in Christian Ethics* 13, 1 (2000).

[53] In the paradigmatic cases of responsibility discussed in Bonhoeffer's essay on "telling the truth" – most notably, the parent's responsibility for the child – there is (what is supposedly) a clear imbalance in the levels of responsibility, which is reflected for Bonhoeffer in a corresponding reduction of the sphere of privacy of (in this example) the child in relation to the parent. "The life of the small child lies open before the parents and the child's word should reveal everything that is hidden and secret," where the converse is by no means true. *Ethics*, p. 326, *DBW* 16, p. 619.

ment. The second is that taking responsibility for the other is, on a Christological understanding, necessarily oriented toward the other's own free responsibility.

Privacy in the Penultimate

Keeping God's secrets

"There must be a point to it . . . that the inner life of another is by nature inaccessible to us, and that no one can see into our inner being. We must obviously be meant to keep it for ourselves and not share it with another."

After reflecting for a long time Ulrich had answered, "Except with God – or with a human being given to us by God, who can keep as silent as God does." (Bonhoeffer, *Fiction from Tegel Prison*[54])

Good people do not know why they are as they are, and they don't *want* to know. The ultimate secret of every human being is . . . God. We should allow the other to have that. (Bonhoeffer, *Fiction from Tegel Prison*[55])

The first of the above quotations from the fiction Bonhoeffer wrote in prison[56] was referred to in the discussion of spiritual care, above (chapter 4). Its immediate context is a discussion between two friends[57] about the advisability or otherwise of personal confession. Beyond this immediate context, however, it offers a useful starting point for wider reflection on the issue of privacy. It places the concern for privacy and reserve within the context of the "natural:" "inner life is by nature inaccessible . . . we must obviously be meant to keep it for ourselves." This recalls the "orders of preservation" around which Bonhoeffer's essay on speaking the truth, discussed above, is structured. Within this framework of thought, people are disunited, from one another and from themselves, because they are

---

[54]   *Fiction from Prison: Gathering up the Past*, eds. Renate and Eberhard Bethge with Clifford Green, trans. Ursula Hoffmann (Philadelphia: Fortress, 1981) , p. 92, *DBW* 7, p. 133. I have chosen this translation rather than *DBWE* 7, p. 128, because ". . . can be trusted to keep a secret like God" seems to lose shades of meaning from ". . . *so schweigen kann wie Gott.*"

[55]   *DBWE* 7, p. 49, *DBW* 7, p. 47.

[56]   The fiction is roughly contemporaneous with the essay on "telling the truth" – see the letter to Bethge of 18 November 1943 (*Letters and Papers*, p. 129), which discusses both the novel and the essay; and see also the editors' introduction to *Fragmente aus Tegel*, *DBW* 7, pp. 7–13.

[57]   Christoph, the character generally thought to reflect Bonhoeffer's own character and views most closely, and Ulrich.

estranged from God; privacy is part of what preserves them in and despite our fragmentation, and for this reason if for no other it is to be respected and guarded. The response that follows does not contradict this claim, but rather deepens and extends its implications.

The inner life that is "by nature inaccessible" is, according to Ulrich's response, to be shared "with God, or with another human being given to us by God, who knows how to keep silent as God does." Notice, again, that in this response the reality of privacy is affirmed. It may not be the case that there is that of ourselves which we are not to share "with anyone," but nor is it the case that everything can be shared "with everyone." Here, however, the silence of the other is interpreted as a gift of God – a gift that, without annulling the "natural" ordering that establishes the inner life as private, redetermines it as ordered toward the "ultimate" reality given in Christ. The privacy of the inwardness that is naturally one's own is redefined in terms of the relationship of "being heard" – heard by the God who keeps silent and by the other who "keeps silent as God does."

The context of the second quotation, from the second scene of the Tegel drama fragment, is a conversation between the best friend (Ulrich) and the girlfriend (Renate) of the central character (Christoph) about the latter's sudden air of secrecy and withdrawal. Ulrich argues passionately that friendship should result in complete openness; Renate responds with the equally passionate claim that secrecy can be an essential part of friendship. It is she who concludes the discussion with the suggestion that "the ultimate secret of every human being is God" – one of very few explicit references to God, in a work marked for the most part by the deliberate adoption of a "secular" terminology and subject matter.

What is being said about privacy here? On the face of it, the quotation implies that knowledge is being treated as a possession; we let the human being "have" his secret and do not attempt to steal it, bring it into the public realm, or otherwise deprive him of it. The claim Renate is making, however, is that the person does not *himself* fully know or recognize the "ultimate secret" that makes him what he is. The ultimate secret that we "allow the other to have" is *God* – not, let it be noted, "his religion" or his particular idea of his relation to God,[58] but God as Godself. This is the one secret that cannot possibly be thought of as a

---

[58] Which might commonly be regarded as a peculiarly "private matter," the knowledge of which could not rightly be demanded by anyone else. (Why else was the question about religion, included for the first time on the census in Britain in 2001, the only optional question?)

"possession" within the control of the one whose secret it is – and yet it is said here to be *his* secret, his most important secret. This passage, then, appears to provide the basis for an understanding of privacy that begins from a divinely given, unthematizable, "ultimate" reality of personal existence.

Renate is not speaking, in this passage, about the boundaries of speech demanded by the social order; on the contrary, she is discussing friendship, and the questions of "publicity" and the public realm do not appear.[59] Significantly, in the conversation with Ulrich she defines the limitations of speech not in terms of space – the "spheres" of existence that must be kept separate from each other by the maintenance of reserve – but in terms of time.[60] Privacy and reserve within friendship are connected with patience, with waiting for the other, and of being present without enforcing speech or demanding a premature clarity.[61]

To consider the "ultimate secret" in these terms, and to treat it as the basis for the protection of privacy, is, then, to call into question the set of assumptions about human "autonomy" on which many other discussions of privacy are based. Clearly, it re-emphasizes the claim that comprehensive knowledge of the other, whether in order to execute judgment or in order to take complete responsibility for him or her, is not a possibility. At the same time, the "ultimate secret" is not some ultimately detached core of individuality. Simply to keep my inner life "to myself" can, the previous chapter suggested, bring about either the abrogation of responsibility or an inescapable subjection to the terrors of a guilty conscience.

It is the latter experience of the divided self that was explored above in the discussion of the "Pharisee" – whose failure, let it be noted, lies not in the conflict between public righteousness and private wickedness but in the private conflict of self-judgment, which has its repercussions in

---

[59]   In the light of the previous chapter's discussion of friendship it should be noted that the Tegel fiction explicitly considers at several points the possibility of friendship across class and other social boundaries. The drama fragment has the tense encounter between Christoph and the proletarian Heinrich (*DBWE* 7, pp. 62–71); the novel has several instances, from the earnest conversation between "Brüderchen" and his playmate about their families' lifestyles (pp. 95–6) to Major von Bremer's account of the beginning of his friendship with Hans Brake (pp. 150–66).

[60]   "Words have their proper time . . . There are things that sometimes one must keep silent about for a while before one can talk about them, even between friends, even between husband and wife" (*DBWE* 7, p. 48, *DBW* 7, p. 46).

[61]   "Both of us simply have to be present for him . . . [people] sometimes have to give each other a long time, until the right word has grown and ripened . . . We must have a lot of patience with one another" (*DBWE* 7, pp. 47–8, *DBW* 7, pp. 46–7).

his public behavior. That which ultimately frees a person from the judging knowledge of others – the presence of an ultimate secret that he is permitted to keep – is also that which frees him from his own judgment; he cannot know his own ultimate secret. What is innermost is not only "my own;" or rather, it is "my own" precisely in that it is given to me.[62]

Rather than being the sphere of self-reflection – "what you keep to yourself" – the private as the "ultimate secret" is at once the sphere of complete other-centeredness and of free responsibility. "Being known by God" interrupts and challenges my dialog with myself – that dialog by which I possess my private thoughts – as much as it interrupts and challenges those dialogs by which others know me. God as the "ultimate secret" never appears as one who could form the basis for my judgment of myself; the ultimate secret never becomes a possession.

What are the implications of this for attitudes to the privacy of others? How do we allow the "ultimate secret of every human being" to be kept? We have already seen that this "ultimate secret" is neither ours to take or leave alone nor the other's to keep. The "ultimate secret" implies, as suggested above, both a negative and a positive imperative concerning the protection of privacy. On the one hand, it prohibits the claim to possess full knowledge of the other. This in itself sharpens the theological critique of a society in which the gathering, storage, and circulation of "personal information" is a growing industry. Every claim to knowledge *about* a person is confronted by the claim that before all such knowledge she is known by God in Christ. This prevents, equally, the passing of definitive judgment, and the claim to be the fully responsible healer or educator who as such is entitled to complete knowledge of the other. Whatever responsibility I have is always mediated responsibility.

On the other hand, and positively, it suggests that the simple identification and isolation of an area of private space is in itself no answer; a right understanding of privacy in theological ethics requires a discussion of the relationships within which privacy is formed, preserved, and developed. I receive myself from another, from God; to let me "keep" this ultimate secret is to permit me again to receive who I am. The relations of

---

[62] Falls-Corbitt and McLain, "God and Privacy," make the suggestion, which they admit runs counter to many theological insights, that God respects a "right to privacy" – that is, that God does not know our thoughts unless they are consciously brought before God. The objections to God's "unqualified" omniscience put forward by these authors assume a close association between listening and judgment. The all-knowing God they present is familiar as the God of the Panopticon; and they substitute, for this, life *etsi deus non daretur*. The challenge our discussion puts to their analysis must be: does being left unqualifiedly alone with the "contents of my consciousness" (their phrase) necessarily liberate me?

privacy are reconstituted, within Christian ethics, as the relations through which this occurs.[63]

Can all of this result in a positive theological significance for privacy – as against its common interpretation as a correlate of negative freedom? Clearly the negative significance of privacy – the need to acknowledge that a person cannot be reduced to a data image, and that comprehensive knowledge of the other is not a given possibility – retains its importance. It should be possible, however, again following the pattern of earlier chapters, to identify the positive significance of the "ultimate secret," the foundation of privacy in the relation of the person to God as the one who hears. Such a positive interpretation of privacy opens up further possibilities for dialog with contemporary writers on the subject.

Privacy and the new

One of the features of divine omniscience as "hearing knowledge" discussed in the first section, to which further reference has not yet been made, is its relation to the possibility of novelty. As noted above, the reference in the Tegel drama fragment to the "ultimate secret" of every human being follows a discussion of the importance of patience – as the relation to the other that awaits the right time for speech, that does not force immediate self-disclosure. The connection between privacy and the possibility of creativity or novelty is here, in the drama fragment, expressed initially in purely secular terms as a general fact of human experience, but is given its full significance by the subsequent claim that the "ultimate secret" is God. This suggests a basis for further development of a theological response to contemporary questions of privacy.

Recent philosophical discussions have often given privacy an orientation toward the future by drawing a close connection between privacy and creativity or the new.[64] Privacy is linked with the formation of inti-

---

[63]   I have already referred to the famous "Finkenwalde rule," prohibiting members from discussing a fellow student in his absence; it was imposed to enable the members of the community to stop watching or passing judgment on each other, and thus "*den Bruder ganz frei stehen lassen, so wie Gott ihn ihm gegenübergestellt hat.*" It should be noted, also, that the protection of "privacy" begins here with a prohibition on irresponsible speech. Its accuracy or inaccuracy is irrelevant; the criterion is its capacity, or lack thereof, to express the relation to each other in which the members of the community are placed before God.

[64]   Schoeman, *Privacy and Social Freedom*; Edward J. Bloustein, "Privacy as an Aspect of Human Dignity: An Answer to Dean Prosser," in Schoeman, ed., *Philosophical Dimensions of Privacy*.

mate relationships, the consideration of possibilities before action is taken, and the development of character or of world view. Schoeman, in his historical analysis of privacy, suggests that it has generally had a dual function – the concealment of activities that are seen as *inherently* private, and the provision of opportunities for creativity and innovation. There is widespread agreement, explicit or implicit, with Bloustein: "without relief from public scrutiny our opinions, being public, tend never to be different."[65]

The protection of privacy is, if this aspect is taken seriously, a form of "forgiveness in advance," and has a function similar to that of forgiveness. It permits the emergence of the new, severing a chain of identifiable causes and inevitable consequences. To preserve privacy is to liberate a person from the "tyranny of actuality" – the way in which an act or word that enters the public sphere becomes both ineradicable and uncontrollable.[66]

If the deprivation of privacy may be compared, as discussed above, to the attempt to reduce a person to a fully comprehensible mute object, the preservation of privacy recognizes and secures the person's freedom for future speech or action. Putting it in these terms, however, reminds us that the privacy that secures the possibility of creativity cannot be understood simply as the protection of already-existing information. Nor can privacy as a condition for creativity be understood apart from the relationships within which privacy is enacted.

Such an understanding of privacy's importance brings it very close to my earlier discussion of the nature of "hearing knowledge" – and suggests that God's omniscience, understood as "hearing knowledge," can be seen to underlie (by no means to "violate") relationships of privacy. God's act of hearing can be understood as the granting of time for innerworldly creativity, change, and growth – which is possible not only on the basis of the world's immanent resources, but out of the future granted to it by God.

If it is the case that people can change, and go on changing, in ways that are significant for and determined by their relation to God, such that their changed lives can be called the lives of free and responsible persons, it must also be the case that there is something in the divine economy that corresponds to privacy. God gives forgiveness in advance – not only liberating from the tyranny of past actuality, but creating a space wherein a different set of future possibilities can arise. To exercise the patience that maintains

---

[65] Bloustein, "Privacy as an Aspect of Human Dignity," p. 188.

[66] The terminology is Arendt's, used in the context of a discussion of forgiveness as that which provides a remedy for the irreversibility of action (Hannah Arendt, *The Human Condition*, 2nd edn. (Chicago: University of Chicago Press, 1998), p. 236).

privacy is to reflect God's patience, in knowing the world through being present to it in a way that grants it time. It is also to acknowledge that the future granted to the other – the possibilities of creativity or change – can exceed any set of expectations I might place upon it.

Recognizing the "ultimate secret" as the basis of privacy, then, involves recognizing that both the silences that keep us from the public eye, and the hearing silences that reshape privacy by mediating the presence of God to the other, are oriented toward the promise of transformation. This both intensifies our responsibility to maintain them and relativizes our responsibility for their ultimate consequences.

Privacy and glory

To say that privacy has a place within the divine economy of salvation, however, raises the question of its possible ultimate significance – its significance for the *telos* of persons in relation to God. In the first section of this chapter, I suggested that one possible reason for a theological reluctance to debate the limits and significance of privacy might be claims concerning eschatological participation in the community "without reserve" that is the life of the Trinity. My final suggestion is that, on the contrary, the mystery of the immanent Trinity may be a focus for theological reflection on privacy.[67]

Is it possible that privacy is, in the last analysis, about glory? The suggestion is initially surprising. What is more public or less reserved than glory? Glory, as the antithesis of shame, is commonly understood as an attribute of a public persona or action, pertaining to its appearance and recognition. At the same time, it should be recalled that "glory" in the Bible is almost invariably used with a possessive – your glory, his glory, the glory of the Lord. The glory I have is inseparable from its being mine.[68] Glory is "had" as well as "given" or "taken."

The theological assertion from which any discussion of God's glory, in this "intrinsic" sense, must start is that God is Trinity, in God's self, from

---

[67] Bonhoeffer's sermon for Trinity Sunday (*DBW* 13, pp. 359–63) discusses the mystery of the Trinity in terms of a mystery that is the opposite of "not knowing" – "the better we know something, the more mysterious it becomes to us" (p. 360). I am not, in this section, rejecting the approach of "social trinitarianism" per se or without exception, although I *would* suggest that visions of innerdivine community can be used to mask some of the genuine concerns raised in debates over privacy.

[68] David F. Ford and Frances Young, *Meaning and Truth in 2 Corinthians* (London: SPCK, 1987), p. 239 and *passim*.

eternity, and that this eternal being of God as Trinity is what determines the trinitarian form of God's work in creation. From eternity God is, God loves, God has life, God relates Godself to Godself. Several interconnected defenses of the importance of the doctrine of the immanent Trinity are of relevance for a theological understanding of privacy. Without the assertion that God is triune from eternity, we are forced to assert that God needs the world in order to be God; God's freedom and prevenience are in question; God is perhaps only the sum of the "data" that can be gathered concerning God.

At the same time, if the immanent Trinity is denied, God's truth and trustworthiness are in question: to say that God is triune in Godself is to say that, in God's communication of Godself to the world, what is communicated is truly God. And this is to say, further, that God's being is such that it makes itself known. The mystery of the immanent Trinity is to be distinguished from the terrifying mystery of the *deus absconditus*. God does not in this sense have a "private sphere" of inner-divine information defended from the world; but God is nonetheless glorious in God's triune being "before the world was."[69]

What does it mean to be conformed to the image of the God who is thus glorious? It can mean, I suggest, that we also have our immanent glory as a gift of God; which in turn means that we have our glory before, apart from, perhaps despite, whatever relations we enter in the world. But it is also precisely for this reason that the privacy of others is to be respected. It is God who ultimately sees and hears, and who thus determines shame and glory. More than this, the person in whom the image of God is recreated is given her own glory.

This chapter, in the context of reflection on contemporary questions about "responsible silence," has suggested further implications of the claim that "God hears" by considering the concept of God's knowledge that this claim implies. Developed on the basis of the biblical motif of divine hearing and of the interpretation of the resurrection put forward earlier, the concept of "hearing knowledge" includes compassionate attention to the particular, judgment and the exposure of injustice, and salvific action. I have contrasted "hearing knowledge" with the understanding of knowledge (or "information") as property, implied in contemporary privacy debates and elsewhere.

The application of this different understanding of knowledge to ethical questions of privacy can be developed within the structure of preservation, judgment, and transformation – or incarnation, crucifixion, and res-

---

[69] Jn 17:5.

urrection – that shapes Bonhoeffer's ethics. His own extended discussion of privacy demonstrates that a Christological and social understanding of knowledge and truth-telling may mean that truthfulness demands the maintenance of privacy and reserve. However, as it stands, this discussion has little to say about the disruption or transformation of existing relations of privacy. The former calls for reflection on the connection between divine omniscience and judgment; the crucifixion is read as the unveiling of, and judgment on, institutions of privacy that lead to silencing. The latter calls for further reflection, in the context of the privacy debate, on the resurrection as determinative of God's act of hearing – and of the asking and answering of the questions "Who hears? Who is heard?"

Four points about the place of privacy within my broader discussion of the Christological reconfiguration of communication emerged from the subsequent consideration of Morton's questions as they relate to issues of privacy. Firstly, knowledge of one another, in the context of a Christian ethics, is inseparable from responsibility for one another, and that in turn must be understood from our "being known" by God in Christ. This places limitations on knowledge and responsibility, but at the same time it enables God's "hearing knowledge" of persons to be mediated by them to one another. This leads to the second point, which is that privacy is never solitary and non-dialogical; the transformation of privacy involves being freed from the self-judging or self-justifying dialog with oneself. The third point is that a theological understanding of privacy reinforces and deepens the assertion that privacy allows creativity and change, by setting it in the context of eschatology. Finally, I suggested that an analogy can properly be drawn between the importance of privacy for Christian ethics and the theological importance of the doctrine of the immanent Trinity.

If the "assigned purpose" and the criterion for truthfulness for both our words and our silence, and thus for the social and institutional relations within which they are located, is to "correspond to the real as it exists in God," to preserve and respect privacy is not necessarily to fail in truthfulness. It can be both to attest truly the division and godlessness of the world and to participate in its becoming truthful, before and with the God who is both ultimate truth and ultimate mystery.

Chapter Eight

OPENINGS

On the "More than Speakable"

How much can be said of silence – of any silence, or of anyone's silence? Throughout my discussion, I have been attempting to allow silences to appear, as "presences" with "history" and "form," without being passed over as absences. I have been considering silences that cannot be equated with acts of speaking but are not on that account to be regarded as either empty or non-specific. Silences within theological texts, the silences kept by listeners, the silences of those who are not or cannot be "heard to speech," silences that maintain privacy or reserve – all call for responses that acknowledge them, not as *un*speakable in the sense of lying "beyond the limits" of thought or speech, but as *more than speakable*.

Bonhoeffer "heard" his world as a world for which God was not necessary, but also as a world in which God was not speakable. He perceived not only the hubris that silences all voices beyond the limits of its single narrative, but also the battle of competing voices, within which the hearing of the word of God is impossible. Reading within and beyond his theology, here, I have sought ways to think about a God who is "more than necessary" – as Jüngel understands it[1] – but who is also *more than speakable*: whose relation to the world, grounded in God's own reality, does not depend on the exercise of the power of speech. It is not only the case that God is not confined by the existing categories of the thinkable, which

---

[1] See Jüngel, *God as the Mystery of the World: On the Foundation of the Theology of the Crucified One in the Dispute between Theism and Atheism*, trans. Darrell L. Guder (Grand Rapids: Eerdmans, 1983), p. 24. The account of God as "more than necessary" is linked, in Jüngel's work, to an account of God as "speakable" (p. 226), but also, as I have already indicated, to categories that reduce only with some conceptual strain to "speakability" or the speech event – God's self-identification as love, God's patience.

decide God's "necessity" or non-necessity. It is also the case that God is not confined by, but rather transforms, the existing categories of communicative action.

To say that God is "more than speakable" is not to deny the positive claims made when God is referred to as a speaker; it is not to return God to the "whereof we cannot speak." Calling God a speaker asserts a relation between God and world that transforms the world, a relation that is approached through the question "Who is God?" answered with reference to the person of Christ. It is precisely such a relation that my analyzes of God's silence have attempted to indicate. Saying that God is *more* than speakable, indeed, calls for the question "Who is God?" to be asked and answered in relation to God's communicative action and to the patterns of speaking and hearing that it produces.

The focus from which I have developed all my accounts of silences − both the silence of God and innerworldly silences − as "more than speakable" is the silence of the resurrection. The resurrection, as the intensification of the Christological incognito, specifies God's unknowability as the unknowability of a living person − and hence as "more than speakable." Bonhoeffer's description of the resurrection as the answer to δος μοι που στω further identifies it as intrinsically incomprehensible or mysterious, while not reducing it either to something unspecified or to a speech-act indefinitely withheld.

The terms I have used in discussing the resurrection as reality for and of God indicate its character as "more than speakable" − self-identification as love; glory as pertaining intrinsically to who God is; the act of hearing that both acknowledges God's own Word and opens up that acknowledgment to others. Likewise, the terms I have used of God's relation to the world suggest the "more than speakable" − patience, and the hearing of the world that comprises affirmation, condemnation, and transformation. In exploring the "realization" of the resurrection in lived existence, I have pointed to aspects of human life and communication in which the "more than speakable" is apparent − listening, wisdom and the capacity for discernment, friendship.

The account of the theological ethics of communication, set out here, considers how the "more than speakable" reality of the resurrection is conformed to in practices of communication − practices that are themselves "more than speakable" and that allow the "more than speakable" to be heard as such. My account has emphasized the importance of the resurrection as *common* place to stand, not according sovereignty to any particular act of speaking, but sustaining, judging, and transforming the innerworldly common places to stand that make communication possible.

In close connection with this, I have suggested that the formation of the hearing mind – or the learning of wisdom – must be considered as integral to an ethic of communication. "Hearing with God's ears" is not merely a preliminary to "speaking God's words," but an equally significant aspect of communicative action conformed to God's self-communication. Practices of responsible silence – such as the silence of a listener – can be signs for others of the silence of God as "more than speakable;" but they must also be understood as themselves open to transformations not anticipated in advance.

What, from all this, can be said about the ethics of communication in the early twenty-first century? It seems that our age has moved beyond the recognition that words can be regarded, metaphorically, as "weapons," toward a global and multilateral war of words – a war that, for all its apparent detachment from bodies and the violence done to them, has real and (very much) embodied casualties.[2] To ask about keeping God's silence, in this time, is to ask about communicative non-violence that, like the non-violence learned and practiced by Christians among others for centuries, will not produce a passive acceptance of the consequences of violence. "Benumbment," acquiescence in one's own silencing, and joining the war of words are all equally ways of answering evil with evil; and they are all, I would argue on the basis of this discussion, denials of the basic character of God's communication. What is called for, it seems, is the kind of non-violence that interrupts the cycle of violence and simultaneously enacts an alternative possibility – the communicative equivalent, perhaps, of turning the other cheek.[3]

My discussion of practices of silence in the sixth chapter might suggest that I am putting forward certain rather marginal "ecclesial" practices as normative for this kind of communicative non-violence. The point about these practices, however, is that they function by being self-subverting and self-relativizing, by doubly referring beyond themselves – to the world that interrupts or places demands on them (consider the spiritual carer's confrontation with the "cultured despiser") and to God as their "more than speakable" source and end. As Fiumara's work suggests – one can, and should, learn about "listening techniques," and about specific ways of resisting the war of words, outside church-communities; one can and

---

[2] Whether they are the workers caught up in and concealed by global "brand wars" or the rather better publicized suicidal casualties of "media battles."

[3] See the (now well-known) discussion of Matt 5:38ff., in Walter Wink, *Engaging the Powers: Discernment and Resistance in a World of Domination* (Minneapolis: Fortress, 1992), pp. 175–84. The point is that to turn the other cheek having been hit on the *right* cheek is the refusal of a back-handed blow and hence of the other's claim to superiority.

should, indeed, use them critically with regard to a church-community's own attempts to assert and maintain its "own message" or its "brand identity" on the communicative battleground.

It is, to put it simply, a matter of increasing urgency that Christians and church-communities should start thinking about how they can listen best, and follow disciplines that form them and others as listeners. It is clearly, to put it more simply still, a matter of enormous urgency that as many people as possible should stop allowing themselves to be made fools of, and should stop regarding it as a valid aim to make fools of others; and it is not clear that theologians, church-communities, or individuals have often acknowledged how they can help or hinder this change, or how pervasive its significance could be.

Again in Fiumara's work, there are salutary reminders of the links between the failure of listening – the halving of the *logos* – and the failure to recognize and act on local and global ecological crises. To focus on conveying the single message of an authoritative voice – or to permit others to do the same – is to prevent oneself from hearing, not just the plurality of competing voices, but their coexistence in a common space. To call, as a theologian, for a return to listening in this situation is not to presume the reduction of the contradictions and oppositions within nature and human society to some universal harmony – which would itself amount to the imposition of a single voice.[4] It is, however, to call for the individual and collective education of persons into responsible ways of knowing and acting that reflect God's hearing of the whole of creation. Feminist theology's emphasis on *connection* as a neglected theological and ethical concern is not – as the words and actions of its proponents make clear – about the retreat into a warm fuzzy world of (quintessentially "feminine") relationality. It is about learning to perceive intractable complexity and to resist (by speech in a different mode, but also by silent action) the lie that denies that complexity.

In such a time, when understandings and practices of communication pose so many social and ethical challenges, it may seem unduly parochial to turn at this point to the question of theology's *own* ethics of communication – to ask what it means for talk about God to recognize and conform to the reality of God as "more than speakable." I have shown in earlier chapters that the ways in which "God-talk" is communicated can themselves be part of the wider social problem. This might itself be

---

[4] Just as to advocate non-violence from a Christian perspective, contrary to the perceptions of some, is not to claim that the total cessation of violence is either imminent or forseeable.

sufficient reason for examining them here; but more important is the recognition that a "theory into practice" model of theological ethics is itself fraught with ethical and theological difficulties. The theologian who claims the right to tell everyone else how to behave, without hearing her own words in relation to her own situation, is already complicit in a "*logos* that does speak and hardly listens."

Beyond this, again, the institutions within which theology is produced – the academic institutions of various kinds – are themselves locations where many of the problems raised here come to a head. Here a range of standpoints and voices are brought into conflict. Here, as the nature and purpose of education is debated, the question of how people can learn wisdom rather than folly is crucial. Here the relationship between the "who" of an author or speaker and those "who hear" is variously enacted and understood. In the last section of this chapter, then, I consider some implications of this discussion for theology's own ethics of communication, not in order to foreclose the wider debate but in order to place it within a particular context.

Opening Theology

At the end of chapter 4, I discussed the Markan and the Johannine accounts of the resurrection "appearances" – both of which, in different ways, allow the reality of the resurrection to appear as "more than speakable." The consideration of theology's own ethics of communication has often taken as a starting point another testimony to the resurrection – the Lukan account of the encounter on the road to Emmaus, and its consequences. The resurrection in Luke's account is clearly not "unspeakable"[5] – but nor is its reality exhausted in the ways in which it becomes "speakable."

> . . . two of them were going to a village called Emmaus . . . and talking with each other about all these things that had happened. While they were talking and discussing, Jesus himself came near and went with them, but their eyes were kept from recognizing him. (Lk 24:13–16).

Here, a communicative situation that has reached an impasse – despite some appearance of progress, and despite there still being a great deal to

---

[5] A possible attempt to avoid speaking about it directly (24:18: "'Are you the only stranger in Jerusalem who does not know the things that have taken place?'") is met with a direct challenge (24:19: "'What things?'").

say – is transformed by the hidden and living presence of the one who is its subject matter. Jesus first appears in the conversation as a listener – to an account of "the things that have taken place" (24:19–24). The account is, it would seem, accurate as information, but reveals, as Jesus' response shows, a failure to hear with God's ears – a narrowness of perception and attention condemned as "foolish" (24:25). The interpretation of scripture that follows (24:26: "he interpreted to them the things about himself in all the scriptures") teaches a different hearing of both the scripture and the given facts. This new hearing becomes possible as the "reality" of the resurrection begins to "realize" itself through the presence of Christ in this process of communication.

I suggest that listening to this account, in turn, can deepen understanding of what it means to do theology in the presence of the God who is "more than speakable" – and whose act of hearing, as in the conversation on the road to Emmaus, both disrupts and transforms attempts to talk about God. At an early stage in my discussion, I raised the question of whether treating the resurrection as central produced a closure in theology – a triumphalism that denied suffering or a reassertion of the sovereignty of divine speech that silenced many human voices. Throughout the Lukan account, the transformation brought about by the presence and action of the risen Christ is described in terms of *opening* – the opening of eyes,[6] the opening of the scriptures,[7] the opening of minds.[8] The theme of fulfillment – "Everything written about me in the law of Moses, the prophets, and the psalms must be fulfilled" (24:44) does not exclude, but rather brings about, the "opening." God's fulfillment of God's own Word – and the perfect hearing, displayed in Jesus' acts of interpreting – is the source of the "power from on high"[9] that begins a transformative movement within the world.

The ideas of opened eyes (and ears), the opened text, and the opened mind help us to identify aspects of the practice of theology that point, like the practices of silence discussed earlier, toward a communicative situation beyond folly and the "war of words." It is important in this that the opening of eyes, of minds, and of the scriptures occurs through and in relation to the living presence of Christ. This specific relation, because it is a relation to a living presence, does not make a practice or situation

---

[6] 24:31: "Their eyes were opened, and they recognized him."
[7] 24:32: "They said to each other, 'Were not our hearts burning within us . . . while he was opening the scriptures to us?'"
[8] 24:45: "Then he opened their minds to understand the scriptures."
[9] 24:49.

any less "open" to transformations not anticipated in advance. Being "opened" in this sense means becoming part of the continuing realization of a given but hidden reality – the risen Christ whose identity and continuing activity is clearly recognized, but who withdraws from sight and from comprehension.[10] Speaking of "opened eyes and ears" points toward an extension of perception – and of the capacity for discernment and recognition that I have discussed elsewhere as "hearing with God's ears." I have discussed "hearing with God's ears" in terms of the three Christological moments of incarnation, crucifixion, and resurrection – moments to which repeated reference is made in this Lukan passage.[11]

"Hearing with God's ears" in theology or elsewhere, in terms of the pattern I have outlined, means, firstly, learning the patient and compassionate attention to the complexities of a particular situation that corresponds to the action of God in taking on the fallen creation. Secondly, it means learning to "do justice" – in the recognition that the compassionate hearing of those who have been unjustly silenced itself already implies an act of judgment. I would argue, in relation to both of these points, that theological speech that *silences those whom God hears* fails to correspond to God, as much as does theological speech that indirectly or directly *silences God*. Calling attention to past and continuing acts of violent silencing, finding ways of hearing the silenced, and repenting of the silencing performed by one's own speech need not be a secondary or subsequent concern of theology.

Thirdly, and most significantly, however, "hearing with God's ears" means hearing in a way that opens up the possibility of creativity neither spurious nor false. If the injunction to "hear with God's ears" becomes the basis for a theological program, it becomes important to recall the ground of this practice of listening in God's act of listening. I have shown, in my fourth and fifth chapters with reference to Bonhoeffer's thought, how the resurrection as reality *of and for God* opens practices of silence to transformations that cannot be anticipated in advance – transformations both of the persons involved and of the relationships between them. The spiritual carer's practice of silence is taken beyond the overcoming of limited problems within a fixed set of social and ecclesial relationships, toward changed ethical discernment and friendship as its "ultimate possibility and grace." In the same way, the theological practice that begins with the attempt to "hear [the silenced] into speech" may find its own goals, techniques, and interpretations of silence redefined. In the Lukan

[10]   24:31: upon recognition, "he vanished from their sight."
[11]   24:19–24, 44, 46.

account, when the capacity for recognition is extended, it is the risen
Christ who is recognized.

Thinking about the relationship between theology and feminist theory, as
discussed in several chapters of this book, it is apparent that feminist theologians have contributed toward a relearning of listening within theology in all
three of these aspects. Methodologically and in terms of content, feminist
theology has sought to draw attention to, and hold attention on, a wide
range of concerns formerly neglected, and to challenge the patterns of
communication that have resulted in that neglect. Furthermore, the feminist
theological enterprise has reached beyond the critical or anti-idolatrous
move to put forward a new theological vision, albeit one that is self-
consciously partial and provisional. The challenge to feminist theology that
arises from my account of God's silence is to maintain and think through,
alongside its commitment to recognize the embodied location of speech and
to speak and listen responsibly, a commitment to the reality of God's act of
speaking and hearing as the ultimate context for all these acts of speaking
and listening. This should not mean a narrowing of focus or a refusal of
any ongoing conversations – quite the reverse. It should, however, guard
feminist theology against reducing theological discourse to a battle of
competing "discursive strategies," and against any temptation to absolutize
its own standpoint. The goals, techniques, and interpretations of feminist
theology are themselves open to redefinition and transformation when
placed within this context.

One particular form of hearing central to theological work is also
central to the Lukan passage discussed above – the "hearing" of texts, and
in particular of biblical texts. What would be the implications of naming
God as the hearer of the Bible as it is read, heard, and interpreted? Firstly,
I suggest, it draws attention to God's continuing activity in relation to the
text, which forms the basis neither for arbitrary reinterpretation nor for
the possession of its definitive meaning by any one group of hearers. The
text is "opened" – not simply "open" to be appropriated without reference to the living presence of the one who opens it, hears it, and is heard
in it, but not "closed" so that any particular reading is the utterance of a
divine "last word." The *silences* of and in biblical texts – like the silences
around the resurrection appearances, discussed earlier – can themselves be
understood as indications of this "openedness."

A further implication, for practices of biblical interpretation, of understanding the scriptures as *heard* by God, is that a hearing of the world
informs a hearing of the text. God's act of hearing encompasses what is
not explicitly said or named here, and to hear these silences is also to
"hear with God's ears." The "minds opened to understand" in the Lukan
passage can understand scripture in relation to what they have seen and

heard; and the presence of the risen Christ mediates this understanding. Perhaps, then, the "opened mind" in interpretation is attentive to the complexities of a lived situation as well as to the details of a text. The text itself is only heard rightly when it makes possible a fuller hearing of the reality to which it points – which in turn implies a fuller hearing of the world within which its hearers are placed.

Feminist commentary, in identifying particular "silences" in the Bible, calls for responsible rereadings that challenge previous assumptions about the significance of speech and silence. Morton's questions, which have determined much of the course of my enquiry 'Who hears? Who is heard?" are challenges no less for biblical interpretation than for other fields of discourse – and the same problems, of how to avoid a reimposition of authoritative speech or a cacophony of competing voices, arise with them.

Asking who is heard in the Bible, feminist – and non-feminist – scholars find in the biblical texts all the subtly different forms of the dumb and garrulous silencing of women, discussed in my first chapter. We can trace in these texts the failure to acknowledge the actions, speech, or even the existence of women in a given context; the assimilation of both sexes to a projected male norm; and the definition of women as "mute objects" of description and analysis, which reflects their status as objects of ownership and victims of all forms of violence. The exercise of reading the "silences of scripture" acquires in this situation a particular ethical significance.

Asking who hears the Bible, feminist commentary brings to light the problem, not only of the absence of women's voices within the Bible, but of the absence of women among the implied addressees or hearers. For at least some of these texts, it is claimed, the obvious response to Morton's questions is that *God* is heard and *men* hear – and that women subsequently become hearers of the men's words about God.[12] Is it in fact the case that scripture only admits women as hidden listeners, inside the

---

[12] One of the most important and extended readings that takes up the question of the male addressees of scripture (from a Jewish perspective) is Judith Plaskow, *Standing again at Sinai: Judaism from a Feminist Perspective* (San Francisco: Harper Collins, 1990), esp. pp. 25–74. On the problems of feminist *reading* – especially the "reading as a woman" of texts of which the implied reader is male – see Patrocinio P. Schweickart, "Reading Ourselves: Toward a Feminist Theory of Reading," in *Speaking of Gender*, ed. Elaine Showalter (London: Routledge, 1989); and, for the application of this to biblical interpretation, The Bible and Culture Collective, *The Postmodern Bible* (New Haven: Yale University Press, 1995), pp. 60–2; Esther Fuchs, *Sexual Politics in the Biblical Narrative: Reading the Hebrew Bible as a Woman* (Sheffield: Sheffield Academic Press, 2000), chapter 1. See also Judith E. McKinlay, *Gendering Wisdom the Host: Biblical Invitations to Eat and Drink* (Sheffield: Sheffield Academic Press, 1996).

tent with Sarah, overhearing the conversations about them by which they have already been defined as non-speakers?[13] If the intended hearers of these words are men, it might seem that feminist readings can only be made "against the grain," as critiques of the patriarchy intrinsic to the texts – the incredulous laughter of the eavesdropper, who will resist any attempt to reintegrate her into this story as its compliant and silent object.

How can a reading of scripture sensitive to these problems avoid the unsatisfactory alternatives of explaining away, or reading out, the sexism of a text, on the one hand, and rejecting large sections of scripture, on the other? Saying of the text that God hears it opens up, I shall suggest, a number of possibilities implicitly contained in feminist biblical interpretation. First of all, it undercuts any claim that the text as such performs the decisive and final silencing of women. To say this would reinforce the model of communication that renders the listener a passive recipient of the powerful word.[14] Naming *God* as the hearer of this text focuses on God's continuing activity in relation to it, which forms the basis neither for arbitrary reinterpretation nor for the possession of its definitive meaning by any one group of hearers.

A further implication of such an approach to biblical interpretation, as noted above, is that a hearing of the world shapes and informs a hearing of the text; God's act of hearing encompasses what is *not* explicitly said or named here, and to hear these silences is also to "hear with God's ears." This becomes particularly important, perhaps, in the reading of texts that record, and often in their structure repeat, violence against women – the "texts of terror." Can the texts of terror themselves be mediators of God's continued hearing? As commentators such as Phyllis Trible record, women whose stories resemble those of the victims of "terror" express their experience through self-identification with the characters of the texts, and in doing so recognize themselves in relation to God.[15] The reality of God's act of hearing is manifested as the story of the violence is spoken before God; and the "hearing" of contemporary stories in the texts of terror gives all who hear the texts an indication of what it means to learn to

[13] See Genesis 18:9–15.
[14] This already suggests that the demand for feminist theology to make a new "canon" or refuse the interpretation of the Bible is misplaced. This is not only, as has often been argued, because the Bible retains its social and political "power" whether or not women participate in its interpretation (Elizabeth Schüssler Fiorenza, *In Memory of Her: A Feminist Theological Reconstruction of Christian Origins*, 2nd edn. (London: SCM, 1994), pp. 28–30, following Cady Stanton). It is also because the activities of the text's *hearers* are integral to whatever "power" it possesses.
[15] See Trible, *Texts of Terror*, p. 28.

"hear with God's ears." The search for a transforming way of interpreting the texts of terror becomes one with the hope for the transformation of existing practices of violent silencing. Because the story of Hagar's suffering (for example) does not have a straightforwardly "happy ending," it cannot be used to silence a contemporary "daughter of Hagar"[16] by foreclosing her account of unresolved suffering. It can only be used to *hear* her, learning to "hear with God's ears" – and learning, thus, to understand her as one who is heard by God.

My suggestion in this discussion, following a reading of the Lukan text, has been that the story of Christ as incarnate, crucified, and resurrected is itself only heard rightly when it can "hear others to speech."[17] Theology's own acts of hearing are shaped by the assurance that *this* story is heard by God, and determines God's whole act of hearing. Practices of biblical interpretation such as the "hearing" of the silences of women in the Bible can be heard as making apparent both the theological basis and the ethical implications of this claim.

My final comments relate to the hearing of theological texts – a hearing that, I have suggested, properly relies on an assumed but not comprehended common "place to stand." I want to suggest that reading with "minds opened to understand" (to recognize, to hear things in relation to one another, to make judgments) involves reading in ways that maintain an awareness of this common place to stand. This means, certainly, being prepared in a critical reading to expose and challenge attempts to secure a "place to stand" by silencing other voices. It also means, however, being open to the possibility that the practice of theology can itself be a *locus* of innerworldly creativity, sustained, as friendships are, by its maintenance – in the "penultimate" – of an unspoken and generative common ground.

It is possible, as I noted in my introduction, to read any theological text for its silences – what issues are avoided, what doctrines are not emphasized or not mentioned, what boundaries of the defined sphere of

---

[16] See Trible, *Texts of Terror*, p. 1.

[17] It is noteworthy that Trible uses both New Testament texts about Christ, and texts from the "Old Testament" that are often interpreted Christologically, to frame her readings of the texts of terror. What does it mean to remember, with Trible, the fact that the scriptures "opened" in Luke 24 (perhaps, the "things about [Jesus] in all the scriptures," v. 27) include the stories of Hagar, of the Levite's concubine, of Jephthah's daughter, and of the rape of Tamar – among many others? It may remind us that the "opening" of the scriptures by and in relation to Jesus cannot mean their absorption without remainder into his known story (the male Jesus is not the target of the specific gendered violence of the texts of terror; and the victims of that violence are not yet resurrected); and at the same time, it may remind us of the need to recognize all of these unresolved "sad stories" within a just and compassionate act of divine hearing.

academic theology are not crossed. The question then becomes – how should these silences be read? A suspicious reading – such as feminist theology has often taken as a starting point – will interpret the marked and unmarked silences of "absences" within a text as attempts to secure a "place to stand" – attempts that can be frustrated by drawing attention to the silences or by calling them into question.

The suspicious or anti-idolatrous reading may often be a necessary move; it may well be that silence is an indication of failures of hearing, such as Bonhoeffer identified in the silence of the churches under Nazism, and such as feminist thinkers identify in past and present theology. In the end, however, a purely suspicious reading of theology's silences, and its expression in refutation or critique, tends toward the reinforcement rather than the conversion of a distorted communicative situation. Using a theologian's silences against him in this way could be the theological equivalent of a denial of privacy – a refusal of patience, a refusal to allow the other's silence to convey, not absence, but the gift of future possibilities given in God's act of hearing. This does not mean that acts of silencing – the "silencing of God" or the silencing of creaturely voices – can or should be "passed over" in a way that repeats them or denies the responsibility of those who perform them. It does mean that the interpretation and critique of theological silences – like, in the end, Bonhoeffer's treatment of "the fool," and like the work of feminist readers who continue to engage with a tradition that seems to silence them – must "convey the ultimacy not of judgment but of love."

Would I have liked to leave the last few pages of this book blank, as suggested by several people when they first learned what its subject matter was to be? Even such a curiously signalled silence could have a wide range of meanings and implications. The blank page that attempted to gesture toward the "more than speakable" mystery of God would, I suggest, only do so insofar as it also constituted an opening toward the work of the reader or hearer. That in turn would only make sense if the communicative activity toward which the reader or hearer was called were understood to be patterned according to God's communicative activity. Perhaps, even without the blank pages, the end of a book can be an invitation to a shared keeping of God's silence.

BIBLIOGRAPHY

Works by Bonhoeffer

Act and Being: Transcendental Philosophy and Ontology in Systematic Theology, trans. H. Martin Rumscheidt, *DBWE* 2. Minneapolis: Fortress, 1996.

Akt und Sein: Tranzendentalphilosophie und Ontologie in der systematischen Theologie, *DBW* 2. Munich: Kaiser, 1988.

Barcelona, Berlin, Amerika: 1928–1931, DBW 10. Munich: Kaiser, 1992.

Berlin: 1932–1933, DBW 12. Munich: Kaiser, 1996.

Brautbriefe Zelle 92: Dietrich Bonhoeffer, Maria von Wedemeyer, 1943–1945, ed. Ruth-Alice von Bismarck and Ulrich Kabitz. Munich: Beck, 1993.

The Cost of Discipleship, trans. R. H. Fuller. London: SCM, 1959.

Creation and Fall, trans. Douglas S. Bax, *DBWE* 3. Minneapolis: Fortress, 1997.

Discipleship, trans. Barbara Green and Reinhard Krauss, *DBWE* 4. Minneapolis: Fortress, 2001.

Ethics, ed. Eberhard Bethge, trans. Neville Horton Smith. London: SCM, 1955.

Ethik, DBW 6. Munich: Kaiser, 1992.

Fiction from Prison: Gathering up the Past, eds. Renate and Eberhard Bethge with Clifford Green, trans. Ursula Hoffmann. Philadelphia: Fortress, 1981.

Fiction from Tegel Prison, trans. Nancy Lukens, *DBWE* 7. Minneapolis: Fortress, 2000.

Fragmente aus Tegel, DBW 7. Munich: Kaiser, 1994.

Gemeinsames Leben und Gebetbuch der Bibel, DBW 5. Munich: Kaiser, 1987.

Illegale Theologenausbildung: Finkenwalde, 1935–1937, DBW 14. Munich: Kaiser, 1996.

Illegale Theologenausbildung: Sammelvikariate, 1937–1940, DBW 15. Munich: Kaiser, 1996.

Konspiration und Haft: 1940–1945, DBW 16. Munich: Kaiser, 1995.

Lectures on Christology, trans. Edwin Robertson. London: Fount, 1978.

Letters and Papers from Prison, ed. Eberhard Bethge, trans. Reginald Fuller et al. London: SCM 1971.

Life Together and Prayerbook of the Bible, trans. Daniel W. Bloesch, *DBWE* 5. Minneapolis: Fortress, 1996.

London: 1933–1935, DBW 13. Munich: Kaiser, 1994.

Nachfolge, DBW 4. Munich: Kaiser, 1994.

Ökumene, Universität, Pfarramt: 1931–1932, DBW 11. Munich: Kaiser, 1994.

Sanctorum Communio: eine dogmatische Untersuchung zur Soziologie der Kirche, DBW 1. Munich: Kaiser, 1986.

Sanctorum Communio: a theological study of the sociology of the Church, ed. Clifford J. Green, trans. Reinhard Krauss and Nancy Lukens, *DBWE* 1. Minneapolis: Fortress, 1998.

Schöpfung und Fall, DBW 3. Munich: Kaiser, 1989.

Spiritual Care, ed. and trans. Jay C. Rochelle. Philadelphia: Fortress, 1985.

Widerstand und Ergebung, DBW 8. Munich: Kaiser, 1998.

Zettelnotizen für eine Ethik, DBW 6 Erganzungsband. Munich: Kaiser, 1993.

Other Works Cited

Abromeit, Hans-Jürgen. *Das Geheimnis Christi: Dietrich Bonhoeffers erfahrungsbezogene Theologie*. Neukirchen: Neukirchner Verlag, 1991.

Adams, Nicholas. "Imagining God's Reign: Ideal Speech and Our Common Future," PhD. University of Cambridge, 1997.

Agamben, Giorgio. *Language and Death: The Place of Negativity*, trans. Karen Pinkus and Michael Hart. Minneapolis: University of Minnesota Press, 1991.

Altenähr, Albert. *Dietrich Bonhoeffer – Lehrer des Gebets: Grundlagen für eine Theologie des Gebets bei Dietrich Bonhoeffer*. Würzburg: Echter Verlag, 1976.

Anderson, Pamela Sue. *A Feminist Philosophy of Religion: The Rationality and Myths of Religious Belief*. Oxford: Blackwell, 1998.

——and Clack, Beverley, eds. *Feminist Philosophy of Religion: Critical Readings*. London: Routledge, 2004.

Arendt, Hannah. *Eichmann in Jerusalem: A Report on the Banality of Evil*, 2nd edn. London: Penguin, 1994.

——. *The Human Condition*, 2nd edn. Chicago: University of Chicago Press, 1998.

Austin, J. L. *How to Do Things with Words*. Oxford: Oxford University Press, 1971.

Balthasar, Hans Urs von. *New Elucidations*, trans. Mary Sherry. San Francisco: Ignatius, 1986.

Banisar, David. *Privacy and Human Rights 2000: An International Survey of Privacy Laws and Developments*. Washington DC: EPIC and Privacy International, 2000.

Barth, Karl. *Die Lehre vom Wort Gottes (Die Christliche Dogmatik, 1)*. Munich: Kaiser, 1927.

——. *Das Wort Gottes und der Theologie*. Munich: Kaiser, 1929.

——. *Church Dogmatics 2/1: The Doctrine of God*, trans. T. Parker et al. Edinburgh: T. & T. Clark, 1957.

Barthes, Roland. "The Death of the Author," trans. Richard Howard, in *The Discontinuous Universe: Selected Writings in Contemporary Consciousness*, ed. Sallie Sears. New York: Basic, 1972, pp. 7–12.

Basso, K. H. "To Give up on Words: Silence in Western Apache Culture," in *Language and Social Context*, ed. Pier P. Giglioli. Harmondsworth: Penguin 1972.

Bauckham, Richard. *The Climax of Prophecy: Studies in the Book of Revelation*. Edinburgh: T. & T. Clark, 1993.

Bauman, Richard. *Let Your Words Be Few: Symbolism of Speaking and Silence among Seventeenth-Century Quakers*. Cambridge: Cambridge University Press, 1983.

Beattie, Tina. "Carnal Love and Spiritual Imagination: Can Luce Irigaray and John Paul II Come Together?," in *Sex These Days: Essays on Theology, Sexuality and Society*, eds. Jon Davies and Gerard Loughlin. Sheffield: Sheffield Academic Press, 1997, pp. 160–83.

Begbie, Jeremy S. *Theology, Music and Time*. Cambridge: Cambridge University Press, 2000.

Benhabib, Selya. *Situating the Self: Gender, Community and Postmodernism in Contemporary Ethics*. Cambridge: Polity, 1992.

——ed. *Feminist Contentions: A Philosophical Exchange*. London: Routledge, 1995.

Benn, Stanley I., and Gerald Gaus. *Public and Private in Social Life*. London: Croom Helm, 1983.

Bethge, Eberhard. "My Friend Dietrich Bonhoeffer's Theology of Friendship," in *The Changing Face of Friendship*, ed. Leroy S. Rouner. Notre Dame: Notre Dame, 1994, pp. 133–54.

Bethge, Renate. "'Elite' and 'Silence' in Dietrich Bonhoeffer's Person and Thoughts," in *Ethical Responsibility: Bonhoeffer's Legacy to the Churches*, eds. John D. Godsey and Geffrey B. Kelly. Lewiston: Edwin Mellon, 1981, pp. 293–306.

Beuchtel, Albrecht. *In dem Anfang war das Wort: Studien zu Luthers Sprachverständnis*. Tübingen: Mohr, 1991.

Bible and Culture Collective. *The Postmodern Bible*. New Haven: Yale University Press, 1995.

Bilmas, Jack. "Constituting Silence: Life in the World of Total Meaning." *Semiotica* 98, 1–2 (1994), 73–87.

Bloustein, Edward J. "Privacy as an Aspect of Human Dignity: An Answer to Dean Prosser," in *Philosophical Dimensions of Privacy: An Anthology*, ed. Ferdinand D. Schoeman. Cambridge: Cambridge University Press, 1984, pp. 156–202.

Bobert-Stützel, Sabine. "Liebt ein Freund mehr als ein Bruder? Zur Problematik der Verhältnisbestimmung von Bruderschaft und Freundschaft bei Dietrich Bonhoeffer unter pastoraltheologischen Aspekt," in *Theologie und Freundschaft*, eds. Christian Gremmels and Wolfgang Huber. Munich: Kaiser, 1994, pp. 89–109.

Bons-Storm, Riet. *The Incredible Woman: Listening to Women's Silences in Pastoral Care and Counselling*. Nashville: Abingdon, 1996.

Braidotti, Rosi. *Patterns of Dissonance: A Study of Women in Contemporary Philosophy*, trans. Elizabeth Guild. Cambridge: Polity, 1991.

Brewer, John. "This, That and the Other," in *Shifting the Boundaries: Transformation of the Language of Public and Private in the Eighteenth Century*, eds. Dario Cataglione and Lesley Sharpe. Exeter: University of Exeter Press, 1995.

Burtness, James H. "Als ob es Gott nicht gabe: Bonhoeffer, Barth und Das Lutherische *Finitum Capax Infiniti*," in *Bonhoeffer und Luther*, ed. Christian Gremmels. Munich: Kaiser, 1983.

——. *Shaping the Future: The Ethics of Bonhoeffer*. Philadelphia: Fortress, 1985.

Butler, Judith. *Excitable Speech: Towards a Politics of the Performative*. London: Routledge, 1997.

Caird, G. B. *A Commentary on the Revelation of St John the Divine*. London: Black's, 1966.

Carr, Anne E. *Transforming Grace*. San Francisco: Harper & Row, 1990.

Cecchetti, Ignio. "Tibi Silentium Laus," in *Miscellanae Liturgica in Honorem L. K. Mohlberg*, vol. 2. Rome: Edizione liturgiche, 1949, pp. 521–70.

Chopp, Rebecca. *The Power to Speak: Feminism, Language, God*. New York: Crossroad, 1989.

Church of England Board of Social Responsibility. *Cybernauts Awake! Ethical and Spiritual Implications of Computers, IT and the Internet*. London: Church of England Board of Social Responsibility, 1999.

Coakley, Sarah. "The Eschatological Body: Gender, Transformation and God." *Modern Theology* 16, 1 (2000), 61–73.

Cooey, Paula. *Religious Imagination and the Body: A Feminist Analysis*. Oxford: Oxford University Press, 1994.

Crichton, J. D. *Christian Celebration*. London: Chapman, 1971.

Cyprian. "On the Advantage of Patience," trans. R. E. Wallis, in *Ante-Nicene Fathers*, vol. 13. Edinburgh: T. & T. Clark, 1869, pp. 21–39.

Dalferth, Ingolf. "God and the Mystery of Words." *Journal of the American Academy of Religion* 60 (1992), 79–103.

Daly, Mary. *Beyond God the Father: Towards a Philosophy of Women's Liberation*. London: Women's Press, 1986.

Daube, David. *The Exodus Pattern in the Bible*. London: Faber & Faber, 1963.

Dauenhauer, Bernard. *Silence: The Phenomenon and Its Ontological Significance*. Bloomington: Indiana University Press, 1980.

Davies, Oliver. "Revelation and the Politics of Culture," in *Radical Orthodoxy? A Catholic Enquiry*, ed. Lawrence Hemming. Aldershot: Ashgate, 2000, pp. 112–25.

——. *A Theology of Compassion: Metaphysics of Difference and the Renewal of Tradition*. London: SCM, 2001.

——and Turner, Denys, eds. *Silence and the Word: Negative Theology and Incarnation*. Cambridge: Cambridge University Press, 2002.

Day, Thomas. *Dietrich Bonhoeffer on Christian Community and Common Sense*. New York: Edwin Mellon, 1982.

Dean, Jodi. "Discourse in Different Voices," in *Feminists Read Habermas*, ed. Johanna Meehan. London: Routledge, 1995, pp. 205–29.

DeCew, Judith Wagner. *In Pursuit of Privacy: Law, Ethics and the Rise of Technology.* Ithaca: Cornell University Press, 1997.

Derrida, Jacques, and Levesque, Claude. *The Ear of the Other: Autobiography, Transference, Retranslation – Texts and Discussions with Jacques Derrida.* New York: Random House, 1985.

Dogherty, Joseph. "Silence in the Liturgy." *Worship* 69 (1994), 142–54.

Dumas, André. *Dietrich Bonhoeffer: Theologian of Reality*, trans. R. M. Brown. London: SCM, 1971.

Dumas, Monique. "Le Sacre et l'Autre Parole Selon un Voix Feministe," in *Silence, the Word and the Sacred*, ed. E. D. Blodgett. Wilfred Laurier University Press, 1980, pp. 149–60.

Ebeling, Gerhard. *Introduction to a Theological Theory of Language*, trans. R. A. Wilson. London: Collins, 1973.

Eckhart, Meister. *Deutsche Predigten und Traktaten*, trans. J. Quint. Munich: Carl Hanser, 1955.

——. *German Sermons and Treatises*, trans. M. O' C. Walshe, 2 vols., vol. 2. London: Watkins, 1981.

Elshtain, Jean Bethke. *Public Man, Private Woman: Women in Social and Political Thought.* Princeton: Princeton University Press, 1981.

Engelhardt, H. Tristram. "Privacy and Limited Democracy: The Moral Centrality of Persons." *Social Philosophy and Policy* 17.2 (2000), 120–40.

Erikson, Victoria Lee. *Where Silence Speaks: Feminism, Social Theory and Religion.* Minneapolis: Fortress, 1993.

Falls-Corbitt, Margaret, and F. Michael McLain. "God and Privacy." *Faith and Philosophy* 9 (1992), 369–86.

Feil, Ernst. *The Theology of Dietrich Bonhoeffer*, trans. Martin Rumscheidt. Philadelphia: Fortress, 1985.

——. "Freundschaft – ein Thema der Theologie?," in *Theologie und Freundschaft*, eds. Christian Gremmels and Wolfgang Huber. Munich: Kaiser, 1994, pp. 110–34.

Fell, Margaret. *Women's Speaking Justified, Proved and Allowed of by the Scriptures [. . .]* London, *c.* 1666.

Fiorenza, Elizabeth Schüssler. *In Memory of Her: A Feminist Theological Reconstruction of Christian Origins*, 2nd edn. London: SCM, 1994.

——. *Jesus: Miriam's Child, Sophia's Prophet.* New York, 1994.

Fischer, John Martin, ed. *God, Foreknowledge and Freedom.* Stanford: Stanford University Press, 1989.

Fiumara, Gemma Corradi. *The Other Side of Language: A Philosophy of Listening*, trans. Charles Lambert. London: Routledge, 1990.

Floyd, Wayne Whitson. *Theology and the Dialectics of Otherness: On Reading Bonhoeffer and Adorno.* Lanham: University Press of America, 1988.

Floyd, Wayne Whitson, and Charles Marsh, eds. *Theology and the Practice of Responsibility: Essays on Dietrich Bonhoeffer.* Valley Forge: Trinity Press, 1994.

Ford, David F. *Self and Salvation: Being Transformed*. Cambridge: Cambridge University Press, 1999.

Ford, David F., and Frances Young. *Meaning and Truth in 2 Corinthians*. London: SPCK, 1987.

Foucault, Michel. *Discipline and Punish: The Birth of the Prison*, trans. Alan Sheridan. Harmondsworth: Penguin, 1979.

Frey, R. G. "Privacy, Control and Talk of Rights." *Social Philosophy and Policy* 17, 2 (2000), 45–67.

Friedman, David. "Privacy and Technology." *Social Philosophy and Policy* 17, 2 (2000), 186–212.

Frye, Marilyn. "The Possibility of Feminist Theory," in *Women, Knowledge and Reality*, eds. Ann Garry and Marilyn Pearsall, 1996, pp. 34–47.

Fuchs, Esther. *Sexual Politics in the Biblical Narrative: Reading the Hebrew Bible as a Woman*. Sheffield: Sheffield Academic Press, 2000.

Fulkerson, Mary McClintock. *Changing the Subject: Women's Discourses and Feminist Theology*. Minneapolis: Fortress, 1994.

Funamoto, Hiroki. "Penultimate and Ultimate in Dietrich Bonhoeffer's Ethics," in *Being and Truth: Essays in Honour of John Macquarrie*, eds. Alistair Kee and Eugene T. Long. London: SCM, 1986, pp. 376–92.

Garrett, S. R. "The Patience of Job and the Patience of Jesus." *Interpretation* 53, 3 (1999), 254–64.

Garry, Ann and Pearsall, Marilyn, eds. *Women, Knowledge and Reality*. New York: Routledge, 1996.

Gawronski, Raymond. *Word and Silence: Hans Urs Von Balthasar and the Spiritual Encounter between East and West*. Edinburgh: T. & T. Clark, 1995.

Gehl, Paul F. "An Answering Silence: Medieval and Modern Claims for the Unity of Truth Beyond Language." *Philosophy Today* 30, 3 (1986), 224–33.

———. "Competens Silentium: Varieties of Monastic Silence in the Medieval West." *Viator.* (1987), 125–60.

Gerber, Scott D. "Privacy and Constitutional Theory." *Social Philosophy and Policy* 17, 2 (2000), 165–85.

Gibbs, Robert. *Why Ethics?* Princeton: Princeton University Press, 2000.

Gilkey, Langdon. "The Political Meaning of Silence." *Philosophy Today* 27, 2 (1983).

Gilligan, Carol. *In a Different Voice: Psychological Theory and Women's Development*, 2nd edn. Cambridge: Harvard University Press, 1993.

Godlove, Terry. "Making Pauses Pregnant." *Philosophy Today* 27.2 (1983), 132–7.

Green, Clifford J. "Two Bonhoeffers on Psychoanalysis," in *A Bonhoeffer Legacy: Essays in Understanding*, ed. A. J. Klassen. Grand Rapids: Eerdmans, 1981, pp. 58–75.

———. *Bonhoeffer: The Sociality of Christ and Humanity*. Missoula: Scholars Press, 1972.

Grey, Mary. *Redeeming the Dream: Feminism, Redemption and Christian Tradition*. London: SPCK, 1989.

——. *The Wisdom of Fools?: Seeking Revelation for Today.* London: SPCK, 1993.

Grisbrook, W. Jardine. "Silent Prayer," in *New Dictionary of Liturgy and Worship,* ed. J. G. Davies. London: SCM, 1986, pp. 492–3.

Grosz, Elizabeth. *Sexual Subversions: Three French Feminists.* Sydney: Allan & Unwin, 1989.

Habermas, Jürgen. "Transcendence from Within, Transcendence in This World," in *Habermas, Modernity and Public Theology,* eds. Don S. Browning and Francis Schüssler Fiorenza. New York: Crossroad, 1992, pp. 226–50.

Hamilton, William. "Dietrich Bonhoeffer," in *Radical Theology and the Death of God,* eds. Thomas J. J. Altizer and William Hamilton. London: Penguin, 1968.

Hampson, Daphne. *Theology and Feminism.* Oxford: Blackwell, 1990.

Haraway, Donna. "Situated Knowledges: 'The Science Question in Feminism' and the privilege of partial perspective." *Feminist Studies* 14, 3 (1988), 575–99.

Harding, Sandra. *Whose Science? Whose Knowledge? Thinking from Women's Lives.* Milton Keynes: Open University Press, 1991.

Harris, Charles. "Liturgical Silence," in *Liturgy and Worship,* ed. W. K. Lowther Clarke. London: SPCK, 1932, pp. 774–82.

Hart, Kevin. *The Trespass of the Sign: Deconstruction, Theology and Philosophy.* Cambridge: Cambridge University Press, 1989.

Hartsock, Nancy. "The Feminist Standpoint: Developing the Ground for a Specifically Feminist Historical Materialism," in *Discovering Reality: Feminist Perspectives on Epistemology, Metaphysics, Methodology and Philosophy of Science,* eds. Sandra Harding and Merrill B. Hintikka. Dordrecht: Reidel, 1983, pp. 283–310.

——. "The Feminist Standpoint Revisited," in *The Feminist Standpoint Revisited and Other Essays.* Boulder: Westview, 1997, pp. 227–248.

Hasker, William. *God, Time and Knowledge.* Ithaca: Cornell University Press, 1989.

Heidegger, Martin. *Discourse on Thinking,* trans. John M Anderson and E Hans Freund. New York: Harper & Row, 1966.

Hell, Silvia. *Die Dialektik des Wortes bei Martin Luther.* Innsbruck: Tyrolia-Verlag, 1992.

Heyward, Isabel Carter. *The Redemption of God.* Lanham: University Press of America, 1982.

Hohmann, Martin. *Die Korrelation vom Altem und Neuem Bund: Innerbiblische Korrelation statt Kontrastkorrelation.* Berlin: Evangelische Verlagsanstatt, 1978.

Holyer, Robert. "Towards an Eschatology of the Past." *Theology* 89 (1986), 209–17.

hooks, bell. "Choosing the Margin as a Space of Radical Openness," in *Women, Knowledge and Reality,* ed. Ann Garry and Marilyn Pearsall. London: Routledge, 1996, pp. 48–55.

Horst, J. "Μακροθυμια." trans. G. W. Bromiley, in *Theological Dictionary of the New Testament,* ed. G. Kittel. Grand Rapids: Eerdmans, 1967.

Hunt, Mary E. *Fierce Tenderness: A Feminist Theology of Friendship.* New York: Crossroad, 1991.

Hunter, Anne-Marie. "Numbering the Hairs of Our Heads: Male Social Control and the All-Seeing God." *Journal of Feminist Studies in Religion* 8, 2 (1992), 7–27.

Ihde, Don. *Listening and Voice: A Phenomenology of Sound.* Athens: Ohio University Press, 1976.

Inness, Julia C. *Privacy, Intimacy and Isolation.* Oxford: Oxford University Press, 1992.

Irigaray, Luce. "Equal to Whom?" *differences* 1, 2 (1989), 59–76.

——. *Marine Lover of Friedrich Nietzsche*, trans. Gillian C. Gill. New York: Columbia University Press, 1991.

——. "Divine Women?," in *Women, Knowledge and Reality*, eds. Ann Garry and Marilyn Pearsall, 1996, pp. 471–84.

Jaggar, Alison M. *Feminist Politics and Human Nature.* Brighton: Harvester, 1983.

Jantzen, Grace. *Becoming Divine: Towards a Feminist Philosophy of Religion.* Manchester: Manchester University Press, 1998.

Janz, Paul. "Redeeming Modernity: Rationality, Justification and Penultimacy in the Theology of Dietrich Bonhoeffer," PhD. University of Cambridge, 2000.

John of Damascus. *An Exact Exposition of the Orthodox Faith*, Nicene and Post-Nicene Fathers, second series, vol. 9. Edinburgh: T. & T. Clark.

Jones, Serene. *Feminist Theory and Christian Theology: Cartographies of Grace.* Minneapolis: Fortress, 2000.

Joy, Morny. "Levinas: Alterity, the Feminine and Women." *Studies in Religion* 22, 4 (1993), 463–85.

Jüngel, Eberhard. *Gott als Gehemnis der Welt: Zur Begründung der Theologie des Gekreuzigten im Streit zwischen Theismus und Atheismus*, 2nd edn. Tübingen: Mohr, 1977.

——. *God as the Mystery of the World: On the Foundation of the Theology of the Crucified One in the Dispute between Theism and Atheism*, trans. Darrell L. Guder. Grand Rapids: Eerdmans, 1983.

——. *Theological Essays*, trans. John Webster. Edinburgh: T. & T. Clark, 1989.

——. "Gottes Geduld – Geduld der Liebe?," in *Wertlose Wahrheit*. Munich: Kaiser, 1990, pp. 183–93.

Kasper, Walter. *The God of Jesus Christ.* London: SCM, 1984.

Kerr, Fergus. *Immortal Longings.* London: SPCK, 1997.

Kierkegaard, Søren. *Christian Discourses*, trans. Walter Lowrie. Oxford: Oxford University Press, 1939.

——. *For Self-Examination*, trans. Walter Lowrie. Oxford: Oxford University Press, 1941.

——. *Fear and Trembling; Repetition*, trans. Edna H. Hong and Howard V. Hong. Princeton: Princeton University Press, 1983.

——. *The Point of View for My Work as an Author*, trans. Howard V. Hong and Edna H. Hong. Princeton: Princeton University Press, 1998.

Kochelmans, Joseph J., ed. *On Heidegger and Language.* Evanston: Northwest University Press, 1972.

Krötke, Wolf. "Der begegnende Gott und der Glaube Zum Theologischen Schwerpunkt der Christologievorlesung Dietrich Bonhoeffers," in *Bonhoeffer-Studien*, eds. Wolf Krötke and Albrecht Schönherr. Berlin: Evangelische Verlagsanstatt, 1985, pp. 25–35.

Kuhlmann, Helga. "Die Ethik Dietrich Bonhoeffers: Quelle oder Hemmschuh für Feministisch-Theologisch Ethik?" *Zeitschrift für Evangelische Ethik* 37 (1993), 106–20.

Kurzon, Dennis. "The Right of Silence: A Socio-Pragmatic Model of Interpretation." *Journal of Pragmatics* 23, 1 (1995).

Laney, James T. "An Examination of Bonhoeffer's Ethical Contextualism," in *A Bonhoeffer Legacy: Essays In Understanding*, ed. A. J. Klassen. Grand Rapids: Eerdmans, 1981, pp. 294–313.

Lang, Berel. *Heidegger's Silence*. London: Athlone, 1996.

Lange, Frits de. *Waiting for the Word: Dietrich Bonhoeffer on Speaking about God*, trans. Martin N. Walton. Grand Rapids: Eerdmans, 2000.

Le Doeuff, Michèle. *Hipparchia's Choice*, trans. Trista Selous. Oxford: Blackwell, 1989.

Lehmann, Paul L. *Ethics in a Christian Context*. London: SCM, 1963.

Levin, David. *The Listening Self: Personal Growth, Social Change and the Closure of Metaphysics*. London: Routledge, 1989.

Levinson, Stephen C. *Pragmatics*. Cambridge: Cambridge University Press, 1983.

Lewis, C. S. *The Four Loves*. London: Collins, 1977.

Liguš, Jan. "Dietrich Bonhoeffer: Ultimate, Penultimate and Their Impact," in *Bonhoeffer's Ethics: Old Europe and New Frontiers*, ed. Guy Carter. Kampen: Kok Pharos, 1991, pp. 59–72.

Littell, Marcia Sachs, ed. *Liturgies on the Holocaust: An Interfaith Anthology*. Lewiston: Edwin Mellon, 1986.

London Yearly Meeting. *To Lima with Love: The Response from the Religious Society of Friends (Quakers) in Great Britain to the World Council of Churches Document "Baptism, Eucharist and Ministry."* London: Quaker Home Service, 1987.

Lowe, Walter. "Bonhoeffer and Deconstruction: Towards a Theology of the Crucified Logos," in *Theology and the Practice of Responsibility*, eds. Wayne Whitson Floyd Jr. and Charles Marsh. Valley Forge: Trinity Press, 1994, pp. 208–21.

Lyon, David. *The Electronic Eye: The Rise of Surveillance Society*. Cambridge: Polity, 1994.

McFadyen, Alistair. *The Call to Personhood: A Christian Theory of the Individual in Social Relationships*. Cambridge: Cambridge University Press, 1990.

——. *Bound to Sin? Abuse, Holocaust and the Christian Doctrine of Sin*. Cambridge: Cambridge University Press, 2000.

McFague, Sallie. *Models of God: Theology for an Ecological Nuclear Age*. London: SPCK, 1987.

McKinlay, Judith E. *Gendering Wisdom the Host: Biblical Invitations to Eat and Drink*. Sheffield: Sheffield Academic Press, 1996.

Mackinnon, Catherine. *Towards a Feminist Theory of the State*. Cambridge: Harvard University Press, 1989.

Mackinnon, Donald. *Explorations in Theology 5*. London: SCM, 1979.

Malone, Mary T. *Women and Christianity*, vol. 1. Blackrock, Co. Dublin: Columba, 2000.

Marsh, Charles. *Reclaiming Dietrich Bonhoeffer: The Promise of His Theology*. Oxford: Oxford University Press, 1994.

Mathewes, Charles. "A Tale of Two Judgements: Bonhoeffer and Arendt on Evil, Understanding and Limits, and the Limits of Understanding Evil." *Journal of Religion* 80, 3 (2000), 375–404.

Meehan, Johanna, ed. *Feminists Read Habermas: Gendering the Subject of Discourse*. London: Routledge, 1995.

Meilaender, Gilbert. *Friendship: A Study in Theological Ethics*. Notre Dame: Notre Dame, 1981.

Mensching, Gustav. *Das Heilige Schweigens; eine Religionsgeschichtliche Untersuchung*. Giessen: Töpelmann, 1926.

Milbank, John. *Being Reconciled: Ontology and Pardon*. London: Routledge, 2003.

Miles, Margaret R. "The Rope Breaks When It Is Tightest: Luther on the Body, Consciousness and the Word." *Harvard Theological Review* 22, 3/4 (1984), 239–58.

Minnich, Elizabeth Karmack. *Transforming Knowledge*. Philadelphia: Temple University Press, 1990.

Mitchell, Nathan. "Silent Music." *Worship*. (1993), pp. 261–7.

Moberly, R. W. L. "Solomon and Job: Divine Wisdom in Human Life," in *Where Shall Wisdom Be Found? Wisdom in the Bible, the Church and the Contemporary World*, ed. Stephen C. Barton. Edinburgh: T. & T. Clark, 1999, pp. 3–18.

Moltmann, Jürgen. "Open Friendship: Aristotelian and Christian Views of Friendship," in *The Changing Face of Friendship*, ed. Leroy S. Rouner. London: Routledge, 1994, pp. 29–42.

Morey, Anne-Janine. "The Literary Physician," in *In Good Company: Essays in Honour of Robert Detweiler*, eds. David Jasper and Mark Ledbetter. Atlanta: Scholars Press, 1994, pp. 183–97.

Mortley, Raoul. *From Word to Silence*, vol. 2, 2 vols. Bonn: Hanstein, 1986.

Morton, Nelle. *The Journey Is Home*. Boston: Beacon, 1985.

Moulton, Janice. "A Paradigm of Philosophy: The Adversary Method," in *Women, Knowledge and Reality*, eds. Ann Garry and Marilyn Pearsall, 1996, pp. 11–25.

Muers, Rachel. "The Mute Cannot Keep Silent: Barth, Von Balthasar and Irigaray on the Construction of Women's Silence," in *Challenging Women's Orthodoxies in the Context of Faith*, ed. Susan Frank Parsons. Aldershot: Ashgate, 2000, pp. 109–20.

——. "Silence and the Patience of God." *Modern Theology* 17, 1 (2000), 85–98.

Mugerauer, Robert. *Heidegger's Language and Thinking*. Atlantic Highlands: Humanities Press, 1988.

Neher, André. "Shaddai: The God of the Broken Arch," in *Confronting the Holocaust: The Impact of Elie Wiesel*, ed. Alvin H. Rosenfeld and Irving Greenberg. Bloomington: Indiana University Press, 1978, pp. 150–8.

Nesti, Arnaldo. "Silence as Elsewhere." *Social Compass* 42, 4 (1995), 421–31.

Nickson Ann L. *Bonhoeffer on Freedom: Courageously Grasping Reality*. London: Ashgate, 2002.

Ochs, Peter. *Peirce, Pragmatism and the Logic of Scripture*. Cambridge: Cambridge University Press, 1998.

O'Donovan, Oliver. *Resurrection and Moral Order: An Outline for Evangelical Ethics*. Leicester: Inter-Varsity Press, 1986.

——. "The Concept of Publicity." *Studies in Christian Ethics* 13, 1 (2000), 18–32.

Ong, Walter. *The Presence of the Word: Some Prolegomena for Cultural and Religious History*. New Haven: Yale University Press, 1967.

Pangritz, Andreas. *Dietrich Bonhoeffers Forderung einer Arkansdisziplin*. Cologne: Pahl-Rugenstein, 1988.

Panikkar, Raimundo. *The Unknown Christ of Hinduism: Towards an Ecumenical Christophany*. London: Darton, Longman & Todd, 1981.

Pateman, Carol. "Feminist Critiques of the Public/Private Dichotomy," in *Public and Private in Social Life*, eds. Stanley I. Benn and Gerald Gaus, 1983.

Peck, William Jay. "From Cain to the Death Camps: An Essay on Dietrich Bonhoeffer and Judaism." *Union Seminary Quarterly Review* 28, 2 (1973), 158–75.

Petrey, Sandy. "Speech Acts in Society: Fish, Felman, Austin and God." *Texte* 3 (1984), 43–61.

Picard, Max. *The World of Silence*, trans. Stanley Godman. London: Harvill, 1948.

Plant, Stephen John. "Uses of the Bible in the "Ethics" of Dietrich Bonhoeffer," PhD. University of Cambridge, 1993.

Plaskow, Judith. *Sex, Sin and Grace*. Lanham: University Press of America, 1980.

——. *Standing again at Sinai: Judaism from a Feminist Perspective*. San Francisco: Harper Collins, 1990.

Propp, William. *Exodus*. Anchor Bible Commentaries. New York: Doubleday, 1999.

Pseudo-Dionysius. *Mystical Theology, in the Complete Works*, trans. Colm Luibheid. New York: Paulist, 1987.

Punshon, John. *Encounter with Silence: Reflections from the Quaker Tradition*. London: Quaker Home Service, 1987.

Quaker Faith and Practice: The Book of Christian Discipline of the Religious Society of Friends (Quakers) in Britain. London: Quaker Home Service, 1994.

Rachels, James. "Why Privacy Is Important," in *Philosophical Dimensions of Privacy: An Anthology*, ed. Ferdinand D. Schoeman. Cambridge: Cambridge University Press, 1984, pp. 290–99.

Rahner, Karl. *Foundations of Christian Faith*, trans. William V. Dych. New York: Crossroad, 1999.

Rich, Adrienne. *The Dream of a Common Language: Poems 1974–1977*. New York: W. W. Norton & Company, 1978.

——. *Of Lies, Secrets and Silence: Selected Prose 1966–1978*. London: Virago, 1980.

Ricoëur, Paul. *Oneself as Another*, trans. Kathleen Blamey. Chicago: University of Chicago Press, 1992.

Rochelle, Jay C. *Spiritual Care*. Philadelphia: Fortress, 1985.

Rosenberg, Alexander. "Privacy as a Matter of Taste and Right." *Social Philosophy and Policy* 17, 2 (2000), 68–90.

Ruegger, Heinz. *Kirche als seelsorgerliche Gemeinschaft: Dietrich Bonhoeffers Seelsorgeverständnis im Kontext seiner bruderschaftlichen Ekklesiologie*. Bern: Lang, 1992.

Ruether, Rosemary Radford. *Sexism and God-Talk*. London: SCM, 1983.

Russell, Letty M. *Human Liberation in a Feminist Perspective: A Theology*. Philadelphia: Westminster, 1974.

Rutherford, Jonathan. *Men's Silences: Predicaments in Masculinity*. London: Routledge, 1992.

Saiving, Valerie. "The Human Situation: A Feminine View." *Journal of Religion* (1960), pp. 100–12.

Sargisson, Susan. *Contemporary Feminist Utopianism*. London: Routledge, 1996.

Sarot, Marcel. *God, Passibility and Corporeality*. Kampen: Kok Pharos, 1992.

Scharlemann, Robert. "Authenticity and Encounter: Bonhoeffer's Appropriation of Ontology." *Union Seminary Quarterly Review* 46, 1–4 (1992), 253–65.

Schindler, Regine. "Verhaftet und Verlobt: Zum Briefwechsel zwischen Dietrich Bonhoeffer und Maria von Wedemeyer, 1943–5," in *Theologie Und Freundschaft*, eds. Christian Gremmels and Wolfgang Huber. Munich: Kaiser, 1994, pp. 154–69.

Schoeman, Ferdinand D., ed. *Philosophical Dimensions of Privacy: An Anthology*. Cambridge: Cambridge University Press, 1984.

——. *Privacy and Social Freedom*. Cambridge: Cambridge University Press, 1992.

Schweickart, Patrocinio P. "Reading Ourselves: Towards a Feminist Theory of Reading," in *Speaking of Gender*, ed. Elaine Showalter. London: Routledge, 1989.

Scott, Jamie S. "'From the Spirit's Choice and Free Desire': Friendship as Atheology in Dietrich Bonhoeffer's *Letters and Papers from Prison*." *Studies in Religion* 22, 1 (1993), 49–62.

Simoni, Henry. "Omniscience and the Problem of Radical Particularity: Does God Know How to Ride a Bike?" *International Journal for the Philosophy of Religion* 42, 1 (1997), 1–22.

Solberg, Mary M. *Compelling Knowledge: A Feminist Proposal for an Epistemology of the Cross*. Albany: State University of New York Press, 1997.

Sölle, Dorothee. *Christ the Representative: An Essay in Theology after the Death of God*, trans. David Lewis. London: SCM, 1967.

Soskice, Janet Martin. "Response," in *Swallowing a Fishbone? Feminist Theologians Debate Christianity*, ed. Daphne Hampson. London: SPCK, 1996, pp. 125–8.

——. "Friendship," *Paper presented at the Consultation on the Future of the Study of Theology and the Religions*. Cambridge, 2000.

Spjuth, Roland. *Creation, Contingency and Divine Presence in the Theologies of Thomas F. Torrance and Eberhard Jüngel.* Lund: Lund University Press, 1995.

Steiner, George. *Language and Silence: Essays 1958–1966.* Harmondsworth: Penguin, 1969.

Steinke, Robin Joy. "Confessing and *Status Confessionis*: A Study in the Theology of Dietrich Bonhoeffer," PhD. University of Cambridge, 1998.

Stephen, Caroline E. *Quaker Strongholds.* London, 1890.

Surin, Kenneth. *The Turnings of Darkness and Light.* Cambridge: Cambridge University Press, 1989.

Taliafero, Charles. "Does God Violate Your Right to Privacy?" *Theology* 92 (1989), 190–6.

Tannen, Deborah, and Muriel Savile-Troike. *Perspectives on Silence.* Norwood, NJ: Ablex, 1985.

Tertullian. "Of Patience," trans. S. Thelwall, in *Ante-Nicene Fathers*, vol. 11. Edinburgh: T. & T. Clark, 1869, pp. 205–30.

Thistlethwaite, Susan Brooks. *Sex, Race and God: Christian Feminism in Black and White.* London: Chapman, 1990.

Thomson, Judith Jarvis. "The Right to Privacy," in *Philosophical Dimensions of Privacy: An Anthology*, ed. Ferdinand D. Schoeman. Cambridge: Cambridge University Press, 1984, pp. 272–89.

Tong, Rosemarie Putnam. *Feminist Thought: A More Comprehensive Introduction.* Oxford: Westview, 1998.

Trible, Phyllis. *Texts of Terror: Literary-Feminist Readings of Biblical Narratives.* Minneapolis: Fortress, 1984.

Turner, Denys. *The Darkness of God: Negativity and Christian Mysticism.* Cambridge: Cambridge University Press, 1995.

Vanhoozer, Kevin. *Is There a Meaning in This Text? The Bible, the Reader and the Morality of Literary Knowledge.* Leicester: Apollos, 1998.

Walker, Michelle Boulos. "Silence and Reason: Women's Voice in Philosophy." *Australasian Journal of Philosophy* 71, 4 (1993), 400–24.

Ward, Graham. "In the Daylight Forever? Language and Silence," in *Silence and the Word: Negative Theology and Incarnation*, ed. Denys Turner and Oliver Davies. Cambridge: Cambridge University Press 2002.

Warren, Samuel D., and Louis D. Brandeis. "The Right to Privacy (the Implicit Made Explicit)," in *Philosophical Dimensions of Privacy: An Anthology*, ed. Ferdinand D. Schoeman. Cambridge: Cambridge University Press, 1984, pp. 75–103.

Watson, Francis. *Text and Truth: Redefining Biblical Theology.* Edinburgh: T. & T. Clark, 1997.

Webster, John. *Eberhard Jüngel: An Introduction to His Theology.* Cambridge: Cambridge University Press, 1986.

——. "Justification, Analogy and Action: Passivity and Activity in Jüngel's Anthropology," in *The Possibilities of Theology: Studies in the Theology of Eberhard Jüngel in His Sixtieth Year.* Edinburgh: T. & T. Clark, 1994, pp. 106–42.

West, Angela. *Deadly Innocence: Feminism and the Mythology of Sin.* London: Cassell, 1995.

West, Charles C. "Ground under Our Feet: A Reflection on the Worldliness of Dietrich Bonhoeffer's Life and Thought," in *New Studies in Bonhoeffer's Ethics*, ed. William Jay Peck. Lewiston: Edwin Mellon, 1987, pp. 235–73.

White, Stephen K. *Political Theory and Postmodernism.* Cambridge: Cambridge University Press, 1991.

Whitford, Margaret. "Irigaray, Utopia and the Death Drive," in *Engaging with Irigaray: Feminist Philosophy and Modern European Thought*, ed. Carolyn Burke. New York: Columbia University Press, 1994, pp. 379–400.

Wiesel, Elie. *Night (& Dawn; The Accident; Three Tales)*, trans. Stella Rodway. London: Robson, 1974.

Wilberg, Peter. *Being and Listening: Counselling, Psychoanalysis and the Heideggerian Philosophy of Listening.* London: Third Ear, 1998.

Williams, Rowan. "The Suspicion of Suspicion: Wittgenstein and Bonhoeffer," in *The Grammar of the Heart*, ed. Richard H. Bell. London: Harper & Row, 1988, pp. 36–53.

——. *On Christian Theology.* Oxford: Blackwell, 2000.

Wink, Walter. *Engaging the Powers: Discernment and Resistance in a World of Domination.* Minneapolis: Fortress, 1992.

Wittgenstein, Ludwig. *Tractatus Logico-Philosophicus*, trans. D. F. Pears and B. F. McGuinness. London: Routledge, 1961.

Wolterstorff, Nicholas. *Divine Discourse: Philosophical Reflections on the Claim That God Speaks.* Cambridge: Cambridge University Press, 1995.

Woolf, Virginia. *A Room of One's Own.* London: Penguin, 1945.

Wyschogrod, Edith. *An Ethics of Remembering: History, Heterology and the Nameless Others.* Chicago: University of Chicago Press, 1998.

Young, Frances. "A Time for Silence – Dare We Mention Prayer?," in *Dare We Speak of God in Public?*, ed. Frances Young. London: Mowbray, 1995, pp. 133–50.

Young, Iris M. *Justice and the Politics of Difference.* Princeton: Princeton University Press, 1990.

Zimany, Roland Daniel. *Vehicle for God: The Metaphorical Theology of Eberhard Jüngel.* Macon: Mercer University Press, 1991.

Žižek, Slavoj. *The Ticklish Subject: The Absent Centre of Political Ontology.* London: Verso, 1999.

INDEX

Abraham 6, 7

Acts of the Apostles 97

actus directus 111, 112

Adam and Eve 191–2

Adorno, Theodor 7

Apache culture 9

apophatic theology 12, 28–9, 31

Arendt, Hannah 127–8, 128n12, 129n16, 168–9, 169n68

atheism 26, 27–8, 31

Augustine, Saint 2

Austin, J. L. 109, 110

Barth, Karl: *Act and Being* 118–19n40; human subject 26; patience 94n71, 97n75

Barthes, Roland 25n9

Bentham, Jeremy 198n43

benumbment: Fiumara 102, 128; folly 138; resistance 56, 125; self-imposed 68, 175; silencing 215

Bethge, Eberhard 73, 137, 173–4

Bible 221–2, 223; *see also individual books*

Bloustein, Edward J. 209

Bonhoeffer, Dietrich: Advent sermon 93; baptismal address 124; character sketches 127, 130, 131–4; *counter-logos* 118; discernment 99–100, 170–1, 172, 179–80; ethics 88, 89, 151; evil 128n12; feminism 89; folly 126–30; future 82–3; German Church 75, 174n83, 224; God's silence 82; Holy Spirit 91n60; knowing/acting/judging 201–2; penultimate 86–91, 101, 137;

pneumatology 91n60; privacy 212; resurrection 18, 79–80, 83–4, 92–3, 95–6, 100; speech 189; spiritual care 19; suffering 136; Tegel prison 73, 124, 130, 131–4, 188–93, 204; Trinity 210n67; truth-telling 107, 204–5; ultimate 93–4; word 107

Bonhoeffer's works: *Act and Being* 111; "After Ten Years" 127, 139, 156; *Christology* lectures 74, 95–6, 103–4, 105, 106, 114, 116, 189–90; *Creation and Fall* 80n22; *Discipleship* 81–2, 116, 125; *Ethics* 73, 83, 85, 87, 90–1, 122, 127, 139, 170, 171, 191, 202; *Letters and Papers from Prison* 71, 74–5, 79, 86, 122, 158; *Life Together* 143, 144, 150, 153, 155, 158, 161, 164; *Sanctorum Communio* 81, 162n51; *Seelsorge* lectures 144, 154, 162, 163, 165–6, 167, 172–3; *Spiritual Care* 161; Fiction from Tegel Prison 131–4, 136–7, 205, 206; "What is Meant by 'Telling the Truth?'" 188–93

Buddhism 8, 29

Burtness, James H. 87n46

Butler, Judith 40n43, 42n49, 113–14

Calvin, Jean 196n38

Chopp, Rebecca 32n20

Christology: Crucifixion 78; ethics of communication 105; God's silence 14–15; incarnation 78, 197; *incognito* 76–7, 78–9, 80–1, 84, 85, 100, 101, 214; Jesus Christ 73, 106; *logos* 63–4;

Christology: Crucifixion (cont'd)
mediation 19, 163, 202; omniscience
197; resurrection 78–9, 100, 214;
silence 104; silence of unknowability
86; truth-telling 200
church–community 122–3, 215–16
Cixous, Hélène 43n50
communication 3, 8, 12–13, 19;
breakdown 125; distorted 124;
friendship 19, 173; Jesus Christ 161,
164; Kierkegaard 161n41; mediation
164, 179, 181; negation 9n17;
oppression 72; place to stand 122, 165;
silence 4–5, 12–13, 61; silencing 76; *see
also* ethics of communication
communities: *ecclesia audiens* 111; at foot
of cross 81–2; ministry of listening 155;
transformation 152; truth 121, 145
complicity in silencing 17–18, 39, 42,
48–9, 90
Confessing Church 75
confession 160, 174n85
congregation 139n42, 146; *see also*
worship
conscience: Heidegger 168; Jesus Christ
as 168, 169; Kant 168, 169n68;
otherness 169; Ricoeur 167–8; voice of
God 170
consciousness-raising 50, 51, 52
control/knowledge 198
counter-logos 105–7, 117, 118
creation: God 11–12, 97–8; resurrection
96–7, 98n79; speech 11
creativity 177–8, 208
Crucifixion 77–8; cry of despair 116;
incarnation 81, 201; privacy 212;
resurrection 79, 81–2; truth 193;
violence 200
cultured despiser 160–1

Daoism 8
data image 199
Dauenhauer, Bernhard: deep silence 6, 11;
phenomenon of silence 22, 52, 147;
terminal silence 7, 8
decision-making technique 170–1
depersonalization 61, 71, 127–8
Derrida, Jacques 140n44

Descartes, René 31; subject 153, 187
discernment 19, 99–100, 170–1, 172,
179–80

ecclesia audiens (community of believers)
111
Eckhart, Meister 10
Eichmann, Adolf 127–8, 129n16, 168–9,
169n68
elenchus (conviction of sin) 156n28
Eliot, T. S. 2
Emmaus 217–18
Ephesians 98n78
Erfanhrung (lived experience) 74–5n10
Erikson, Victoria Lee 38n39
eschatology: ethics 42; feminism 42;
Fiumara 63; listening 59; privacy 183;
resurrection 80, 82
ethics: Bonhoeffer 88, 89, 151;
eschatology 42; friendship 178;
penultimate 89; privacy 211–12;
responsibility 85
ethics of communication: Bonhoeffer 16;
Christology 105; discernment 19;
feminism 45–6; God 18; Habermas 36;
hearing mind 215; listening 49;
resurrection 214; selfhood 112;
speaker/hearer 69
evil 127–9, 188
exclusion of women 37–8
Exodus 194–5, 196
expressivist models 44
exteriority 68

Falls-Corbitt, Margaret 207n62
family relationships 175, 193
female body 43n50
female societies 41
feminism: alternative approaches 37–8;
Bible 221; Bonhoeffer 89; breaking the
silence 38–43; critiques 41; eschatology
42; ethics of communication 45–6;
experience 66n26; listening 15–16;
privacy 186, 199n46; representation
141n46; silence 13, 221; silencing of
women 32–3, 35–8, 64, 186–7,
199n46; standpoint epistemology 134–5,
136; voice 39, 40, 70; worship 149

feminist theology: connection 216; God's silence 220; hearing to speech 51; identity 64; lesbians 175n86; listening 220; primary speech of God 47; silence 224; voiceless people 19, 45; vulnerability 117; Word of God 112

Finkenwalde community 154, 173n80, 208n63

Fiumara, Gemma Corradi 49–50; benumbment 102, 128; critiqued 62; eschatology 63; listening 18, 53–4, 57–8, 215–16; listening self 126; logocentrism 125; *logos* 63; *The Other Side of Language* 53; philosophy of listening 59, 112; postmodernism 55–6n12; silencing 54–5; theology 60–1

folly: benumbment 138; Bonhoeffer 126–30; as evil 127–9; spiritual care 167; view from below 128–9; wisdom 126, 217

forgiveness 209–10

Foucault, Michel 198n43

freedom: finitude 9, 140; love 176; *necessitas* 174–7; negative 184, 208; omniscience 193; silence 140; silence of God 75

friendship: communication 19, 173; creativity 177–8; ethics 178; *necessitas* 174–5, 176; openness 205; penultimate 177; privacy 205; reserve 206; resurrection 176; spiritual care 145, 204; Tegel fragment 206n59; women 175n86

Friends, Society of *see* Quakers

future/past 82–3, 91, 95n73

Gadamer, H.-G. 54

gender identity 39

gender roles 68–9n35

Genesis 6, 195–6

German Church 75, 174n83, 224

Gibbs, Robert 67n30

gift/Holy Spirit 99

Gilkey, Langdon 9n17

Gilligan, Carol 37

glory 210–12

God: creation 11–12, 97–8; death of 77–8; future 91; hearing 19, 119, 195–6, 197; hearing knowledge 20, 212; hearing silence 201; hearing to speech 69; hiddenness 143, 144; Israel 194, 195, 196; Jesus Christ 197; Jüngel 213; knowledge 183, 194; listening 63–4, 102; listening silence 15; love 29n17, 145, 149–50, 176; more than speakable 213–14, 224; mystery 27, 28–9; patience 93, 125–6, 214; privacy 206, 207n62; remembrance 196; secrecy 205–6, 208; self-acknowledgment 96–7; self-recognition 198; silencing 24, 25, 27, 31, 43, 224; speech 13, 14, 29–30, 46–7, 63–4, 102; temporality 82, 198; truth 212; unspeakability 28, 52, 58; voice 170; Word 15, 73, 119; *see also* God's silence; omniscience

"God-trick" 135, 141

God's silence 11–12; Bonhoeffer 82; Christian theology 71–2; Christology 14–15; depersonalization 71; Eckhart 10; feminist theology 220; freedom 75; Godself 12, 95; hearing 97–100; hearing to speech 50–3; Jüngel 31; Morton 52; patience 92–5; responsibility 75

God-talk 26, 216–17

grace 79, 93, 176–7

Grey, Mary 47n56, 51n4, 60n16

Habermas, Jürgen 36, 67n30

Hagar 195, 223

Hannah, Song of 195n35

Haraway, Donna 135

hate speech 113–14

healing/knowledge 197n41

hearers 69, 113, 114–15, 119, 173

hearing: deep 50; God 19, 119, 195–6, 197; with God's ears 152, 164–7, 168, 179, 215, 219, 220, 222–3; God's silence 97–100; knowledge 197–8; liberatory 142; love 183; Luther 111n22; obedient 112; passive/active 110, 140; reciprocity 62–3; responsibility 120, 196; Ricoeur 64; self-forgetfulness 111, 112; spiritual care 172; standpoint epistemology 141–2

hearing mind 61n18, 124, 157, 215

hearing to speech: feminist theology 51; God 69; God's silence 50–3; Morton 18, 50, 52–3, 66, 124, 145, 151, 166; philosophy of listening 60; political 50, 63, 124, 166; silencing 139–40; spiritual carer 162–3; unknowability 100
Heidegger, Martin 54, 58, 61, 62, 168
Hitler, Adolf 168
Holy Spirit 45n51, 85, 91n60, 99, 121, 156

identity 39, 64, 65, 81
incarnation: Christology 78, 197; Crucifixion 81, 201; Jesus Christ as Word 119–20; privacy 200; resurrection 201
incognito: Christology 76–81, 84, 85, 100, 101, 214; Jesus Christ 115, 116
individuals 187, 199
information 183–4n4, 185–6, 189, 194, 198–9, 211
institutions 192–3, 199n46, 217
insult 113–14
intellectual property 185n11
intentionalist models 44
interiority 99
intimacy 6, 197, 208–9
intuition 58
Irigaray, Luce 33–4, 40, 42n49, 43n50
Isaac 6
Ishmael 195–6
Israel 194, 195, 196

Jaggar, Alison M. 36n31
Jesus Christ: Christology 73, 106; communication 161, 164; conscience 168, 169; counter-logos 105–6; exaltation 95–6, 97; God 197; Holy Spirit 85; identity 81; incarnate/crucified/resurrected 73–4, 76–7, 83, 106, 219, 223; incognito 115, 116; logos 103, 106–7, 108–9; mediation 162, 179, 181; moment of death 116, 197; mystery 92–3; panoptic gaze 200; Pharisee 202; reconciliation 86–7, 202; silence 76–7, 116–17; silence of unknowability 85, 120; as ultimate reality 205; unknowability 76–7, 94; as

verbum internum 97–8n77; vindication 141; as Word 117, 118, 119–20, 121–2
John, Gospel according to 97, 178, 180–1, 217
John of Damascus 31
judgment 99–100, 195n35, 202, 212
Jüngel, Eberhard: addressing word 30n18, 109–10, 120–1n43; God 213; God as the Mystery of the World 26–30, 109–10; God's patience 93n70; God's silence 31; Godself 26; insult 113–14; perlocutionary-attractive effect 109–10, 111; silence 31, 43, 44, 46, 52, 224; silencing of God 29, 31, 44, 46, 52; speech 47

Kant, Immanuel 168–9, 188–9
Kasper, Walter 98n77
keeping silent: collective worship 151; communal 153, 181; Fiumara 55; interruption 58, 147; liturgy 147, 148–9; non-violence 215; privacy 182
Kierkegaard, Søren 6–7, 34, 111–12, 161n41
knower/knowledge 197n42
knowledge: commodified 185n13; control 198; God 183, 194; healing 20, 183, 197n41, 200, 202–3, 208, 209, 211–12; and hearing 197–8; judgment 195n35; knower 197n42; panoptic 199; property 185n11, 201; responsibility 201–4; suffering 141; see also omniscience

Le Doeuff, Michèle 41
Leah 196
Lehmann, Paul L. 169n69
lesbians 24, 175n86
Levesque, Claude 140n44
Levinas, Emmanuel 66n29, 67, 68
liberal feminism 36, 37
liberation theology 45
listeners 18, 68, 160
listening 62, 63; active 57, 144; Bonhoeffer 17; causality 57n15; with ears of God 143; eschatology 59; ethics of communication 49; failure 63, 216; feminism 15–16; feminist theology 220;

Fiumara 18, 53–4, 57–8, 215–16; God 63–4, 102; Holy Spirit 121; learning to 53–4; responsibility 62, 132–4, 137; risk-taking 57; silencing 54; speech 57; suppressed 56; transformative 58; weak 56–7; *see also* philosophy of listening
listening self 126, 140, 152
liturgy 6, 7, 147, 148–9, 150
logocentrism 125
logology 103, 105
logos: Christology 63–4; *counter-logos* 105–7; deified 64n23; divine/human 108, 109; Fiumara 63; halved 54, 60, 63, 102, 129, 139, 216; Jesus Christ 103, 106–7, 108–9; non-listening 56; reconciled 121, 138, 179; transformed 122–3; truthfulness 124–5; *see also* Word
love: discernment 171; eternity 13; freedom 176; God 29n17, 145, 149–50, 176; Godself 171–2; hearing 183; secrecy 203; speech 30
Luke, Gospel according to 44n51, 217–18, 219–20, 223
Luther, Martin 111n22

McFadyen, Alistair 39n40
Mackinnon, Donald 179
McLain, F. Michael 207n62
Mark, Gospel according to 115n31, 131, 180, 217
Matthew, Gospel according to 111, 115n31, 215n3
meaning-making 7, 8, 13, 105
mediation: Christology 19, 163, 202; communication 164, 179, 181; Jesus Christ 162, 179, 181
men: Christian theology 32–3; voice 72, 221–2; world view 65
ministry of listening 155, 167
monastic life 145
monastic writers 11, 31
Morey, Anne-Janine 54n9
Morris, Charles 104n4
Mortley, Raoul 13, 15
Morton, Nelle 18; competing voices 221–2; gender roles 68–9n35; God's silence 52; hearing to speech 18, 50–4, 66, 124, 145, 166; *The Journey is Home*

49, 50, 51; privacy 212; reciprocity in hearing 62–3; silencing 72; speakers 113
Moses 194, 195
Muers, Rachel 95n72
mystery 27, 28–9, 81, 92–3, 155–6
mystical theology 11, 31
mysticism 27, 150

Nazism: Bonhoeffer 125, 129, 130; German Church 75, 122, 224; resistance 134
necessitas 174–5, 176
negative theology 12, 31
Neher, André 78n17
Neoplatonism 13
New Hermeneutics 109
non-speakers 221–2
non-violence 215
Numbers 195

Ochs, Peter 197n41
omniscience: Christology 197; freedom 193; hearing knowledge 200, 208; information 194, 198; judgment 212; privacy 182, 199–200
opening in resurrection 218–19, 220–1
openness 205
oppression 44, 72, 135
orthodoxy/orthopraxy 151
other: conscience 169; hearing/heard 98; privacy 207; responsibility 204; Ricoeur 169n69; self 167; women 54

Pangritz, Andreas 175n87
Panopticon 198, 199–200
parables 115n31
pastor/parishioner 163, 165–6n61, 173–4
pastors-in-training 154–5, 158
patience: forgiveness 209–10; God 93, 125–6, 214; God's silence 92–5; Jüngel 93n70; philosophy of listening 94–5
Pentecost 51
penultimate: Bonhoeffer 86–91, 101, 137; ethics 89; friendship 177; silence 91; ultimate 86–91, 183; unpredictability 130

perlocutionary-attractive act 109–10, 111, 113–14, 119
personal mystery 81
personal/political 186
2 Peter 93
Pharisee 202, 206
phenomenological approach 4, 7, 8
phenomenon of silence (Dauenhauer) 52, 147
philosophy of listening: addressing self 67; Fiumara 59, 112; hearing to speech 60; patience 94–5
philosophy of religion 194
place to stand (resurrection) 19; communication 122, 165; friendship 176; future 83; God's will 95; Haraway 135; right judgment 99–100; *Seelsorge* 167; standpoint theory 134, 141, 142; transformation 85–6, 143, 173, 218; unknowability 214
Plaskow, Judith 221n12
Plato 54
pneumatology 91n60
predestination 193
privacy: Bonhoeffer 212; creativity 208; Crucifixion 212; deprivation of 209; eschatology 183; ethics 211–12; feminism 186, 199n46; friendship 205; glory 210–12; God 206, 207n62; Godself 183; hearing knowledge 209; history of 209; incarnation 200; individualism 187; information 183–4n4, 198–9; institutions 192–3, 199n46; intimacy 208–9; invasion of 201; keeping silent 182; Morton 212; omniscience 182, 199–200; other 207; property ownership 184–6; protection 202–3, 209; public sphere 203n52; relationships 190n27, 203–4; rights to 184, 186, 187, 198; secrecy 207, 210; shame 191–2; social order 191; unknowability 19–20
propaganda 127–8
property/knowledge 185n11, 201
property ownership 184–6
Proverbs 126, 128, 131, 137
psalmists 196
Psalms 103

Pseudo-Dionysius 11, 31
public/private sphere 186–7, 191, 193, 203n52

Quakers 9, 145–6, 147–8, 150, 151, 152–3n16
quietism 126

Rachels, James 190n27
reciprocity 62–3
reconciliation 86–7, 202
relationships 190n27, 203–4, 219
remembrance 196
representation 141n46
resignification 152
resistance 56, 125, 134, 215–16
responsibility: congregation 139n42; ethics 85; free 94; God's silence 75; hearing 120, 196; knowledge 201–4; listening 62, 132–4, 137; other 204; resurrection 90; truth-telling 203n53; Word 118–19
resurrection: Bonhoeffer 18, 79–80, 83–4, 92–3, 95–6, 100; Christology 78–9, 100, 214; community at foot of cross 81–2; creation 96–7, 98n79; Crucifixion 79, 81–2; Emmaus 217–18; eschatology 80, 82; ethics of communication 214; future/past 82–3, 95n73; God's Word 73; Godself 101, 191; incarnation 201; John, Gospel of 180–1; Mark, Gospel of 180; mystery of 155–6; opening 218–19, 220–1; responsibility 90; silence 95; silence of unknowability 91–2; soteriology 80; standpoint epistemology 134, 141, 142; transformation 85–6, 143, 173, 218; truth 193; unknowability 72–3, 82–3, 84; *see also* place to stand
Revelation 1–2, 3, 4, 5
Rich, Adrienne 31, 39; "Cartographies of silence" 21, 22–4
Ricoeur, Paul: conscience 167–8; hearing 64; *Oneself as Another* 65, 67–8; other 169n69; solicitude 66
rights to privacy 184, 186, 187, 198
risk-taking 57, 151–2, 197
Romanticism 33

Rosenberg, Alexander 185n12, n13
Rutherford, Jonathan 69n35

Saiving, Valerie 136
Sarot, Marcel 197n42
Satan 194
Schleiermacher, Friedrich 31
Schoeman, Ferdinand D. 209
secrecy: God 205–6, 208; love 203;
    privacy 207, 210; totalitarianism 201;
    truth-telling 188–9; ultimate 206, 207,
    208, 210
Seelsorge (spiritual care) 144, 154–8,
    165–6
self: addressed 67; divided 206; ethics of
    communication 112; listening 126, 140,
    152; otherness 167; speech-acts 68
self-benumbment 115
self-creation 158–9
self-forgetfulness 111, 112
self-recognition 198
semiotics 104n4
sexual difference 40
shame 191–2, 211
Shoah 7
silence: breaking of 38–42, 66n28;
    Christian theology 13; Christology 104;
    communication 4–5, 12–13, 61;
    congregation 146; consent 8; deep 5–6,
    7, 11; feminism 13, 221; feminist
    theology 224; finitude/freedom 140;
    Heidegger 61, 62; instrumentalization
    147, 148; Jesus Christ 76–7, 116–17;
    Kierkegaard 111–12; liturgy 150;
    mysticism 150; practices of 9, 153–4,
    158n33, 161, 215; reinterpreted 58;
    resurrection 95; social contexts 22–4;
    speech 2, 42, 47–8, 146–7; utterance
    5–6; worship 143–4, 145–7, 150–1,
    179; see also God's silence; keeping
    silent; Quakers
silence, types: deep 5–6, 7, 11; hearing
    201; intervening 5, 6; listening 3, 15;
    more than speakable 213; originary 58,
    62; passive 43–4, 49; penultimate 91;
    personalized 49–50; subjective/objective
    154; terminal 6–7, 8, 78; theological 2,
    3; truthful 190

silence of unknowability 66, 68–9, 144,
    167; Christology 86; God 18; Jesus
    Christ 85, 120; resurrection 91–2; risk
    151–2; spiritual carer 180
silenced people 24, 49, 90, 219–20
silencing: benumbment 215;
    communication 76; complicity 17–18,
    39, 42, 48–9, 90; Fiumara 54–5;
    garrulous/dumb 26, 28, 30, 32–3, 43,
    55, 65–6; God 24, 25, 27, 29, 31, 43,
    44, 46, 52, 224; hearing to speech
    139–40; Jüngel 31, 43, 44, 46, 52, 224;
    lesbians 24; listening 54; Morton 72;
    oppressive 44; responses to 20; unjust
    120; violence 10, 52, 66n27, 223
silencing of women 136; Bible 221–2;
    complicity 17–18; dumb/garrulous 43;
    feminism 32–3, 35–8, 64, 186–7,
    199n46; God as speaker 14; theology
    42, 45
Simeon 196
sin 156–7
social conservatism 89, 192
social order 189, 191
solitary confinement 9
Solomon 61n18
soteriology 80
space 40n43
speaker–hearer relationship 69, 113, 119,
    173
speech: active 43–4, 49; Bonhoeffer 189;
    created things 11; God 13, 14, 29–30,
    46–7, 63–4, 102; Jüngel 47; listening
    57; love 30; silence 2, 42, 47–8, 146–7;
    women 36, 44
speech-acts 68, 104, 108, 110, 165
speechless people 38n39; see also silenced
    people
spiritual care 19, 145, 167, 172, 180, 204
spiritual carer 161–4, 169, 180, 219
standpoint epistemology 134–5, 136,
    141–2, 217
Steiner, George: Language and Silence 7
story-telling 50
subject: Barth 26; Cartesian 153, 187;
    identity 65; universal 33
suffering 136, 141, 197n41
surveillance 184, 200

temporality 82, 198
texts, violent 222–3
theology 2, 3; ethics 13–14; feminism
  17–18, 43, 220; Fiumara 60–1;
  institutions 217; mystical 11, 31;
  negative 12, 31; silencing of women
  42, 45; *see also* feminist theology
theopaschism 193
totalitarianism 9, 201
transformation: communities 152;
  inwardness 145; listening 58; *logos*
  122–3; resurrection 85–6, 143, 173,
  218
Trible, Phyllis 222, 223n17
Trinity 210, 210n67, 211
triumphalism 98n79, 218
truth: community 121, 145; Crucifixion
  193; God 212; *logos* 124–5; resurrection
  193; Satan 194; trustworthiness 211
truth-telling: Bonhoeffer 107, 204–5;
  Christology 200;
  Crucifixion/resurrection 193;
  responsibility 203n53; secrecy 188–9

ultimate: Bonhoeffer 93–4; justification
  94; penultimate 86–91, 183; secrecy
  206, 207, 208, 210
unknowability: hearing to speech 100;
  Jesus Christ 19, 76–7, 94; place to
  stand 214; resurrection 72–3, 82–3, 84;
  Trinity 210n67; *see also* silence of
  unknowability
utterance 5–6, 104–5, 109; *see also* speech

violence 10, 66n27, 200, 222–3
voice: competing 221–2; different 39, 40,
  45, 48; feminism 39, 40; of God 170;
  identity 64; men 72, 221–2; standpoint

epistemology 217; voiceless people 19,
  45; women 70, 221–2, 223; *see also*
  silencing
Von Wedemeyer, Maria 175, 176–7, 178

war of words 108n16, 114, 116, 215–16
Whittier, John Greenleaf 10–11
Williams, Rowan 85n43, 159–60
wisdom 61n18, 124, 126, 136–7, 138,
  217
Wittgenstein, Ludwig 23, 30, 31, 54, 55;
  Tractatus Logico-Philosophicus 21, 22
women: abused 9; empowerment 36;
  excluded 37–8; experience 66n26;
  female body 43n50; friendship 175n86;
  as hearers 113; Kierkegaard 34; non-
  speakers 221–2; other 54; as place to
  stand 137; speech 36, 44; voice 70,
  221–2, 223; wisdom 136–7, 138; *see
  also* feminism; silencing of women
Woolf, Virginia 34–5
Word: Christian theology 76; feminist
  theology 112; God 15, 73, 101, 119;
  God's hearing 119; hearers 114–15;
  hearing mind 157; Jesus Christ 117,
  118, 119–20, 121–2; responsibility
  118–19; vulnerability 149; weakness of
  116–17
word: as address 30n18, 107–8, 109–10,
  111, 120–1n43; Bonhoeffer 107;
  hearers 115; mangled 115; worship
  150–1
worship: collective 151; ecumenical 152;
  silence 143–4, 145–7, 149, 150–1;
  words 150–1; *see also* congregation
Wyschogrod, Edith 66n28

Zechariah 44n51